The Silence of the Miskito Prince

The Silence of the Miskito Prince

HOW CULTURAL DIALOGUE WAS COLONIZED

Matt Cohen

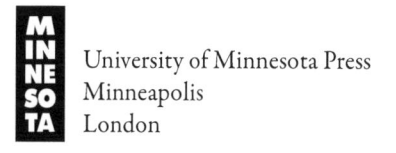

University of Minnesota Press
Minneapolis
London

The University of Minnesota Press gratefully acknowledges the financial assistance provided for the publication of this book by the University of Nebraska–Lincoln.

Open access edition funded by the National Endowment for the Humanities.

Portions of the Introduction and chapter 5 are adapted from "'Between Friends and Enemies': Moving Books and Locating Native Critique in Early Colonial America," in *The World, the Text, and the Indian: Global Dimensions of Native American Literature,* ed. Scott Richard Lyons, 103–27 (Albany: State University of New York Press, 2017). Portions of chapter 2 are adapted from "Believing in Piety: Spiritual Transformation across Cultures in Early New England," in *Religious Transformations in the Early Modern Americas,* ed. Stephanie Kirk and Sarah Rivett, 161–79 (Philadelphia: University of Pennsylvania Press, 2014). Portions of chapter 5 are adapted from the author's review of *Eloquence Embodied: Nonverbal Communication among French and Indigenous Peoples in the Americas* by Celine Carayon, *NAIS* 8, no 1 (2021): 198–200.

Excerpts from "In Mystic," from *Conflict Resolution for Holy Beings: Poems,* by Joy Harjo, copyright 2015 by Joy Harjo. Reprinted by permission of W. W. Norton & Company, Inc.

Copyright 2022 by the Regents of the University of Minnesota

The Silence of the Miskito Prince: How Cultural Dialogue Was Colonized is licensed under a Creative Commons Attribution-NonCommercial-NoDerivatives 4.0 International License (CC BY-NC-ND 4.0): https://creativecommons.org/licenses/by-nc-nd/4.0/.

Published by the University of Minnesota Press
111 Third Avenue South, Suite 290
Minneapolis, MN 55401–2520
http://www.upress.umn.edu

Available as a Manifold edition at manifold.umn.edu

ISBN 978-1-5179-1394-6 (hc)
ISBN 978-1-5179-1395-3 (pb)

A Cataloging-in-Publication record for this book is available from the Library of Congress.

Printed in the United States of America on acid-free paper

The University of Minnesota is an equal-opportunity educator and employer.

Contents

Acknowledgments *vii*

Introduction *1*
1 Cosmopuritanism *21*
2 Believing in Piety *49*
3 Waiting for the Beginning *79*
4 Rethinking Reciprocity *103*
5 Beyond Understanding *129*

Notes *159*
Index *197*

Acknowledgments

The Silence of the Miskito Prince has been a long time in the making, and many folks contributed to its coming into being. It was written in the lands of the Ponca, Pawnee, Otoe, Omaha, Ho-Chunk, Kaw, Lakota, and Dakota people. My earnings from the book will be returned to these tribes. If you are a U.S. taxpayer, thank you, too: the National Endowment for the Humanities granted me a fellowship in 2017 to support the writing. Of course the opinions I express here cannot be attributed to that helpful institution.

I'm grateful to Doug Armato for his patient support of this book, and for long walks and good talks in Austin and Seattle. He picked amazing readers, whose challenging suggestions improved the book. Zenyse Miller, Mike Stoffel, and Ana Bichanich were perfect guides during the production process. You will be as grateful as I am to Karen Hellekson for firm but elegant copyediting; and my thanks to Dan Fielding for creating an excellent index for a book that ranges widely.

My department at the University of Nebraska–Lincoln is delightful and supportive. Marco Abel, its chair, has been a reassuring supporter of all my work, and Jaime Long and Mirhuanda Meeks have been stellar (and refreshingly hilarious) administrators of its tangled bureaucracy. My faculty colleagues are a joy to work with; for their help with the ideas in this book particularly, I thank Tom Gannon, Brie Owen, Joy Castro, Roland Végső, Caterina Bernardini, Steve Ramsay, Chigozie Obioma, Ken Price, Melissa Homestead, Rachael Shah, and Julia Schleck. My graduate theory class in 2019 did not perhaps know that some of the key concepts here were being tried out on them; for great conversations, thanks go to Sarwa Abdulghafoor, Alexandra Bissell, Maura Bradshaw, Luke Folk, Gretchen Geer, Samantha Gilmore, Paul Grosskopf, Phill Howells, Molly

McConnell, Reagan Myers, Susie Rand, Carson Schaefer, Ashlyn Stewart, and Will Turner.

Former colleagues at the University of Texas at Austin also made this book imaginable; indeed, Evan Carton posed the query about understanding that started the project during the question-and-answer period after my job talk there. Conversations with Michael Winship, Lars Hinrichs, Phil Barrish, Ann Cvetkovich, Hannah Wojciehowski, Jim Cox, Luis Cárcamo-Huechante, Lisa Moore, Doug Brewster, J. K. Barret, Trish Roberts-Miller, Jorge Cañizares-Esguerra, and Heather Houser have shaped the book, and Elizabeth Cullingford was a great chair. I miss my colleagues in UT's Native American and Indigenous studies program (and Shannon Speed, who has also moved on), who exemplify how to do this work in the academy. The work of brilliant UT doctoral students Ty Alyea, Alejandro Omidsalar, and Aubrey Plourde informed this book in a range of ways.

The community of early Americanist scholars welcomed me long ago despite my ignorance and other rough edges, and has continued to nurture me generously as I catch up. Thanks for that early welcome are especially due to Ralph Bauer, Karen Kupperman, and Dennis Moore. Audiences at several conferences of the Society of Early Americanists, the Omohundro Institute for Early American History and Culture, and the American Society for Eighteenth-Century Studies, as well as focused symposia like Sarah Rivett and Stephanie Kirk's "Religious Transformations" meetings and Marcy Norton and Ralph Bauer's "Entangled Trajectories: Integrating Native American and European Histories" gathering, were a great help. Particular thanks go to the organizers of those events and to Kris Bross, Matt Brown, Kathleen Donegan, Edward Gray, David Hall, Chris Looby, Laura Mielke, Kenneth Mills, Alyssa Mt. Pleasant, Gordon Sayre, David Shields, Cristobal Silva, Fredrika Teute, Bryce Traister, Abram Van Engen, Priscilla Wald, Caroline Wigginton, and Hilary Wyss. In Vermont, Jonathan Beecher Field has been both a gracious host and a helpful reader, and thanks also go to Meredith Neuman and Ivy Schweitzer for the provocative conversations about patience and understanding we had in that ancient, verdant place. Yael Ben-Zvi and Germaine Warkentin shared relevant work in progress with me; and a postmodernism seminar (of all things) I took with James Axtell at William & Mary long ago had a delayed but meaningful impact on the writing of this book.

Another pivotal set of conversations happened at Scott Lyons's "Globalizing the Word: Transnationalism and the Making of Native American Literature" symposium at the University of Michigan. His wisdom and that of Gerald Vizenor, Sean Teuton, Jace Weaver, and the other participants were a great gift. For formative conversations and warm friendship, I am grateful to Hannah Alpert-Abrams, Pastor Tim Anderson, Micah Bateman, Stephanie Bettman, Katie Chiles, Lauren Coates, Steffi Dippold, Betty Donohue, Tom Ferraro, Erica Fretwell, Jeff Glover, Lauren Grewe, Robert Gross, Jay Grossman, Kirsten Gruesz, Robert Gunn, Sandra Gustafson, Molly Hardy, Christy Hyman, Todd Lapidus, Russ Leo, Linda Garcia Merchant, Rob Mitchell, Andrew Newman, Kinohi Nishikawa, Phil Round, Gordon Sayre, Orin Starn, Tim Sweet, Robert Warrior, Marta Werner, Kelly Wisecup, and Edlie Wong. Conversations with Lisa Brooks and Paul Chaat Smith gave me both healthy trepidation and courage. John Miles always seems to know just when to text me. Jace Everett and Caleb Smith are brothers and, in different ways, key fomenters of the ideas in this book and how I approached writing it.

Of course, much of what I've learned about both how to talk with people and how people talk about people can be attributed to my friends from way back. I love you all! But a few folks particularly influenced this book. Thank you to Jenny Hammat, Debby Rutledge Mennuti, Marty Scarbrough, Janet Whaley, Jenny Bates, Catie Bates Robertson, Brad Weier, Jen Wamsley, Jennifer Johnson Kehoe, Christine Lipat, Melissa Muscio, Lizzi Lahoz, Mignon Keaton, Billy Cullop, William Brown, and Jim Turley. Jason Woods and his family, Pam, Ronnie, and April, have shaped my ways deeply. On the other end of the spectrum, a bully or three taught me some things as well, but I reckon they can remain nameless.

Fred Gray passed away during the writing of this book, and I sorely wish he could be here to ask me hard questions about it. Julie, thank you for your support, and I hope the typeface is harmonious. My uncles David Earnest and Richard Steiger have provided joy and high textual standards. The spirits of both my grandmothers hover over this book; it could not have been conceived without them. Without my beloved mother and father, who read the whole thing, and my brother Dan, it could not have been written. Nikki Gray and the Brown Prancer mulled, wrote, and revised every page with me, and I can never thank them enough for their love.

Introduction

> Properly speaking, then, language is sacred. It will not suffice to say that the verbal and the sacred are related; they are indivisible.
> —N. Scott Momaday, *The Man Made of Words*

> Failure stalks in every word.
> —Laura Riding, *The Telling*

Somewhere east of Jamaica, in 1775, aboard an English merchant ship, a formerly enslaved person and an Amerindian man sat together, poring over an illustrated book. The subject was at once grand and grim—a series of vivid woodcuts depicting the violent martyrdoms of Protestant saints—but the company was surely welcome for both men. Olaudah Equiano, recently freed through his own industry and with the help of friends interested in his religiosity, had sought out the young Miskito to draw him into the Christian fold. Yet on a long journey, and aboard a vessel, the *Morning Star,* creaking with both weather and the jibes, subtle and crude, of their white fellow passengers, fellowship and curiosity beckoned as well. Like Equiano, Prince George of the Miskito tribe had an unusual past, for thanks to the peculiarities of that tribe's long relationship with Britain, the man spoke, dressed, and was named like an Englishman. Surely, given such preparation, the heart of the Miskito prince could be won for the supreme God?

The lessons went well at first. George was an eager learner, and Equiano, a passionate recent convert himself, used his own experience as a guide. Yet the notion of hell was a stumbling block for the Miskito prince. What would an afterlife be without one's friends, Christian or otherwise? Equiano pressed him: the glories of the afterlife were only for the godly. Their fellow passengers pressed George too. Why listen to the

African, when there was the ready raucous sociability with them to be had on board? Eventually Prince George turned away from both parties. "He became ever after," Equiano tells us in his narrative, "during the passage, fond of being alone."[1] The two went to a church service once they arrived in Jamaica, but it seemed clear that the desired conversion was not to be had. Equiano, ever industrious, carried on: "Our vessel being ready to sail for the Musquito shore, I went with the Doctor on board a Guinea-man, to purchase some slaves to carry with us, and cultivate a plantation," he writes. "I chose them all my own countrymen."

This episode, a brief one in Equiano's expansive narrative, shimmers with difficulty for today's student of colonial America. Regarded as a hero by many, Equiano wrote a narrative that is arch, earnest, and rare—one of the few works that is today regularly assigned across history courses and both English and American literature surveys. The story of his struggle out of slavery through literacy, then into the British political sphere is at once a touchstone of the era and a rebuke to past narratives of the Enlightenment. What to make, then, of this journey on the *Morning Star*, in which first his rhetoric and then his morality seem, to latter-day eyes, to falter? What to make of the ex-slave involved in enslavement, this former heathen now piously colonizing a young Amerindian leader's mind, refusing George's ethos of reciprocity and fellowship? In the end, Equiano's patience and persuasiveness seem to have reached their limits with the prince, with whom he fails to forge a lasting bond despite being a fellow cosmopolitan traveler in the crucible of the Black Atlantic. What is to be understood by the silence of the Miskito prince?

The difficulties posed by these questions are matters of both history and historiography. One problem is how to recover the contexts of moments like this from the colonial record—to dig through the archives and the published accounts, to listen to the oral histories of descendants, and to piece together the fabric of cosmologies clouded by time. Such recovery, in the case of the enslaved and the colonized people of the Atlantic, is often unachievable by mainstream, empirical means. Another problem is to confront the fact that what we today are able to read or feel in those archives and accounts is partly a function of what we desire to learn from such narratives and what we want others to think about them. Who are to be the heroes or models here? What is the template for improving relations across the boundaries of language, belief, and habit? Prince George's silence—the deliberate choice of isolation by a colonized Indigenous person—and Equiano's choice to describe his acts of colonization, proselytization, and slave trading stand as emblem and enactment of the challenge of writing about colonial history while we are still living within it.

There was a time when the writing of such histories was intended to extend colonialism. Things have changed. Now when scholars tell the story of colonial America, they often intend to reveal the injustices of the past. James Brooks summarizes the state of affairs among scholars of Native history as demonstrating "a scholarly generation's commitment to emphasize indigenous actors as agents rather than 'people without history' who inevitably succumb to the expansion of global mercantile capitalism," people for whom "emerging markets and military alliances often served their own strategic ends."[2] The racism, classism, and sexism of today, recent scholarship reveals, emerged out of the imperial contests and settler colonial incursions of the past, along with their religious and economic effects. Yet Equiano's well-intentioned attempt to convert Prince George hovers over these attempts to reveal the truth as well. There is often as much silence as sound in the disciplinary channels between Indigenous studies and history today. What language, what stories, and what silences, if any, can bring about an end to colonization?

Above, in phrasing some queries provoked by Equiano's account of the *Morning Star* voyage, I used five concepts that this book will interrogate: cosmopolitanism, piety, patience, reciprocity, and understanding. Each of these words has been crucial to the scholarly attempt to improve the present by means of describing the past. *The Silence of the Miskito Prince* argues that misunderstanding, slippery definitions of cultural reciprocity and patience, and violent forms of cosmopolitanism and piety shaped cross-cultural relations in the seventeenth and early eighteenth centuries. It also argues that they haunt the very conceptual apparatus that scholars, in the last forty years of cultural historical research, have hoped would promote intercultural dialogue. The terms we use when we write about scenes like the one on the *Morning Star* stubbornly seem to depend on differences between entities we have designated as "cultures" and leave unresolved the paradox of violent reciprocities and the failures of understanding to produce peace. How can we tell such histories in a way that invites conversations across group boundaries, engages the complexity of forms of affiliation under colonialism, and bridges the disciplines and desires of Native American and early American studies? What words do we use? By confronting the disturbing dimensions of the common conceptual vocabulary for North American colonial studies, in its long historical depth and through a series of archival explorations, *The Silence of the Miskito Prince* calls for new ways of framing scholarly conversations that use the past to think about relations among peoples today.

The reflections in this book were spurred by my work in early American studies. In a previous book, *The Networked Wilderness,* about the information technologies of the early settlement of New England, I treated Indigenous American communications systems—things like wampum, baskets, paths, stories, and rock carvings—as information technologies because I wanted to argue against the idea that cultures could be described as "oral" or as "literate," much less that the possession of certain technologies indicates cultural or intellectual superiority. During my reading in volumes of historical, anthropological, and literary research on Native America, I found that two continually recurring words—words I went on to use in that book—describe the better future of relations between the academy (and indeed the United States at large) and Indian Country: reciprocity and understanding.

Yet nobody seemed quite to agree on just what reciprocity was. Certainly scholars did agree in positioning that concept at odds across a cultural divide, with reciprocity suggested to be the basis of Indigenous North American ethics, as opposed to a Western individualism that blinded settlers to Native ways. I had also been warned not to trust "understanding" as a scholarly motive by both my poststructuralist literary training (everything is relative; the reality that would ground understanding is perspectival, a social and linguistic construct) and by Sioux writer Vine Deloria Jr.'s hilarious 1969 send-up of anthropology, "Anthropologists and Other Friends."[3] Of the two influences, Deloria's offers the more practical argument for thinking hard about what we mean by understanding and how to live without it. The more I began to think about these terms, the more I began to wonder. How are the relationships assumed by the terms "reciprocity" and "understanding" imagined? How are those terms used, and what are they used instead of? Toward what liberatory or ameliatory end are they invoked, on what occasions, and to what measurable effect? They mediate "cultures," to be sure, whether one is speaking of establishing a reciprocal relationship across human groups or among humans and also with the environment, as in Indigenous views. Take Equiano and Prince George's conversation, for example. Christian ideas of reciprocity and those of the Miskito might have been as much a point of disagreement as potential harmony. Certainly "understanding" is a frequently cited panacea to racial, cultural, and religious conflict, imagined as a thing that scholarship can increase to positive ends. What, though, are "cultures" after reciprocity and understanding take hold? To what extent do we imagine cultural boundaries in part through inscrutability, or at least partly closed economies?[4] As positive but never-quite-achievable ideals, what boundaries do reciprocity and understanding help create or maintain? What do we make of the dark side of these concepts—the possibility, for example, that at some level, or seen from some perspective, the Aztec sacrificial ritual is premised on a concept of reciprocity, or that Palestinians and Jews really do understand each other, but still fight? Did George's silence signal the failure of understanding on the *Morning Star,* or its accomplishment?

The Silence of the Miskito Prince takes up these questions by analyzing the concepts we use to describe solutions to cross-cultural communication challenges and how those concepts emerged from, and continue to evolve within, colonial dynamics. It argues that notions key to the interpretation of Indian–European relations in the colonial period are also meaningful to how we think about and enact relations among human groups today. Two main concepts, reciprocity and understanding, are investigated with three related ones: piety, patience, and cosmopolitanism. These are all key theoretical terms in colonial American studies, but they are seldom treated as theoretical in scholarship of the early part of this period. Together, these terms form a web of ideas about human relationships and about how to improve or mend those relationships, the conflicted history and ethics of which have seldom been interrogated by scholarship that has depended on appeals to these words.

Concepts like cosmopolitanism, reciprocity, piety, patience, and understanding can seem to be timeless, describing behaviors, states, or attitudes that we today might share with people in the past. They seem to leap the barrier between the past we describe and the historiographic act of trying to change the present. History, however, as Édouard Glissant once wrote, is "a highly functional fantasy of the West."[5] Modern coloniality, the ongoing context of deeply embedded inequalities in which we communicate with each other today, is entangled with the historically destructive contexts and structures that count as knowledge. We therefore cannot depend on knowledge as a window onto the colonial past. "Scholars recapitulate the interpretive quandary facing seventeenth-century French Jesuit missionaries in Canada," writes Kenneth Morrison. "How to make sense of the Native American other when an adequate self-understanding was, and is, not commonly available."[6] Morrison's "was, and is" points to the crux of the historiographic problem of understanding under colonization. Hindsight is far from twenty-twenty.

Yet acknowledging one's ethnocentrism can also perpetuate colonialism. One often sees the claim, both within and beyond the academy, that the ways Europeans understood their exchanges with Natives and the ways Indigenous people understood such exchanges were at odds because of deep-seated sociocultural differences, even in the case of diplomatic agreements that endured. Such a claim seems to say two comforting things: first, that was then, this is now, and we know better; and second, the failures of treaties to maintain peace and equality were inevitable products of supraindividual forces. No individual today is to blame; nor are your ancestors. Yet not only do we know both circumstantially and from their recorded admissions that settlers often understood perfectly well what Indigenous expectations of treaties were, but we also know that Indigenous people kept (and keep) telling settler authorities that such violations of treaties were violations of the Western ideas of trust on which mutual understanding's benefit was premised, including Christian doctrines, the violation of which could result in eternal damnation.[7] Sharing a set of values across groups does not prevent parties to an agreement from violating it.

"How we have come to know intimacy, kinship, and identity within an empire born out of settler colonialism," writes Jodi Byrd, "is predicated upon discourses of indigenous displacements that remain within the present everydayness of settler colonialism, even if its constellations have been naturalized by hegemony and even as its oppressive logics are expanded to contain more and more historical experiences."[8] This is to say that how we know what we think we know is not just a product of the histories of resistance to hegemonic nationalism or imperialism or expansionism that the critical academy values; our knowledge is also born of the pervasive normalizations of the imagination of living with colonialism that subsist even in the vocabulary of that resistance. Bridging human communities has a conceptual vocabulary, an imaginary wrought in words whose genealogies we can sketch. The cacophony of competing representations of the "Indian" over time was generated in part by related competitions in the West's lexicon of cross-cultural rapprochement.

In light of this problem of history's fantasticalness, this book attempts to unsettle the present by rendering less presumable some of the terms on which historiography's beneficent mission depends. To do so, I engage in a philological investigation, sometimes comparative, of these terms, whose pasts may indeed seem like another country. Our distance in historical time from the early colonial era constitutes a methodological and evidentiary challenge. Yet it also places a mirror in front of the historian or theorist: the tasks of interpreting the past and acting in the present, when it comes to Native–settler cultural interaction, are shaped by each other, enacted in a language wrought through colonial inequalities.

"There are no terms that can be simple foundations of indigenous resistance," write the editors of the book *Native Studies Keywords*. "These words cannot be taken for granted. Rather, a constant interrogation and reinvention of language and terminology is part of the process of decolonization itself."[9] Such is the spirit of *The Silence of the Miskito Prince*. There is a long history of such interrogations.

In a series of influential essays, historian James Merrell reflects on the fact that the lexicon of American colonial history has not changed much, despite decades of work focusing on indigeneity in the era. Historians keep decentering Native historical perspectives and cosmologies. "The root of the problem lies in the very words used to tell stories about olden times," Merrell writes.[10] Indigenous people have been making this point for a long time, as evidenced by the epigraph by N. Scott Momaday that opens this introduction. From the persistence of the concept of "discovery" to the trope of "barbarism" (problematic whether applied to Europeans or Natives), Merrell finds a retrograde vocabulary. The Keywords book series from New York University Press widens the range of disciplinary areas that may be approached in this way, from American studies to environmental studies and beyond.

The words taken up in *The Silence of the Miskito Prince* are not discussed in Merrell's critiques, or in the keywords addressed in the American cultural studies volume, or in Raymond Williams's foundational *Keywords,* which set the model back in the 1980s. They are neither buzzwords at the forefront of academic conversations today—words like "sovereignty" or "commons"—nor good old saws of the past, like "wilderness" or "encounter." Many of those concepts will make an appearance, but I focus instead on words that function at an even more basic level—words like "understanding" or "patience"—or that inform the imagination of an ideal multicultural world—like "cosmopolitanism" or "reciprocity." That imagination is shaped by these terms both within and beyond academic conversations. Nor is my goal to turn these terms into buzzwords ("cosmopolitanism," for example, has already had a turn or two in the limelight). Instead, these words are methodological portals, ways onto ways. By investigating the colonial histories of these terms and their functions in scholarship that wants to bring us a world beyond colonialism, I offer both a reflection on how we got here and a technique for rethinking many other words that are just as crucial as these, which hold us to our better or worse pasts.

"When we come to say 'we just don't speak the same language' we mean something more general," Williams reminds us: "that we have different immediate values or different kinds of valuation, or that we are aware, often intangibly, of different formations and distributions of energy and interest."[11] In the case of both the linguistic encounters of early America and those that have generated and sustain the period's study today, those distributions of energy and interest have concerned the viability of competing cultural and political regimes. Although none of my central terms appears in it, *Keywords* informs my approach (as it has the approach of many others), with its simple but powerful attentiveness to words with problems of definition that seem inextricably bound up with the problems they have been used to discuss. "Some important social and historical processes occur *within* language," Williams argues, rather than language merely reflecting such processes. In contests over words, in the spectacular or quiet renegotiation of their meanings, change can happen, not least by altering the available imaginative options—what Williams describes as "new kinds of relationship, but also new ways of seeing existing relationships"—within a society sharing a vocabulary.[12]

One of Williams's other key contributions was to put the term "culture"—a form of which appears in this book's subtitle—into question. His inquiry has been extended and deepened in the work of cultural anthropologists since that time. The historical scenes in this book, in which language circulates stories about interactions, offer examples of how colonialism itself unfolds in everyday moments of negotiation or problem solving, and how a kind of inertia builds simultaneously in power relations and in the conceptual vocabularies of relationality itself. The terms that I take up have consequently accrued their meanings within the context of colonial power struggles and the rise of a particular conception of boundary definition among human groups—or cultures—that enabled colonial operations. "Culture is the precaution of those who claim to think thought but who steer clear of its chaotic journey," writes Glissant. "Evolving cultures infer Relation, the overstepping that grounds their unity–diversity."[13] Yet having already been put under erasure in anthropology, Native American studies, and poststructuralist-informed literary studies, "culture" is still a little-questioned placeholder in the discipline of history, particularly in the most popular forms of colonial historiography.[14] So although I begin with the trope of "cultural dialogue," I hope that in the end the reader will see my suggestion that we imagine across definitions of culture—both synchronous ones at the moments in time I analyze here and diachronic ones, as the concept emerged as central to the maintenance of settler power in North America. "Because the components of a culture, even when located, cannot be reduced to the indivisibility of prime elements," Glissant argues, neither a posited culture's internal nor its external dynamics can be defined. "But such a definition is a working model," he insists. "It allows us to imagine."[15] Imagination plays a central role in Glissant's analysis of colonialism's effects on relationality, but also in his theory of what analysis itself might look like in the age of relativism. As we learn from the history of transgroup interactions, we are reminded of the condition of time in which we operate as analysts, necessarily invoking the imagination in a poetic relationship with the past. The terms of colonialism's culturalization of human association were built on redefinitions of relation and responsibility that were the product of struggle among all parties involved, and that substantially involved transformations in language itself.

Williams's other important emphasis is on how historical process-bearing keywords cluster, or interrelate in ways difficult to pull apart, but the analysis of which is aided by beginning with the single word and moving to examples or delineating a few important connections that qualify the isolated reading of a word. The meanings of keywords like "race" and "class," for example, depend on each other in profound yet historically shifting ways. "This is not to impede but to make possible the sense of an extended and intricate vocabulary," Williams explains, "within which both the variable words and their varied and variable interrelations are in practice alive."[16] In this notion of the functional aliveness of words, Williams begins to approach the idea of the sacred quality of words expressed by Momaday. Words have both individual and collective lives, and as such, under a traditional Indigenous cosmology, they are beings we must negotiate both through and with.

Merrell was sure that certain words were preventing historians from conceptualizing a Native-centered history. Others have suggested that even using the words well might not be enough. Robert Berkhofer Jr., writing in the heyday of postmodernism's challenges to the habitual naive realist mode of historical writing, argued that historians should take a reflexive, multicultural approach, borrowing from some of the insights of anthropology and cultural studies. Native thinkers have argued that scholars must go further still, committing their research programs and their time and effort to Native community-guided projects or political activism.[17] Decolonizing the activity of history writing would involve not only changing how we write, speak, and walk in the academic professions but also returning the land to Native people.[18]

One step I can take toward that return is to generate discomfort about a few of the more idealistic, seemingly consensual terms in my field. My approach has been to unsettle the words that link depictions of the past to the imagination of an intercultural future.[19] The problem is not just the persistence of colonial or colonialist language in historiography. More basically, language itself functions a bit like colonization. Its reproductive capacity effects linguistic persistence by assimilating each new person to its norms, which in exchange for recognition demand subjugation and a measure of conformity. Yet just as is the case with colonization, no such assimilation or performance of conformity is ever absolute. As a consequence, the chapters that follow do not attempt to produce an ethnographically accurate understanding, exactly. What I hope to encourage is not so much understanding as a stance.

The Silence of the Miskito Prince has an argument to make in one corner of the academy, for harder thinking in colonial studies about the metaphors we use to describe our ideal pathways to improved intergroup relations. That harder thinking might lead first to an awareness of the ways common historiographic terms and frames maintain colonial relations, and second to goals for and modes of history writing more engaged with Indigenous and other conceptions of relationality and its ethics. I choose the North American, settler colonial, and Indigenous frames in part because they speak to a particularly Anglo-American set of effects or assumptions underwriting the five concepts studied here that impede resistance to ongoing colonization. Those assumptions are certainly at work in other academic and popular contexts, but I have deliberately constrained my focus to paint a richer picture, and I hope that the effort may nonetheless be useful in other domains. My goal is not to produce a countermythology but rather to offer coordinates for interrogating concepts that anchor notions about what the cross-cultural study of colonial America can accomplish, where, and how. There are, and will emerge, other such terms, but I hope the manner of my investigation will provide a path for sensing and questioning them as they begin to cohere.

Notwithstanding that constructive intention, the philological reflections that follow might at times feel, with their endless destabilizations, a bit depressing. I have drawn inspiration from critical traditions, such as queer pessimism and Afropessimism, that are powerfully skeptical about the potentials of liberal reform in societies and under governments deeply structured by racism, homophobia, and xenophobia.[20] Still, I am optimistic about both the capacities of historical storytelling and the chances for new concepts to emerge that would take us into a more relational form of dialogue about colonialism and how settlers can begin to relax their death grips.

Despite the difficulties of creatively navigating a critical vocabulary saturated with colonial power relations, it is possible for historiography to turn toward justice, as well as to turn its readers from their accustomed ways. Achieving those ends requires dismantling some of the expectations of and about historiography, along with its place in the settler colonial political economy. The seamless mastery of a past landscape conveyed by historical narratives—indeed, a mastery required of professional academic historians—is driven by a need to reinforce a sense that some definitive version of the past is actually attainable. History writing and reading are usually pursued as a kind of unifying enterprise—a means of getting readers all on the same page, as it were. The historian sets out to provide a definitive, or at least enduring, account of a past era. But the colonial relation disrupts the coalescence of a common desire that could ground such a consensual enterprise. With a readership made up of those who have settled and those who have been dispossessed, each act of storytelling about the past inscribes a power difference in the present. The link between domination of an imagination of the past and domination of the land is short and strong because stories motivate, justify, and create bonds among some people out of divisions from others and their stories. To turn to the past is not to escape the present but rather to shape the future; it is not merely the content of the story, as this book suggests, but rather the most basic rationalizations for its telling or assumptions about its values that inscribe difference even in the act of attempting to break down difference.

This book has been shaped by a range of intellectual movements. In addition to queer theory and Afropessimism, it participates in approaches and attitudes from queer temporality scholarship, postsecularist religious studies, and Native American and Indigenous studies' interrogations of sovereignty and identity, as well as the unrelenting fugitive irony of Native writers like Gerald Vizenor.[21] Practitioners in these areas are not all, or not always, focused on questions of decolonization; at times they express a separatist antagonism to each others' emphases. Yet their bodies of work share a focus on the persistence of regimes of oppression and the problem of imagining a way out of the representational webs those regimes have spun over a long stretch of time. These approaches' positive contributions can be enhanced through an awareness of the degree to which they have been shaped by colonial contests over power (including resource struggles within the academy) and the settler norms that have both erased common ground in some areas and created a self-serving illusion of it in others.

The ontological turn in anthropology, particularly as it emerges from the work of Andeanists on Indigenous–settler relations in Peru, plays a structuring role in this book. These scholars' focus on translation and the relay among conceptual worlds within that landscape and history has produced fascinating new stances for scholars to take, including Eduardo Viveiros de Castro's notion of controlled equivocation. If equivocation is, as he writes, "a failure to understand that understandings are necessarily not the same, and that they are not related to imaginary ways of 'seeing the world' but to the real worlds that are being seen," then one need not despair at the disjunction. It is possible for "the referential alterity between . . . positions" to be "acknowledged and inserted into the conversation in such a way that rather than different views of a single world (which would be the equivalent to cultural relativism) a view of different worlds becomes apparent."[22] Taking such an approach to the distant past means also treating temporal difference as equally relevant to world crossing as cultural and linguistic difference.

From time to time, I make reference to scholars who are doing that kind of work, in Indigenous studies and beyond. Writing about colonization could be informed by poetry's suspension of "understanding" as a goal, as in the work of Glissant; by the evocative apposition of interpretation and archive, as in the work of Susan Howe; by a collaborative authorial dynamics that decenters scholarly authority, as in Siobhan Senier's work with Northeastern Native archivists and storytellers; by a disruption of historiographic clarity, as in the work of Saidiya Hartman; and by a narrative approach that multiplies perspectives, archives, and interpretations, as in the work of Lisa Brooks.[23] These writers both improvise and unearth the past, to help readers (not quite) understand the past, and as a consequence to understand their present a bit less, all to the end of opening conversational potential. These approaches have created space, directly or indirectly, within the conversation about colonialism for new kinds of reckoning between Indigenous and settler people, or for interpretations that do not require consensus, or for collaborations that may not end in books.

In different ways, all of these critical thinkers warn us, as William Faulkner did, that the past isn't past. That condition is one we live inside as individuals feeling and exercising prejudices, affiliations, blindnesses, and the like, but also in our unequal treatment within legal, economic, religious, and other regulatory systems. But as scholars, too, we are caught in a welter of desire, projections, and misidentification when we study the past. We too often go there looking for a thread to ourselves or our communities rather than looking for something radically other, or something we will never understand. The threads may well be there, but we cannot always see them, even when we find the smoking gun (a telling metaphor) in the archives. To be surprised by identification across the supposed forms of difference that make us who we are, and to be startled at the absence of a thread where we presumed there was one, to someone who seemed to be like us, or to have been related to us, in the past—those emotions might be as significant in shaping a narrative as any methodological parsing of historical data or overarching narrative of social change. In both cases, we turn out to be something other than we thought we were; to induce such emotions is a power both transformative and seductive for the historian to wield.

A wise man once told me never to relinquish the power of irony, that unsettling mode of talk. So these chapters recount contradictions and present possibilities, but they leave much unsaid, or said sideways. In the end, however, the point of this book's linguistic unsettling is to promote a material unsettling. The less comfortable scholars are believing that, in Audra Simpson's words, settlement is "'done,' 'finished,' 'complete'"—a fait accompli on whose canvas academic inquiry unfolds, folds its hands, wrings its hands—the more likely they might be to see how Indigenous sovereignty can benefit us all. Perhaps I'm less a cruel optimist, as Lauren Berlant might have it, than a strategic pessimist.[24]

This book, partly as a consequence of these inspirational scholarly movements, is a product of reflection on what drew me to study its subject. The Puritans initially struck me as interesting aliens, ancestors somehow of the evangelicals that I grew up with in western Kentucky. I became fascinated with the way dissenters insisted on the inscrutability of God's mind with a fundamental, humbling nonknowingness, the implications of which reached into every corner of human existence—politics, economics, sexuality, hospitality, everything. Locked in a struggle with a parent religion that, as the Calvinists saw it, betrayed this commitment to skepticism by emphasizing outward displays of godliness over inward conviction, they profoundly theorized a tension that was at the heart of the development of science, new forms of public governance, perhaps even the feelings—the recognizability—of individuality and of collectivity as many people in the West know them today. With such a generative gift, such a potentially beneficent skepticism, why had the Protestants who settled North America not lived up in deed to what they were supposed to feel at heart?

Some of those settlers were ancestors of my own, on my mother's side. But their beliefs, with the exception of the golden rule—which was big in our household—had eroded by the time my mother raised me. She insisted on a patient inquiry into the other-than-human people around us—the insects, animals, and trees, as well as the Blood River, which I grew up on. Instead of a catechism, I had Shel Silverstein's devastating *The Giving Tree*. My parents, nonworshippers themselves, encouraged my brother and me to attend all of the various churches of the friends with whom we spent weekends, and to think of their congregants as worthy of careful attention and inquiry as well. It would have been hard for me, once I became a student of the past, not to conclude that, by and large, the settlers had neither kept nor lived up to their word, and that the Indigenous people of the continent, by and large, had. Yet if the spiritual leaders of Indian America are right that, in Simon Ortiz's words, the original occupants of the land are engaged in "a long outwaiting" of settler occupation, then it is no less true that evangelicals are and will continue to do the same, although with a different end in mind. All of these stories have power, as Equiano must have known when he opened Foxe's book of martyrs to Prince George, and as Prince George must have known when he began to withhold his voice and companionship.

For those caught in the complex webs of dependency, concern, and necessity that structure the North American economy's daily experience, thinking deeply about the past and the language that brings it to us, or pausing to consider the effect of a word on the large pattern of our daily interactions with other people, seems like a luxury. So in the brief space of reflection offered by this book, I spend time with a few words that are parts of the environment of language in which we tend to think about the colonial American past. Each chapter is a meditation on a concept that is part of the infrastructure of the scholarly imagination. The violent or appropriative cosmopolitanism of settler Protestants and the Pequot tribe alike calls into question the liberatory potential of that term. Piety's centrality to the lexicon of Puritan studies emerges as an obstacle to imagining intercultural cosmologic practices. Patience appears less as a common virtue than as a site of spiritual and political contest, through a reading of the texts and contexts of Roger Williams's debates with the Quakers of Providence Plantations. The embeddedness of the concepts of reciprocity and of intersubjective understanding in deep histories of Western geopolitical and philosophical programs offers a caveat to the use of those terms for describing the colonial past.

Each chapter also asks a common question: what stands between knowing what a term means and the actuation of the ethos for which it seems to stand? Tracing the backgrounds of these words leads us back to their roles in the social-intellectual fabric of the academy today. This dimension of the book led me to keep the chapters short, assignable alongside commonly taught texts from the early colonial period in North America. There is some insider talk from time to time in what follows, but those beginning the study of this period and place have been at the forefront of my mind in writing *The Silence of the Miskito Prince*. Like all elders, those working in this field have their own time-tested ways of teaching these matters. I hope that this book will, even and perhaps especially in its weaknesses, assist their efforts. The settler nonconformists were right about the limits of knowledge, and the catch-22 is that as a result, we can never truly know what any of them thought or felt. But if those of us who study the American past want to live up in deed to our words as they did not, we can think about our words broadly and deeply, as they function across different communities and cosmologies.

"How do individuals and communities reckon with a past of almost unspeakable cruelties and dispossessions, the effects of which have persisted through centuries of racialized thinking and policy-making?" asks Christine DeLucia in a searching study of violence and memory in the Northeast. "How do they—we—conceive of ourselves as complicit in these violences, or as witnesses, victims, survivors of them?"[25] Like Morrison's "was, and is," DeLucia's "they—we" captures the mode in which moral reckoning under ongoing colonization takes place. "In a region still strongly shaped by settler colonialism," DeLucia advises, "'collaborative' arrangements ought to be viewed as pragmatic, time- and site-specific connections that proceed imperfectly, rather than as long-term, finalized agreements to dissolve differences—or as bids for reconciliation, a perhaps premature endeavor in places where cultural contact still seethes and where foundational political dilemmas about the exercise of Indigenous sovereignty remain profoundly unresolved."[26] While the seething region in question here is New England, this approach could be applied to all colonized space.

The notions of cosmopolitanism, patience, understanding, reciprocity, and piety discussed in this book each express the hope and yearning for the good and for justice that many of us feel. As such, in different ways, they reach out across cultures, however defined. They also point to the effects of colonialism on the possibility for clear conversation between peoples, and the ways in which such reaching out may fail by virtue of its own often unrecognized premises. These concepts are also structured by long-evolved power contests rather than consensus. Indeed, at times Native people have appropriated these terms to community-building ends. My intention is not to hamper those uses of any of these terms, especially perhaps the application of reciprocity. Still, given the histories of these words, some reflection on the past they carry seems wise. Perhaps such an exercise can help encourage a habit of awareness of the noncongruity of worlds as well as of their overlaps—an equivocation that opens time and space for agonistic, protracted relations rather than judgment and violence.

If ever there were two groups of people who thought deeply about words and their sacredness, it was the Indigenous people of North America and the religiously motivated settlers who invaded it. The colonial record, from descriptions of the earliest exploratory encounters to Roger Williams's *Key into the Language of America* to the writings of Samson Occom and beyond, shows the mutual curiosity about language that resulted. That shared passion for language and meaning alone did not produce harmonious coexistence—or in some cases sustain coexistence at all. Studying this period both affords its students leverage and demands humility.

Some of the most difficult-to-solve problems of this world, problems in which our daily lives are nested, have been built out of violent reciprocities, rooted in deep understandings. This book is meant as a tool for rethinking some of the key terms that we are using to talk our way out of the dark legacy of violence and inequity. By its own logic, it cannot promise understanding; nor can it offer a prescription for balance. It can, however, carry forward a conversation. Instead of imagining understanding as our goal in the study of the past, we might see an opportunity to build relationships, kinships of many kinds, so we can stay in touch about our changing needs, share grief over the disasters and betrayals of the past, and celebrate the glimpses it gives us of happy partnerships or beautiful creations. In all of this, we make an effort to treat each other well because we enact our mutual dependency in the very search for the past itself—whether, like Equiano and the Miskito prince, we understand each other or not.

1 Cosmopuritanism

> Exile is a model for the intellectual who is tempted, even beset and overwhelmed, by the rewards of accommodation, yea-saying, settling in.... To be as marginal and as undomesticated as someone who is in real exile is for an intellectual to be unusually responsive to the traveler rather than to the potentate, to the provisional and risky rather than to the habitual, to innovation and experiment rather than the authoritatively given status quo.
>
> —Edward Said, *Representations of the Intellectual*

> "Now, then, for the writing," said the cosmopolitan, squaring himself. "Ah," with a sigh, "I shall make a poor lawyer, I fear. Ain't used, you see, barber, to a business which, ignoring the principle of honour, holds no nail fast til clinched. Strange, barber," taking up the blank paper, "that such flimsy stuff as this should make such strong hawsers; vile hawsers, too."
>
> —Herman Melville, *The Confidence-Man: His Masquerade*

The framing of New England's nonconformist settlers, whether Massachusetts Bay Puritans or their more radical separatist neighbors in Plymouth, as puritanical in the modern, negative sense, began early in the national life of the United States. Even as their society was increasingly argued to be the source of Americanness, it was also imagined as a restrictive, judgmental, inward-looking community—that is, as anything but cosmopolitan.

"In this enlightened and liberal age," one of the narrators of Lydia Maria Child's 1824 novel *Hobomok, a Tale of Early Times* tells us, "it is perhaps too fashionable to look back upon those early sufferers in the cause of the Reformation, as a band of dark, discontented bigots."

Mr. Conant, one of the novel's central antagonists, is the model of the "the rigid Calvinist, in that lone place" of New England, who "seemed like some proud magnolia of the south, scathed and bared of its leaves."[1] From the beginning, he evinces the negative traits that would come to embody a Puritan stereotype before the middle of the nineteenth century: a rejection of earthly pleasures and an insistence on human fallibility, and along with these a suspicion of the outside world. "It surely is not strange that I should think often of places where I have enjoyed so much," his daughter, Mary, insists early in the novel as she dreams of the old country,

> "and should now be tempted to ask questions concerning them, of those who have knowledge thereof." "Aye, aye," replied the stern old man, "encamped as you are in Elim, beside palm-trees and fountains, you are no doubt looking back for the flesh-pots of Egypt. You'd be willing enough to leave the little heritage which God has planted here, in order to vamp up your frail carcase in French frippery. But I would have you beware, young damsel. Wot ye not that the idle follower of Morton, who was drowned in yonder bay, was inwardly given to the vain forms of the church of England?"[2]

Thomas Morton, in the hands of Nathaniel Hawthorne, would of course become the famous emblem of resistance to Puritan ways.[3] As resurrections of the settler Puritans became an increasingly popular literary tactic, Child's moralistic, protonationalist nonconformists evolved into later depictions in which "puritan" was used to label those who are judgmental and deprecate the world and its pleasures. The movement of Hawthorne's character Pearl away from Puritan New England to an aristocratic realm of unspecified nationality at the conclusion of *The Scarlet Letter* marks such an evolution in a novel that has helped sustain the popular stereotype.

Hobomok, however, depicts a range of nonconformist characters. It persistently reveals not only their transatlantic connections but also their constant interactions with Native people and with people in other settlements. It is perhaps the title character who is the most cosmopolitan of all, by the conventional definition. Hobomok is multilingual, deeply spiritual, but not sectarian; he is a broker among all the region's nations, both settler and Indigenous. His exile at the end of the novel—not for his sins but for his generosity—bears not only the signature of the vanishing Indian myth but also an echo of the silence of the Miskito prince, George, when he turned away both from Olaudah Equiano's attempts to convert him to Christianity and his shipmates' attempt to turn him from Equiano.

If between the Puritans and worldly men like Morton "jollity and gloom were contending for an empire," as Hawthorne famously put it, the battleground was not merely Indigenous space in New England but rather the whole cosmos.[4] The English settlers of New England were neither isolated nor homogeneous in ways that make it easy to characterize their society as insular. Material and political interconnections with Europe and a range of Native nations contributed to the shaping of New England's sociopolitical order, from long-standing separatist ties with the original émigrés in Leiden to a sustained interest by colonial thinkers in a range of Spanish-language publications from England's most powerful imperial competitor.[5] It has become easy to see how Hawthorne's anxious narratives about prudery and the compression of space and time may have overstated the case. It is still difficult, however, to think about early New English communities in nonparochial terms. An ambient sense lingers that spatial isolation from Europe and the appropriation of Indigenous land, vectored by a stern judgmentalism, produced a historical rupture eventually leading to a democratic "America."

Yet thinking of those people or communities as cosmopolitan may not provide us with what we are looking for, if that is some sort of historical redemption or merely a richer texture to the imagination of American nonconformist life. There is a long-standing, contentious conversation in the humanities about cosmopolitanism. Intensely debated in the 1990s, the question of cosmopolitanism as an alternative to national forms of belonging had been flagging when it was revived by the attacks of September 11, 2001, and the resulting response of the George W. Bush administration. Since the violently xenophobic reign of the forty-fifth U.S. president, it has surged again, across humanities fields. At the same time, early American studies has been flowering intellectually, in part by engaging the same questions that underwrite the cosmopolitanism debate: arguments about ideal forms of transnational political and social identities and how they relate to law, religion, and economics. The rituals and representations that sustained Puritan social formation have long been fertile for investigating the genealogy of U.S. exceptionalism. In the wake of the national trauma of 9/11, a seemingly endless series of mass shootings, and a reinvigorated providentialism in government, scholars of colonial America took up frameworks for understanding U.S. denizens as being bound to the nation by, in Lauren Berlant's words, a spectacular "capacity for suffering and trauma at the citizen's core." Debates about trauma and the nature of the public and private worlds are tantalizing for early Americanists, building on decades of scholarship engaging Sacvan Bercovitch's thesis about the Puritan origins of the American self.[6] There seems to be something about the Puritan experience in the Northeast—about a belief structure that fuses a quest for supernatural grace with pious living deeply rooted in a specific earthly place—that we can trace forward continuously in time.

The nonconformists' homelessness, their search for a nonnational space when they left for the New World, has been an important part of the story. "Nation" was a contested, often typological term in early modern English writing in general, but the Puritans and Plymouth's separatists, who had a conflict-ridden relationship with the Stuart monarchy and the Church of England, were particularly agile in resisting the language of English nationalism. "The respectable, London-based colonial enterprise had emerged as a colony dominated by Puritans who proclaimed their allegiance to King and Church but clearly expected to be free of both," Neal Salisbury says of the Massachusetts Bay settlement.[7] Given that these godly settlers were prenational, perhaps even in a degree anational, more tied as they were to the body of Christ than to a national body, in what relation does cosmopolitanism stand to the genealogy of American political and intellectual order imagined to emerge out of Puritanism?

Today, as religious fervor increasingly shapes public feeling, rhetoric, and policy on the international stage, scholarly debates about cosmopolitanism seem at once more important and more unsatisfying. The debates' terms have come to seem mismatched to today's vocabulary of international relations. Although critics may speak of one or another ideal of cosmopolitanism, they share reference to something that they understand, as

Craig Calhoun puts it, to have taken shape "largely in opposition to traditional religion and more generally to deeply rooted political identities," especially national ones.[8] In the U.S. context, however, cosmopolitanism has been profoundly incubated in the Christian universalist tradition as well as tangled in a web of transnational, translingual dependencies. The recent resurgence of right-wing and fundamentalist leaders and policy across the globe has put increasing pressure on the practical potential of cosmopolitan theory, and scholars of colonial America have offered trenchant reminders that the way the United States understands itself in relation to those outside its imagined national space can be described as a long history of contests shaped in complex and mutual ways by Indigenous, hemispheric, and transcontinental contexts.[9]

The debate over critical cosmopolitanism shares logics with the ways the dissenting groups that first settled New England thought about themselves. In what follows, I look in two directions at once to interrogate cosmopolitanism as a way of talking about the past and imagining the future. Typology was a way of understanding the Bible for many seventeenth-century Christians. Assuming that God had placed prefigurations of the New Testament Christ in the Old Testament, it linked the two through a logic that was metaphorical, rather than causal or successive, as a means of countering the contradictions between those two sets of texts. Here typology functions as a methodological model, one that does not rely on a continuous causal narrative. The appeal of cosmopolitanism, after all, does not merely rest in how, by providing an analytical lens, it can reveal things about the past; it is also one of the supposed virtues of the academy and its denizens. The academy's entanglement with cosmopolitanism as a culture-bridging stance, method, and attachment can obscure the ways in which it is also both authority generating and bound to ideas about what history telling can do in the world. Exceptionalism can work just as powerfully in methodology as it does in narrative.

Although any number of religious groups might be examined to make this argument, including the nonconformists' nemeses, the Jesuits and the Quakers, New England's people of God are particularly suggestive. The notion persists both in the popular imagination and in scholarly writing that the Puritans were in some way set apart from the world.

Whether thought of as God's chosen people or provincials, their social self-differentiation and geographic isolation are considered to have produced influential, if sometimes irrational, departures from European ways. Yet if the dissenting settlers of New England were in fact deeply woven into international currents of thought, theology, and economics, then we are left with a question. How could such a cosmopolitan community have implemented violent suppression of dissent within its bounds and grindingly dispossessed Native Americans beyond them, all while operating under notions of openness and interconnectedness? It was perhaps cosmopolitanism itself that enabled that violence; cosmopolitanism, no less than other means of identification such as nationalism, has a dark side. That should give us pause when we consider cosmopolitanism's potential as a logic of postnational representative political formation, and what it means to summon it as a way of describing colonial-era communities, whether settler or Native. In the space of that pause might enter an appreciation for manners of extralocal thinking that are nonextractive, that respect the loss of territory and of history that have attended travel and settlement, and that confess that we are, to paraphrase Joy Harjo, visitors to contested histories of relation in all places touched by colonialism.[10]

To Be Citizens of the World

Beginning in the early 1990s, cultural critics began to grapple with the strengths and limitations of cosmopolitanism as an approach to political theory that could think past the nation-state as a form. The discussion was fueled by broad conversations about globalization, particularly in the wake of the end of the Cold War. Often in this debate it is unclear by what precise means cosmopolitanism could be effective. Sometimes the vision is idealistic: cosmopolitanism is an ideal of universal citizenship, from which a political order beyond the power of any individual state is to be built and to which any individual might appeal for protection. Other times it is a form of subjectivity or affect, what Rob Wilson calls an "aesthetic of openness toward others."[11] Sometimes it seems merely to be an analytical skill; at still other times, it comprises some combination of all of these orientations and talents. Perhaps as a result of this ambiguity, some scholars worry that the cosmopolitanism advocated by academics is, particularly when cast as a subject-forming project, merely an adaptation to new regimes of economic exploitation: the norms of highly mobile labor and flexible capital accumulation. If we all adopt an open attitude toward other people and places, after all, won't we be less attached to any particular place or people, as well as more accepting of a norm in which employment is highly unstable with respect to place and demographics?

Two responses to such concerns are perennially summoned: a notion of cosmopolitanism as a model for a democratic world order and a competing understanding of "discrepant cosmopolitanisms" emphasizing the local.[12] The idea of "cosmopolitan democracy" underwrites a range of influential scholarship on cosmopolitanism. This notion dates back in its particulars to the seventeenth-century emergence of the law of nations and in its inspiration via classical Greece. Martha Nussbaum has influentially argued for a "national unity in devotion to worthy moral ideals of justice and equality," the enabling condition of which is a democratic concept of civic belonging. Finding the U.S. educational system not up to the task of promoting such a concept, she proposed a Stoic cosmopolitanism as the foundation for a new public pedagogy. Nussbaum's essay was a response to statements by Richard Rorty and Sheldon Hackney that called for a "'national conversation' to discuss American identity" in the midst of the culture wars of the 1990s.[13] Rorty and Hackney make arguments that are familiar to students of early New England's community rituals, invoking a kind of polity-wide mental "chewing the cud," an intellectual day of atonement, as the paradigm for pushing nationalism into a more ethical incarnation. Nussbaum's criticism of the narrow-mindedness of such an approach nonetheless implicitly posits democracy as a universal governmental ideal.[14]

How would representation work in a putatively global democracy? Chantal Mouffe anatomizes the difficulty with post- or extranational governance schemas:

> We should . . . be aware that without a demos to which they belong . . . , cosmopolitan citizen pilgrims would in fact have lost the possibility of exercising their democratic rights of law-making. They

would be left, at best, with their liberal rights of appealing to transnational courts to defend their individual rights when these have been violated. In all probability, such a cosmopolitan democracy, if it were ever to be realized, would be no more than an empty name disguising the actual disappearance of democratic forms of government.[15]

Liberal democracy, it is claimed, requires boundaries, so cosmopolitanism may only safely refer to the establishment of an awareness of connectedness or contingency at the heart of any nationalized mentality. "National consciousness," Frantz Fanon notes, "*which is not nationalism,* is the only thing that will give us an international dimension."[16]

Other scholars have imagined a cosmopolitanism functioning at the level of the local. James Clifford's influential formulation of discrepant cosmopolitanisms argues that one need not identify one's self under a universalist categorization of the human. Clifford relocates human affiliation within those forms of society, local or regional, that provide individuals or groups with strong political commitments. Such distributed and potentially incompatible forms of affiliation would require different mechanisms of politics than, say, representational democracy to come into dialogue with each other. Pheng Cheah and Bruce Robbins label as "cosmopolitics" the attempts to formulate a responsible representative or negotiative schema that could bring such discrepant systems of belonging into order. This use of cosmopolitanism seems most promising ethically and theoretically, yet it is perhaps the least likely to produce material changes in governance.[17] The small number of arguments that synthesize these two approaches, making as their "local" or discrepant gesture a criticism of the academy's position in this debate, often ultimately advocates a tentative, abstract model of global democracy.

The means by which cosmopolitanism, whatever its configuration, could be achieved or implemented are almost never specified in any of these approaches. The many frustrated efforts of the United Nations and the resurgence of xenophobic totalitarianism, underwritten by a rhetoric of salvation, suggest the limited effects the debate has had on its objects. Yet conversations about cosmopolitanism have sustained a belief that humanistic, comparativistic education and experience can at least produce individuals who are less susceptible to the appeals of xenophobia and violent patriotism. One of the key figures in this belief is the exile. The experience of exile and its effect on how one thinks about the world are a centerpiece of one theoretical conversation about how critical subjectivity is formed. It is here that a brief return to the ways in which the English settlers of New England addressed the real-world means of implementing their particular cosmologic visions can be helpful in reflecting on our attachment today to cosmopolitanism as an ideal, and to the idea of the scholar as a kind of exile.

Puritans in "Native" Spaces

In a poetic meditation on his own death, William Bradford describes the terms by which godly church members must find their path:

> *From my years young in dayes of Youth,*
> *God did make known to me his Truth,*
> *And call'd me from my Native place*
> *For to enjoy the Means of Grace.*
> *In* Wilderness *he did me guide,*
> *And in* strange Lands *for me provide.*
> *In* Fears *and* Wants, *through* Weal *and* Woe,
> *As* Pilgrim *passed I to and fro.*[18]

The trope of the wanderer or pilgrim, invoked both by separatists like Bradford and by nonseparating Puritan leaders, draws biblical resonance from descriptions of God's covenant with the Jews such as that in Exodus 6:4: "I made my couenant with them to giue them ye land of Canaan, the land of their pilgrimage, wherein they were strangers."[19] The Plymouth settlers in particular saw their emigration as a do-or-die venture—a venture that Bradford's poem pictures less in terms of a material fear than as a spiritually mortal decision. To leave a place one feels to be one's own is the condition of beginning one's access to "the Means of Grace." The poem celebrates the tension between mobility and groundedness, making the status of "pilgrim"—rootless, in transit—into a morally ideal mode of existence, producing as it does the tension between "weal and woe" prescribed for those who would be godly.

Crucially, Bradford chooses a simile—"*As* Pilgrim"—to express his relationship to the model of mobility he proposes and to distinguish his rootlessness from ritual religious travel to sacred sites or icons. Avoiding metaphor removes an identifiable "proper," concrete meaning through which to imagine the relationship of the subject of the poem to a landscape or nation. It is not merely the "Native place" that is thus deprecated but "strange Lands" as well. Indeed, all "Lands," figured here as state entities (unlike the uncivilized spaces of "Wilderness") remain ever foreign. Bradford's etherealization of the notion of locality exemplifies one of the many modes of imagining the extralocal—the relationships among the global, the metaphysical, the local, and the material—advocated by New England's leaders.[20]

Even those with fringe theological orientations insisted on the interchangeability or enduringly metaphorical status of places. Roger Williams, who was exiled from both Massachusetts Bay and Plymouth Plantation, depicted his rootlessness time and again to suggest parallels to Paul and the struggles of the early church. Williams invokes his traveling from place to place, living in proximity to barbarians and heathens, and surviving (by God's grace) to tell the tale to testify to his spiritual authority. "*I know what it is to* Study, *to* Preach, *to be an* Elder, *to be applauded*," he claims in the preface to one tract, "*and yet also what it is also to tug at the* Oar, *to dig with the* Spade, *and* Plow, *and to labour and travel day and night amongst* English, *amongst* Barbarians!"[21] Such exile had both spiritual and political implications. No nation could, for Williams, legitimately represent itself as Christian. Indeed, Williams's *Key into the Language of America* (1643) famously indicted Englishness by comparison with Narragansett social practices, urging readers to seek membership in the body of Christ's regenerate people rather than relying on national or ethnic membership to supply spiritual foundations—and, by extension, to justify taking land away from another nation.

Exile was one of many domains in which extralocal thinking was crucial. Puritan leaders such as Cotton Mather, influenced by treaty making under the newly international "law of nations" philosophy, reworked basic components of their faith, such as the covenant and the millennium, in the late seventeenth century. The understandings of these components became dependent on a kind of global comparativism and a sense of the availability of all humans to join the Christian universe of souls. From a narrow focus on whether or not Jews were converting to Christianity—one of the predicted signs heralding the millennium—Mather and other Puritan writers expanded to take in evidence from the Ottoman Turks, Catholic political thinkers, and globally minded legal theorists.[22] Just as the sermon "A Modell of Christian Charity" had asked its hearers to imagine themselves with a world audience—warning that their failure to model successful Christian colonization would be "a story and a by-word through the world"—so inversely did the globe become increasingly interesting as evidence of God's attention.[23]

These cosmopolitanisms were all limited in metaphorical and material ways. First, they were constrained by a particularly Christian kind of universalism: the cosmopolis of the Puritan mind was specifically filled with the godly, and conversion was the primary requirement for peaceful coexistence with other peoples. The distinctions made between Christians and non-Christians in "A Modell of Christian Charity" starkly convey this fundamental difference, as the requirements for charity change depending on whether or not its object is in the fold. That prejudice was built out of a vision in which ultimately Christ's return would result in either the purging or conversion of non-Christians. "It will be an Addition unto the pleasure," Mather writes, "to see the *Harmony* which True, Right, Genuine PIETY will produce, in Persons that are in many *Sentiments* as well as *Regions,* distant from one another."[24] Second, the legal premises of treaty law, which spoke to the material distinctions among peoples by jurisdiction, may have been crucial in a few treaty cases with Indigenous groups. As Lisa Brooks has shown, however, it was not treaties but land deeds and deals that were the primary legal operator of Native dispossession in early New England, and that triggered King Philip's War as a result of Plymouth's expansion campaigns. Extralegal means of dispossession—performing missionary work, encouraging drunkenness, creating and exploiting Native indebtedness, and enforcing extended family separation through imprisonment and other means—were pivotal to effecting a program of territorial theft and cultural transformation that looks far from what today is thought of as cosmopolitan.

Bradford's poetic lament voices a tradition of Christian estrangement: "the notion," in Carrie Hyde's words, "that true Christians are pilgrims and strangers in this world and must renounce worldly desires and attainments to ensure their spiritual passage to a heavenly home."[25] The distant colonization of part of America by way of a corporation put self-consciously estranged groups like the Plymouth separatists neither into an unambiguously "English" political position with respect to the maintenance of cultural and political boundaries nor into a position entirely removed from the forms of imperial and commercial belonging that their appeals to the pilgrims-and-strangers model would deprecate. For just as the imagination of Christian nationalism emerged out of the adaptations of a model of heavenly citizenship—allowing Christians to identify "the progress and development of the government with the realization of God's kingdom on earth" despite clear biblical counterindications—so too were the strangers in the wilderness able to co-opt the imaginary space of cosmopolitanism as a distinctly Christian orientation to a shifting geopolitics, despite the seeming contradictions of their policies toward Indigenous people, Quakers, and Catholics.[26] In short, it is not just the material cosmopolitanism of the Puritans that ought to give us pause as we consider the relationship between early settlement and today, but also the imaginary one—call it the cosmopuritanism—that did not sidestep the model of engagement with other nations as equals, but rather replaced it.

Nonconformist leaders appealed to potential church members and justified the parameters of membership in the polity by linking afterworld or metaphysical spatiality to geopolitical spatiality. What these English colonists were building was necessarily as much an ex-tablishment (an imagination of how to be in relationship to the globe) as an es-tablishment (an architecture of an internal self that related to a local community of saints). Envisaging a church member as mobile within a space both material and figurative was accomplished by creating and encouraging tensions between a set of cultural theories and a real geography of church participation (including religious and vernacular architecture and the landscape of New England) particular to the historical moment.[27] Not an ideology and not quite a conspiracy, American nonconformist cosmopolitanism featured the interplay of a range of senses of space, from belonging within the Protestant international body to locally peculiar jurisdictional concepts, synchronizing and unsynchronizing as they emerged in sermons, essays, rumors, warfare, and the allocation of real property.[28]

American nonconformist ideas about global belonging competed for persuasiveness within a much larger social ferment over geopolitical boundaries and individual mobility. Debaters of cosmopolitanism customarily begin by observing that the "first global design of the modern world was Christianity," a project that "preceded the civilizing mission, the intent to civilize the world under the model of the modern European nation-states."[29] This overstates the degree to which what we would call secular cosmopolitanism can be extricated from religious conceptions.[30] Cosmopolitanism was controversial in the English Renaissance. Dynamics of rank and class shaped these debates, but so did suspicions about international political and religious plots against the sovereignty of England and the Protestant cause. Transregional travel, economic relations, and military associations were common, including Queen Elizabeth's progresses through the Low Countries and the migrations of radical religious believers.

Those two cases equally exemplify the distrust of internationalism that characterized the late sixteenth and early seventeenth centuries. For Elizabeth, extranational aristocratic affiliations (even to the point of rebellion) made it difficult to control the dukes of Leicester and Essex, suggesting the benefits of national thinking. Anglicans and dissenters alike shared suspicions about Catholic plots not just to undermine England's power but also to take over the world. Roger Ascham's 1570 pedagogical manual *The School-master* was virulently isolationist, associating foreign travel and instruction with the undermining of English spiritual purity. Another writer "declared 'Rome to be hell itself,'... home to Jesuit-run seminaries from which issued a steady stream of 'Jesuited' Englishmen, heading home to propagate their faith." Travel—even talking or writing about travel—could be polluting.[31]

Yet by the end of the century, a change was underway. A cosmopolitanism less subject to biblical regulation was on the rise. Around the time that members of the Leiden separatist congregation made their move to America, vast travel itineraries on the scale of those in the old fantastic voyages literary genre were becoming a literal possibility. Those in elite circles, at least, could make such journeys to distant countries, and they became part of the machinery of social dominance.[32] Books like Thomas Nashe's *Unfortunate Traveller* (1594) and Thomas Coryate's *Crudities* (1611) parodied attitudes like Ascham's. The potentially corrupting content of these narratives was still a concern: Ralph Bauer observes that in England, "the cultural anxiety about the need to 'police' empirical travel accounts in an expanding world is manifest in a proliferation of manuals aimed at prescribing, formalizing, and regularizing the content and style of travel histories" during this period.[33] These books had an effect on actual travel. As an apprentice in London, eventual Pilgrim leader Edward Winslow likely printed *An Itinerary Written by Fines Morrison, Gent.*, an early travel narrative. Not long after his shop printed the book, Winslow departed on a tour of Europe—one that ended in his conversion from Anglicanism not to Catholicism, as antitravel writers had warned, but to separatist Protestantism in the Low Countries.

The courtly rendition of cosmopolitanism ran parallel to the Puritan logic of temporal homelessness. Unlike Bradford's poem, narratives that valorized foreign travel often did so expressly in the name of England. Thomas Palmer offered *An Essay of the Meanes How to Make Our Trauailes, into Forraine Countries, the More Profitable and Honourable* (1606) to correct "the manifould errors and misprisions, that the greater sort of such as trauaile into forraine Countries, haue theretofore committed." His book offers a rubric for ensuring that English travelers' accounts work "for the good of this kingdom wherein they liue so happily" in "better seruice to his Maiestie." Such travelers must ask themselves if by their travel "they will benefit their Countrie, or themselues."[34] For Palmer, nationalism is the goal of properly conducted and recounted travel.

Palmer's principal categorical distinction in *An Essay* was between voluntary and involuntary travelers, a categorization that still shapes the cosmopolitanism debate today. The Scrooby congregation—which emigrated to Leiden, and some members of which would make up the Plymouth venture—fell between these categories. Separatists involved themselves in an international reform movement even before those who made up much of the Plymouth settlement moved to Leiden. When they left the Low Countries, it was not simply because they thought it was the moment to establish themselves as a discrete, reasonably self-sufficient community. It was also in part because they feared Spanish invasion with the expiration of the Dutch treaty with Spain. When they left, neither material nor intellectual isolation resulted. A print marketplace, economic arrangements with New and Old World entities, sustained familial immigration—strong and sophisticated ties like these with the larger world remained.[35]

The particular uses of cosmopolitanism by early New Englanders were conditioned by their involvement in the socioeconomic and intellectual environment of the Low Countries and the reach of its publishing. The Low Countries were a hot spot for the rapid circulation and intense discussion of ideas at a time when many places in Europe offered little access to texts in languages beyond Latin and local vernaculars.[36] The separatists who settled Plymouth, by a coincidence of their cosmology and their movement from England to the renowned university town of Leiden, had been involved in international intellectual currents. The 1607 edition of *The Confession of Faith of Certayn English People, Living in Exile, in the Low Countreyes,* for example, addresses itself to "the reverend and learned men, Students of holy Scripture, in the Christian Vniversities, of Leyden in Holland, or Sanct-andrewes in Scotland, of Heidelberg, Geneva, and other the like famous schooles of learning in the Low countreys. Scotland, Germany, & France."[37] The purpose of claiming this audience for the profession is

> to have the truth through your help more defended & furder spread abroad . . . partly also moved with love of our native countrey, and of these wherein now we live and others else where; wishing that al may walk with a right foot to the truth of [t]he Gospel, & praying daily vnto God, that the great work of restoring religion . . . by our Gracious Soveraigne and the other Princes of these countreyes & ages . . . he would fully accomplish, to the glorie of his name & eternal salvation in Christ of his elect in al places of the earth.[38]

Described here is a progression through concentric geopolitical scales of potential effect to an ultimately cosmopolitical belonging: from congregation, to land of birth, to foreign nations, to the ethereal body of Christ "in al places."

"So It Is Lawful Now to Take a Land"

While offering a rich metaphorics of salvation, New England's church leaders at the same time tied congregations to the aural space of their words and the zones of mobility that gave access to them. "Although the 'appointed place' of the Puritans seems to be the entire world," Ann Kibbey emphasizes, "in actuality the colonists are limited to the space the Puritan church actually occupies. In refusing the limitations of the concept of sacred place, and by locating the source of spiritual power and truth in the words of ecclesiastical authority instead, the Puritan is bound to the words of the preacher."[39] Such a binding had implications difficult to imagine in the present day. For many New England Congregationalists, the full civic rights of property ownership, for example, were attainable only through the pursuit of grace. As Kibbey points out in the case of John Cotton's Revelation sermons, it is "conversion, and therefore obedience to the minister's rhetoric, that bestows the rights of property."[40] If one lived in, say, the Massachusetts Bay colony, such conversion had to be proved in an individual performance that took the form of a peripatetic spiritual narrative ending with submission upon witnessing God's saving glory. The performance happened in a material space, the church, the occupation of which was structured by codes of hierarchical social organization that made it a proper place within which to tell these radically equalizing stories of grace before a judgmental ministry. Immanent grace was a solution to the problem of defining membership, and a key ingredient in the imagination of social and real spaces.

How did Puritan leaders deliver such a complicated spatial appeal? Many sermons, like Samuel Danforth's famous one of 1670 proclaiming his listeners to be on an "errand into the wilderness" to bring the true church to earth, forged a temporality out of spatial ingredients. Listeners yearning for the reappearance of Christ on earth and hoping to find themselves among the regenerate were offered a future-oriented, even apocalyptic understanding of their place in history. Such sermons also functioned in local, political ways to shape the order of New England space through a sustained appeal to the nonlocal. Leaders appealed to believers through other genres as well. Robert Cushman's "Reasons and Considerations Touching the Lawfulness of Removing out of England into the Parts of America," a 1622 settlement essay by one of the Leiden separatists, exemplifies how the tension between disembodied, distant places and local understandings of the materiality of space was used by religious leaders.

Cushman's essay offers a justification for the physical takeover of American geography from its Indigenous denizens. The essay directs itself beyond those who "[affect] their home-borne countrey so vehemently" toward those who harbor religious reservations about emigration and colonization.[41] Cushman insists that God's call to the Jews in the Bible to travel "from citie to citie," together with the allocation of certain lands as "appropriated vnto a holy people," is no longer in effect as a literal justification for migration and expropriation. The idea of a territorial sovereignty based on divine will is defunct in the wake of Jesus's advent, and consequently, "we are all in all places strangers and Pilgrims."[42] Cushman, like other English writers of his time, regards the conversion of Native Americans as a rationale for settlement, but his argument implies that it is less by missionizing than by creating a shared living space that Natives will come to the true church. His claim for how settlers would legally justify their jurisdiction rests on a now-familiar shell game. Massasoit (or Ousemaquin), leader of the Wampanoags, whom Cushman says is "the Imperial Gouernor" of the territory, would guarantee the homogeneity of consent of his territory, "whose circuits in likelihood are larger then *England* and *Scotland*." The paradox is that although the topographical circuit coheres because of an implied communications chain, one linking "Emperour" to Native subject, yet it is not a circuit: "It being then first a vast and emptie *Chaos*."[43]

Ultimately Cushman's case for territorial expropriation depends on abstracting biblical knowledge analogically, rather than offering either a typological or literal justification from Scripture. "As the ancient patriarchs therefore removed from straiter places into more roomy," Cushman argues, "where the Land lay idle and waste, and none vsed it, though there dwelt inhabitants by them . . . so it is lawfull now to take a land which none vseth, and make vse of it."[44] Already, America belongs to the dissenting religious settlers who choose to work its land. Yet for Cushman the movement is not into an uninhabited, chaotic wilderness. It is rather a migration into a zone where usufruct rights (which during this period were codified in the notion of *vacuum domicilium*) have decayed, but whose population represents an opportunity for the wise-walking godly to effect religious conversion. It is not separation and isolation but convergence, the possibility of performing an infectious godliness, that combines with a legal claim to justify travel and colonization.

Like other leaders, Cushman and Danforth made space one of their explicit subjects. They did so in the interests of preserving dependence on ministerial authority and of expanding New England's economic and political spheres, whose geopolitical well-being was imagined in cosmologic terms. Cushman's essay fused spiritual rationales with physical reasons for separation. The expansionist implications of the metaphor of the spatialized body of Christ manifested themselves in what has been called the declension debate. New England's colonial leaders argued that settlers should remain in close proximity to one another, sometimes even passing laws to limit movement away from the meetinghouse. Such an argument conflicted with the geographically centrifugal logic that tied virtue to expansion in promotional literature like Cushman's. In both cases, however, an etherealization of local history and residents' agency, setting them in a biblical-historical scheme, worked to maintain situated hierarchies of English settler authority.[45] Accompanying each cosmopolitan vision was a local gain.

The geopolitical situation of the settlement complicated appeals to authority. Congregationalist leaders were part of a population at once peripheral in an imperial, mercantilist economic system and locally dominant in efforts to eliminate or reterritorialize Indigenous political entities.[46] Of course, Indigenous American communities had their own powerful notions of how to relate to the extralocal. Those ideas and protocols, rooted in regional intertribal relations and long-distance travel and trade, Jace Weaver has argued, enabled a thoroughgoing transformation of the Atlantic world in the wake of encounter and colonization. "Native resources, ideas, and peoples themselves," Weaver reminds us, "traveled the Atlantic with regularity and became among the most basic defining components of Atlantic cultural exchange." American wealth revitalized Europe; Indigenous technologies and agricultural products transformed the world's senses and sensibilities; Indigenous alliances were not just integral to European political transformations but were also their very medium for centuries in the colonies; and Indigenous languages, mores, arts, and cosmologies forever altered the course of European sciences, philosophy, and religion.[47] Tisquantam's appearance, speaking English to the Pilgrims on their arrival, may have seemed providential to the newcomers, but his multilingualism and worldly hospitality were no miracle. The Algonquians of southeastern New England were among the most crucial of Weaver's "defining components" of exchange in the seventeenth century, possessing time-tested long-distance trade circuits and elaborate protocols for interacting with outsiders, in addition to a range of cosmologic beliefs premised on kinship responsibilities, the redistribution of resources, and the maintenance of a deep connection between landscape and history.[48]

The Pequot War of 1637—the first large-scale conflict in New England between Natives and settlers—suggests how some New England colonies borrowed from Native systems of linking communities together even as they displaced Indigenous control. In the early seventeenth century, the Pequots were the center of a large tributary domain that included the Mohegans, the Western Niantics, and other communities along the Connecticut and Mystic rivers. In the mid-1630s, English traders and settlers moved into this domain, where the Dutch had already begun to make inroads. Two Englishmen and one Pequot man were murdered in the process, straining relations on all sides. As Pequot tribal politics roiled in response, rumors began to spread of attacks coming from all parties. Connecticut and Massachusetts Bay demanded of the Pequots not just compensation for the murders but also political subjugation—a position that quickly led to violence.

The complete destruction of the palisaded village at Mystic and the killing of hundreds of children, women, and elders—as well as the accompanying English celebrations of these deaths as evidence of God's favor—have hitherto been explained in two ways. Either these events are seen as logical extensions of European war practices or, more often, they are a product of an "othering" of the Native in which Puritans measured their "civility" in inverse proportion to and by violent domination of supposed Indian "savagery."[49] Other possibilities become visible when the conflict is understood in terms of international relations. As Lynn Ceci has observed, seventeenth-century Pequots occupied a key geographic zone for the production of wampum. Wampum—cowrie, whelk, and quahog shells handcrafted into beaded belts with complex designs—served more than an exchange function for Indigenous groups. It was simultaneously clothing, document, money, ritual object, and more; consequently, its production was controlled, and access to it was considered valuable. The Pequots and their tributary tribes controlled the most important shell-gathering and bead-production zones in this period, linking their trade networks into a broader set of markets through Dutch, English, and French trade in wampum and furs. The Pequots had been in the forefront of economic and political reconfigurations leading to a new, imperial world economy.[50] After their defeat, the English explicitly took control of the interface between Native wampum production (again, cosmologic as much as economic) and European trade networks, but without replacing wampum production.[51] Native understandings of extralocal relationships were put to work in conjunction with English Puritan cosmology to promote the interests of the Massachusetts Bay colony.

To this point, I have used concepts from the recent debate over cosmopolitanism to suggest the historically and culturally specific relations between a particular way of being in the world and the imagination of space that underwrote it. Calling attention to a cosmography's local situatedness pulls it out of its seemingly natural, often nationalistic, context. The anationality of American congregationalism is interesting to critics of nationalism today, but it is problematic as well. Infamous exclusions and violent removals—of the Pequots from Mystic, but also of Roger Williams, Thomas Morton, and Anne Hutchinson, among others—enabled the inward-looking effects of the Puritan production of space on land allocation and policy. At the same time, they forced the surrounding tribes into new extramural arrangements with each other, with settler empires, and with those empires' cosmographies. If this double-edged conception of relations with others was already an important part of what has been perceived as American particularity, then what light might such a use of it throw on cosmopolitanism as an academic conception or outlook?

Academic Pilgrims

Bradford's poetic description of early New Englanders' notion of the relationship between a subject and the globe resonates across time in an eerily familiar way. That one learns the "Truth" in one's "Native place," but must be "call'd" from thence in order to enjoy "the Means of Grace" is a formula that structures the critical imagination of what is known as exile theory. Homi Bhabha and Edward Said, among others, have argued that to be the best, most insightful critic of culture, one must be an exile, passing "to and fro" in "strange lands" (though rarely, apparently, in the wilderness). Exile theory sutures material spaces with critical powers in a way that ultimately evacuates places of particularities that bind, keeping them forever "strange." Said tells us:

> Because the exile sees things both in terms of what has been left behind and what is actual here and now, there is a double perspective that never sees things in isolation. Every scene or situation in the new country necessarily draws on its counterpart in the old country. Intellectually this means that an idea or experience is always counterposed with another, therefore making them both appear in a sometimes new and unpredictable light: from that juxtaposition one gets a better, perhaps even more universal idea of how to think.[52]

Here a promised, but not quite automatic, revelation is claimed to be brought on through the experience of a particular spatial configuration—a structure of reasoning that Mather and Cushman would have found familiar. The newly acute critical vision is a product of a physical dislocation and a necessarily resulting temporal juxtaposition that, as for the Puritan convert who has experienced grace, renders a different kind of history. Said makes explicit the particular means by which the "universal idea" might become apparent to individuals—or at least, to intellectuals: "The pattern that sets the course for the intellectual as outsider is best exemplified by the condition of exile, the state of never being fully adjusted, always feeling outside the chatty, familiar world inhabited by natives, so to speak, tending to avoid and even dislike the trappings of accommodation and national well-being. Exile for the intellectual in this metaphysical sense is restlessness, movement, constantly being unsettled, and unsettling others."[53] Thus, like the Puritan, the ideal (regenerate?) observer is one "who is always a traveler, a provisional guest, not a freeloader, conqueror, or raider." Better an unsettler than a settler, perhaps. But who, metaphorically and materially, are the "chatty," perhaps "familiar" natives doing the community-maintaining work to welcome, serially, this figure whom Said elsewhere refers to as "undomesticated"? Implied here is a division of intellectual labor based not so much on an experience of space but on a particular relationship to mobility: the idea that movement necessarily produces insight is dangled, but it obfuscates the resources, institutions, or simple luck necessary to producing that subjectivity in fact.

In a crucial and little-remarked-on passage at the beginning of a work that has shaped all early Americanist scholarship since, *The American Jeremiad,* Sacvan Bercovitch traces the intellectual origins of his insight into the form of the jeremiad as the product of just such an exilic experience:

> Indeed, what first attracted me to the study of the jeremiad was my astonishment, as a Canadian immigrant, at learning about the prophetic history of America. Not of North America, for the prophecies stopped short at the Canadian and Mexican borders, but of a country that, despite its arbitrary territorial limits, could read its destiny in its landscape, and a population that, despite its bewildering mixture of race and creed, could believe in something called an American mission, and could invest that patent fiction with all the emotional, spiritual, and intellectual appeal of a religious quest. I felt then like Sancho Panza in a land of Don Quixotes.[54]

This last line takes us back even to the Congregationalists' antagonist, Thomas Morton of Merrymount, who also made reference to Cervantes's fiction as he framed the separatists and Puritans as uncosmopolitan and irresponsibly coercive. Yet Bercovitch does not mention here that he is not just any Canadian immigrant; he is one whose parents named him after the anarchists Nicola Sacco and Bartolomeo Vanzetti. His experience of the shock of American nationalism's imagination of community no less than his methodological facility result as much from a radical upbringing and an uncharacteristically extensive, well-connected education as from the simple act of crossing national borders.

There is no denying the significance of Bhabha's critique of nationalism, or of Said's insistence on overturning "an uncritical alignment between intellectuals and institutions of power which reproduces the pattern of an earlier imperialist history."[55] Indeed, such visions inspire this book. Yet the figure of the exile as authority and cosmopolitanism as a universalist form of commitment are part of the pattern of an earlier imperialist history. Indigenous studies scholars have often identified the self-authorizing logic of cosmopolitan universalism as complicit with imperial projects despite the best intentions of the cosmopolites. George Tinker, Taiaiake Alfred, and Jodi Byrd, writing out of different fields and tribal backgrounds, have made such claims about missionaries, sovereignty negotiations, and Native debates about tribal citizenship.[56] In addition, postcolonialism, at least recently, has run a risk beyond embedding expertise in the exile. Even as it ingrains what Bhabha terms a dialogical cosmopolitanism in transnational methods of cultural study, it simultaneously describes some forms of cosmopolitanism as a necessity for the oppressed. "To survive," Bhabha says, some people "have to learn new moral idioms, strange habits of life, and vernacular ways of speaking and living."[57] Cosmopolitanism thus becomes woven into the social logics of its academic institutionalization by virtue of the scholar's ability simultaneously to identify (in academic publications) such things as "vernacular" or other cosmopolitanisms, to teach university students how to be cosmopolitan, and to embody that cosmopolitanism in one's person. The appeal of this fusion is grounded in the social politics of the profession: in the modern literary and academic sphere, critical cosmopolitanism is a positioning technology, a job skill; scholars and writers can loosen their physical spatial constraints by freeing their intellectual spatial constraints.[58]

Stephen Greenblatt once reported an uncomfortable social moment that shows how cosmopolitanism becomes sewn into the affective fabric of academic work. Sent to pick up Nadine Gordimer and Carlos Fuentes from the airport, Greenblatt is at first understandably giddy at the prospect of having two such well-known and fascinating authors as interlocutors. As the two writers talk in the back seat about mutual friends, shutting Greenblatt out of the conversation, his enthusiasm wanes. Still attentive, Greenblatt decides to intervene when Gordimer suggests, in an assessment of the U.S. president's cosmopolitanism, that Bill Clinton probably read William Faulkner at Oxford, while he was a Rhodes scholar:

> "I doubt that Faulkner was part of the Oxford curriculum," I said. "Clinton probably read it in Arkansas or perhaps at Georgetown." From the backseat there was a terrible silence...
>
> In the comical awkwardness of the remainder of the ride, I mused on why I had felt the urge to intervene. In part, of course, I was simply trying, at a stroke, to win what is called, in a different context, a social promotion.... My suggestion... was probably motivated less by a passion for scholarly accuracy than by an obscure sense that Faulkner was *ours,* not England's. In other words, I was giving expression to the gravitational tug of the old national model of literary history, a model that has, despite significant weakening in recent decades, retained considerable power. All it took was a drop in my class status to make me start waving the flag.[59]

It is the kind of moment in which many academics have participated. Although he frames his response in terms of nationalism, Greenblatt suggests the complex way in which such chauvinisms are relational. One might see this exchange as a contest of cosmopolitanisms: Greenblatt (no mean cosmopolite himself, as the perfecter of a globe-spanning New Historicism) wields the authority of the U.S. professor of English who knows both his president's regional roots and the history of the Oxford curriculum. As he suggests, at issue is class (though perhaps ethnicity and gender were also at work in that "terrible silence" from Gordimer and Fuentes). Between the academy and the literary marketplace, episodes like this are tense, but perhaps less is at stake than in their more common manifestations among university workers, or between scholars and the local communities with which they live. Cosmopolitanism inscribes itself between the anxiety of control over certain kinds of knowledge and the silences or the aggressions we utter in—if there is such a thing—casual conversation.

As Greenblatt's story suggests, alongside the jeremiad as part of the social ritual of consensus in public ceremonies is a cosmopuritanical ideal, part of the social ritual of consensus within the academy. It takes shape both in publications and in the material form of academic sociality: talks, department life, conferences, choices of where to live and whose dinner invitations to return, multilingual repartee. The rhetorical assertion that one cosmopolitanism is better than another, or is threatened by someone else's supposed parochialism, is no less a powerful tool in academic conversations than it is in state justifications of violence, restriction of mobility, and economic oppression. It is not less so now than it was when reservations and removal were first advocated for Native people. Puritan approaches to Indigenous North American worldviews lacked the syncretism of the Jesuits and the insistence on nonviolence of the Quakers. Yet precisely because the cosmologic dynamics were different, to think about the literatures of encounter involving those groups and others—the Iroquois, the Dutch on the Hudson River, or other English colonies—in terms of contests of cosmopolitanisms might contribute to making contemporary debates more thoughtful.[60]

Herman Melville is often thought of as among the most cosmopolitan of U.S. writers. Melville, however, left us a sharply ironic portrait of the cosmopolitan in the character by that name from his last published novel, *The Confidence-Man: His Masquerade.* Part of a wide-ranging condemnation of American credulity and chicanery whose ultimate target is the reader's affection for fiction itself, the cosmopolitan from the start seems too good to be true. He calls himself Frank; he does good things like criticizing "The Metaphysics of Indian-Hating"—the tale of Colonel Moredock, a spiritual inheritor of the sacred violent rage of the colonial army in the Pequot War. "If ever there was such a man as Moredock, he, in my way of thinking, was either misanthrope or nothing; and his misanthropy the more intense from being focused on one race of men," the cosmopolitan pronounces, after having praised "Massasoit, and Philip of Mount Hope, and Tecumseh, and Red-Jacket, and Logan—all heroes."[61] Melville's book, however, warns us, darkly, about the limits of this kind of vision. The human-loving cosmopolitan turns out, for instance, to be equal parts seraph and Satan in the novel's final scene, one of a series of supernatural incarnations of the confidence man. Melville's novel, by hinting that these incarnations may be either good or evil, depending on one's perspective, pivots on how badly we want to believe, on our acceptance of fiction as a palliative, even as a source of our worlds—a disillusionment forged by the ironic cosmopolitan for would-be cosmopolitans.

Consider, by contrast, "In Mystic," a poetic reflection on the Pequot War by U.S. poet laureate Joy Harjo, certainly a well-traveled writer and exemplar of cultural curiosity:

> I do not want to know this, but my gut knows the language
>   of bloodshed.
> Over six hundred were killed, to establish a home for God's
>   people, crowed the Puritan leaders in their Sunday
>   sermons.
> And then history was gone in a betrayal of smoke.
> There is still burning though we live in a democracy erected
>   over the burial ground.
> This was given to me to speak.[62]

This conflict of two ways of thinking about how to relate to others, this failure to let cosmopolitanism rule the day—these lay the groundwork for a tragic U.S. democracy in this poem. Still, the most regenerative step beyond Melville's cynicism about death and fiction might be the way the poem opens. Rather than assume the poet's lyrical privilege of imaginary tourism, Harjo, who is Mvskoke Creek, begins with a protocol of asking permission to enter not just this physical space, but the difficult history hosted and represented by it.

> My path is a cross of burning trees,
> Lit by crows carrying fire in their beaks.
> I ask the guardians of these lands for permission to enter.
> I am a visitor to this history.[63]

The logic of a nonconformist English settler's relation to the world beyond was elaborate, rich with imaginative figuration. Within the imaginary limits it helped to construct, it was a source of community and a comfort, but it was simultaneously part of a larger contest. Without a well-developed sense of their relationship to a larger world, both real and supernatural, the specific means English settlers used to dispossess Indigenous people and others—including witches, Quakers, and dissenters within—would not have functioned as they did. Theirs was, in the grand scheme of things, a sectarian universalism. Cosmopuritanism helped justify attacks on others in order to effect a distinctly transnational body of Christ. Harjo's sense of being "a visitor to this history," of making central that status as a guest in both time and space, prompts us to ask what attitude toward this history makes the most sense, if we really do dream of being able to live together justly, happily, and equitably. On the basis of their effects, perhaps we should think of early American Christian imaginations of the world in terms different than the cosmopolitan. Cosmopuritanism could serve as a revelatory example of cosmopolitanism's material dimensions in the imagination and in resulting social practice. It is a warning and a way of explaining how, for example, today's tyrants, who are profoundly world traveled, with vast international networks of friends, family, and economic interests, can so powerfully wield xenophobia, separating families and excluding refugees in clear violation of their stated Christian principles. The xenophobic citizens of the world today are not a contradiction in terms, and they are not unprecedented. Recognition of the other does not guarantee openness to the other; nor does it preclude the proselytizing, judgmental framework with which the Puritans and many other groups have regarded other religions and cultures over the centuries. Theirs was an openness designed to dispossess, a largemindedness designed to convert.

Recognition of the otherness of the past does not ensure openness to the contradictory lessons it might hold. Early American studies has been anchored in historicism for a long time. The lesson of cosmopuritanism, however, is darker than what we have been learning through historical relativism. Cosmopuritanism reminds us of cosmopolitanism's elastic, Janus-faced quality; it warns us not to try to perfect a definition of cosmopolitanism but continually to interrogate its role in creating authority. When we use seventeenth- or eighteenth-century definitions of the cosmopolis or cosmopolitanism, we can get closer to the mind-sets, goals, and capacities of the people of the time, and we can uncover hidden stories. We can also begin to think of the ways in which those definitions might need to be put alongside non-Western imaginations of external relations because they insufficiently describe the mind-sets, goals, and capacities of all peoples. It is difficult fully to set aside our dreams and valorizations of cosmopolitanism today, our sense of how openness to others is embodied in a world with international legal bodies, human rights, and global media. That which produces good in those dreams and valorizations, including the careful investigation of the historical past and the utterances of our ancestors, whispers to us the power and value of our feeling for openness.

2 Believing in Piety

Fus Harjo was not a good Creek;
The pious members of his clan
Declared his virtues all were weak.
—Alexander Posey, "Fus Harjo and Old Billy Hell"

The most faithful adherents of a clerical mythologizing long since abandoned by its creators and never wholly convincing to its intended victims seem to be on too many occasions the practicing historians of colonial America.
—Stephen Foster, *The Long Argument*

In his story "An Element of Piety," Kiowa writer N. Scott Momaday introduces us to his storyteller's dog, a young black lab named Cacique del Monte Chamiza. Beloved by the family and "good-natured in the extreme," the canine is taken to round out his beneficent character at the feast of St. Anthony, during which the pastor offers a blessing for all the parishioners' animals. Father Cuesta passes "among the faithful, so to speak, touching them with holy water and uttering the formula that would, in a sense, stand forever between them and the perils of paganism." All seems well—until shortly it appears that Cacique's temperament has changed for the worse: "Of late he has assumed a certain posture with respect to others of his kind. He has, I believe, conceived a holier-than-thou notion of himself. An element of piety has entered into his being. And like learning, a little piety is a dangerous thing." Although initially concerned, in the end, Momaday's narrator shrugs, suggesting that "perhaps Cacique has more spiritual change in his pocket than I have in mine. In any case," he concludes, "I am not the stuff of which martyrs are made."[1]

The humor and ambivalence of this story do not obscure its knock on piety. Momaday's writing is in general far from irreverent: the sacred is everywhere, and in some ways books like his *House Made of Dawn* are spiritual road maps in narrative forms. The story, with its touch of self-irony, refracts a long-standing and now well-known Native perspective on what Osage scholar George Tinker terms "missionary conquest." However well-meaning the work of some European missionaries with American Natives was, being saved from "the perils of paganism" usually went hand in hand with being dispossessed of land, sovereignty, and the lifeways that had sustained Indigenous communities for thousands of years. Momaday's storyteller's concluding line, refusing martyrdom, positions piety on the other side of a line marking the distinction of a healthy living-out of the sacred from something more sinister—something that turns good characters into bad attitudes. Momaday and Alexander Posey, the turn-of-the-century Creek author of this chapter's opening epigraph, are far from the only Native thinkers to have taken a stance on the term in this way.

If Indigenous writers have good reason for ironizing or deprecating piety, it is also true that they are part of a larger historical trend. A Google Ngrams search may not be the most scholarly of indicators, but even as a rough proxy for the public presence of "piety" or the "pious," it bolsters a commonsense impression that the word is being eschewed (Figure 1). To take one influential evangelical Christian example, you'll search in vain for the term in the "About" section of the Southern Baptist Convention (SBC) website. Indeed, no form of the word has been used in an SBC resolution since 1941.[2] "The historical trajectory" of the term "piety," as James Garrison describes it, "leads away from epic toward satire. . . . After Dryden the very notion of a pious hero typically signifies either irony or oxymoron."[3] The religious spirit may be on the rise these days, but the letter of "piety" is flagging. Its chances of going viral have never been so low.

Whatever its challenges in public circulation, piety has a central place in the academic study of colonial New England—and by extension in successive schools of thought about the origins of the United States and its purported exceptionalism. It is part of broad arguments, like Max

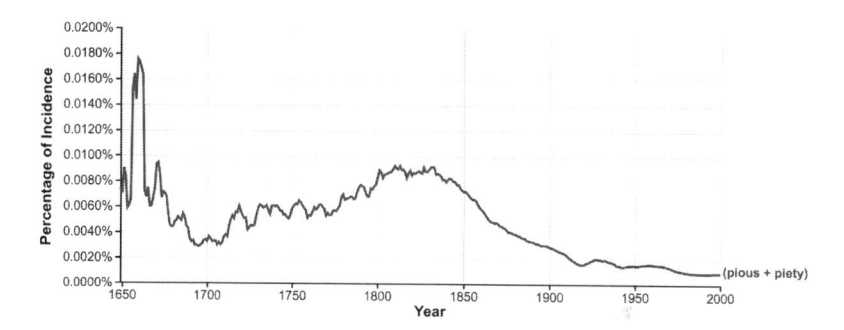

Figure 1. Google Books Ngram Viewer combined search for the words "piety" and "pious" from the years 1649 to 2000. Overall, the percentage appearance of these terms in millions of published books scanned by Google has been decreasing as time passes (http://books.google.com/ngrams).

Weber's, for explaining the deeply felt emotional drive of a certain kind of capitalism. It plays a role for those who argue that the New England Puritan way transformed into a secular republic with a patriotism deeply structured by Protestant piety. It is crucial for arguments about the transformations of religious feeling that ebbed and flowed through a series of spiritual revivals in Northeastern North America.[4] And as Michael Kauffman has observed, Puritanism offers powerful traction for religious studies or postsecular methodology. "The Puritans frequently, almost obsessively, asked themselves" questions like, "What counts as evidence of legitimate religiosity? Should religious belief be measured in terms of behaviors and practices (such as attending a particular church), or emotional responses to sermons, or interpretive protocols of Scripture, or representations of the soul in conversion testimonies?"[5] In short, while the rest of the academy is busy rediscovering religion, the study of belief in colonial New England has long been ahead of the postsecular curve. An analytics of religious belief was indispensable for any kind of cultural study of the settlement of the North American Northeast.[6]

In fact, it was the Puritans' underlying skepticism about knowledge—the conviction that it is never complete, that the purposes of the divine are inscrutable—that drew me to studying English nonconforming Protestants of this period. I certainly was not conventionally pious. Raised by a former Catholic whom the high school priests turned atheist and a former Episcopal-church-attending but never doctrinaire nature lover, my brother and I were encouraged by our parents to attend services with friends whenever we stayed overnight with them. When in Rome—though, this being deeply rural western Kentucky, such catholic attendance drew attention and the desire to convert from the myriad sectarians, evangelical and mainstream, we encountered as a consequence of our parents' policy. I never converted, and I learned quickly that letter, spirit, and action could diverge sharply among Christians of any sort. There were a few admirable folks who followed the model of Christ as well as anyone could, to be sure. But the racism, sexism, and economic exploitation characteristic of the South shaped the appeal, sensation, and practice of Christianity. When I think about how my own seeking has led me to study (among other religious spheres) nonconformist theology and history, it is the particularly porous quality of dissenting theology and practice in the context of American colonization that draws me, methodologically. Shaping this attraction was the experience of trying to find my place in a small town in which religious affiliation for people of all races was welded to social and economic power structures. New England seemed a particularly fertile example of basic and ancient questions. How could followers of Christ as communities commit the atrocities they did, both physical and rhetorical? Why did individual, conscience-bearing humans affiliate with such communities?

Can the meaning of "piety" on which those questions rest, and the series of debates within which they are nested, function sufficiently broadly to explore the dynamics of spiritual cultures under colonialism? What does it mean to speak of "Indigenous piety" in the early period? It might be argued that the most extensive religious transformation of the early settlement period in New England resulted not principally from the arrival of Christianity but from the death and displacement of a massive number of Indigenous people. There is disagreement about the effects of epidemics on the spirituality of those living in the eastern woodlands. Some scholars say Native ways persisted; others that they transformed superficially but stayed structurally intact; still others that they were changed so much by mortality and subsequent colonization that we cannot be sure they share anything deeply significant with the precontact period. We know that the objects associated with what anthropologists and archaeologists interpret to be Indigenous spiritual acts changed, at various times and to varying degrees, many times before contact.

Certainly the religious forms used by the Europeans who settled Northeastern North America changed, some say radically, within just the first century of their residence there. Some scholars insist that the changes had to do with a shifting global economy, a capitalist inclination powered in part by the very religious beliefs held by the settlers. For others, the internal dynamics of the New England way forced changes. Creole believers did not have the same motivation that the original settlers had; theological disagreements among dissenting factions mapped onto evolving social conflicts.[7] The Christianization of Native populations has until comparatively recently been an adjunct to the story of the shift toward worldliness and the decreasing authority of New England's ministers, rather than being understood as part of that shift's engine. This apparent trend toward worldliness and decreasing authority could be viewed as part of a longer, local spiritual history—that is, it is possible that rather than having their faces set toward secularism, with respect to religious feeling, settlers have been becoming more like Natives were becoming. Slightly differently put, what if a Western modernity was not the eschaton of scholarly analysis but instead a partly Native American future, not yet quite visible to us? One of the advantages of such a reframing is that it highlights stumbling blocks to thinking interculturally about religion in early colonial New England.

There is an extensive conceptual vocabulary for describing the effects of the encounter of convictions about the invisible world in the early colonial era. Conversion, syncretism, adaptation, traditionalism, mimicry, assimilation, resistance, appropriation, hybridity, and other terms have all been deployed in an attempt to envision a relationship between what could clearly be called Christian piety and whatever it was Indigenous people were thinking or doing. One of the difficulties with critical terminology in this matter is the complex relationship between piety and historicism. Every time we talk about conversion or forms of belief or identity, we are also talking about the present, the moment of an identity- or belief-bearing person's writing or reading a historiographic narrative. This dynamic is unavoidable—particularly so in times of fear-driven resistance to relativism, to mixed or multiple identities, or to the political category of "identity" altogether. In such times, it is helpful to interrogate the imagination of the past as well as the conceptual vocabularies through which are voiced descriptions of peoples' changes of belief or shifting cultural or political identifications. Rather than focusing on more obviously contested terms like those listed above or positing a new one, I treat the imaginative and historiographic functions of piety itself as a problematic. Piety can be appealing as a conceptual means for grounding respect, whether for another person's religious institution or for that person's deeply felt spiritual experiences, no matter how awful the political experience of a religion might be, under colonialism or other sorts of (often gendered) violence. Such a feeling, generous on its face, presents us with the paradox shared by, for example, the U.S. Constitution's insistence on respect for all religious beliefs. To respect religious belief entails dilemmas because sometimes service to a god demands killing other people, exerting control over their bodies, excluding them from civic ceremonies or employment, or refusing them common goods and services.

A full-fledged liberalism would want us to believe that a Native American could become fully a Christian in the seventeenth century, or a Christian a "white Indian"—and everything in between, however any of those terms might be defined.[8] One of the most subtle scholars of early colonial popular religion, Douglas Winiarski, praises the best intercultural studies of colonial religion because they

> expose the limits of missionary extirpation campaigns, unmask the subtle acts of rebellion through which interpreters translated Catholic dogma into a distinctly Native idiom, excavate the multicultural origins of indigenous saints and Christian communal rituals, and recover the nearly infinite variety of ways in which Native peoples throughout the Americas . . . adopted the religious beliefs and practices of European colonizers yet redeployed those same traditions in the service of thoroughly local and often anticolonial projects.[9]

Talking about religious belief even in this flexible way, however, seems to return us time and again to the same story: Christians (with a few exceptions) came and tried to convert; Natives (with a few exceptions) adapted or resisted. Yet power seems relentlessly to have flowed to the colonizers. As Lisa Brooks points out in her account of the fate of Christian Natives in King Philip's War, no demonstration of conversion or assimilation could reliably protect Indigenous people during that conflict. Piety, regarded as a problematic at the nexus of the past and the moment of historiographic inscription, offers one pathway for thinking about how and why scholars tend to look for a specific kind of end point, identity, or even stance resulting from an encounter with Christianity among Indigenous people, or vice versa. To follow that path requires thinking about how scholarship's seemingly common, agreed-on terms produce differential social effects in the present—everywhere from the grand narratives about civilization or colonization like Sir John Eliott's and Jared Diamond's to the demographics of attendance at scholarly conference panels on religion and power in the Americas.[10]

Although focused on one region and time, this chapter is designed less to make a historical argument than to incite a disciplinary and philological discussion. Among the terms that have tended to divide Native American and Puritan studies, "piety" limns a tension that is ultimately about conceptions of history, both in the academic disciplinary realm and more broadly between groups of people today. Epistemes built on oppositions long dogged the discussion of the mutual effects of European and Indigenous ways: oral and literature "cultures," "religion" and "spirituality," linear history and circular time, interiority and performance. More recently, as Indigenous outlooks have begun to influence the thinking of early Americanists, scholars have begun to imagine a "fluid spiritual world with few boundaries."[11] Each of these ways of thinking about human behavior is revelatory, telling us stories about sacred experience and social power that we might not otherwise have imagined.[12] They give us new perspectives on Indigenous views and ways, even as they disagree about what should serve as evidence or how we should read that evidence. These are not just descriptions, however. Metaphors of fluid identity, no less than epistemes based on opposites, were tools of colonial encounter and settlement. As precipitates of that historical process, they function today in ongoing attempts to contain Indigenous power or presence—as well as that of other "others" positioned as savage by settler patriarchy, including enslaved people, women, and the poor.

I am not arguing against close theological analysis or for decentering devotional practices as an object of study in the early colonial era. My discussion aims at the conditions, assumptions, and unanticipated effects of our wrangling about piety and, to a lesser extent, at provoking a richer methodological imagination for analysis of human relations with the invisible world under colonization. As Denholm Elliott's character puts it, masquerading as an inebriated priest in the film *Trading Places,* "I always say, religion is a fine thing—taken in moderation." I feel the same way about the secular, and about history. The pieties of the historian do not come down to just political or religious ones. I am less concerned with, say, an obsession with piety that yields an antipatriarchal narrative of Anne Hutchinson's trials at the expense of sociohistorical "fact" than with the more fundamental locating of such claims within a set of assumptions about historiographic authority that might alienate the readers who could benefit the most from hearing that argument.

A history of the term "piety" is the chapter's starting point, dramatizing how the concept exerts a centripetal historiographic force through its dependence on both historically specific and transhistorical dimensions. The chapter then turns to the latest generation of scholarship on religion in the early colonial period, which has increasingly taken up the question of how to tell the story of spiritual interculturality. This work shows the power of bringing the study of New English settler colonial piety into a reckoning with frameworks of Native cosmology that Western notions of religion have trouble engaging. In those frameworks, kinship, political considerations, and a complex fabric of Indigenous ideas about other-than-human forces play key analytical roles. By turning to the relations between the material and invisible realms of early colonial New England, the chapter then examines two objects and their environments that are points of conjunction for those worlds, and that also might provoke emergent ways of speaking about the past in the present. These two scenes of early colonial cohabitation offer a means of shifting our imagination of piety, and perhaps the vocabulary we use to approach it, unsettling piety in its function as a sectarian, or even "cultural," boundary marker and helping us see the consequences of the relationship between the history of piety and piety's historiography.

Piety and Historicism

Vine Deloria Jr.'s frequently reprinted and updated *God Is Red* has a chariness about piety—despite its profound spirituality—that prompts us to look deeper into the history of the term for guidance. In it, the terms "pious" and "piety" are associated with usually acerbic accounts of Western religious practice. The same, for both terms, is true of his influential book *Custer Died for Your Sins*.[13] Although he is sensitive to variations among American Indian religious practices, in *God Is Red,* Deloria ambitiously searches for differences between Western and American Indigenous religious foundations in order to teach a lesson about Western failings. His use of "piety" thus reinforces its identification of culture with a certain form of religious feeling—even in a book expressly designed to help bridge orientations toward the sacred. The suggestion here is that piety ill fits Native American notions of a sacred relationship among a person, a people, and the supernatural; or that it is too laden with the history of justifications of genocide and cultural conversion to function in a positive way today. This is worth pondering as scholars navigate the vocabularies for studying early America, notwithstanding the desire to use terms with sensitivity to their living meanings in their historical moments. It suggests that the difficulty with the term may be less a matter of identifying patterns of belief in the past than with the ways in which we situate, authorize, and write our scholarship.

Rooted in the Latin *pietas,* the word "piety" has a long, vexed history. The early modern period saw a split in the English meanings of the word "piety" into "piety" and "pity." The former came to have the connotations we associate with it today, both positive connotations about deep personal religious devotion and negative connotations in which that same sort of devotion becomes bigotry or uncritical worship of an unworthy object. Its function in describing personal spiritual experience has become significant in contradistinction to the way one imagines a relation to state or family. The term "pity" has largely retained its constellation of meanings related to compassion, derived from vernacular uses of the word "piety" (synonymous with the meaning of the Latin word *misericordia*) in various languages of Latin descent from the early Christian era through the sixteenth century.

In the classical tradition, exemplified by Virgil's depiction of Aeneas, *pietas* implies a tripartite devotion to the gods, to one's family, and to one's country. It describes an attitude or relation. It is tied to "an unmistakably Roman ideal of principled conquest," in Garrison's words, "that confers the blessings of order exemplified by the devotion of sons to fathers."[14] In Virgil, it is the occasion not for a formulaic set of actions but rather for depicting complex, tension-ridden decision making by Aeneas as he attempts to manage the different demands of kinship, the civic, and the divine. *Pietas* thus had meanings across domains that in the West increasingly became stratified after the seventeenth century. Puritan controversies over how government and church should interrelate under a commitment to God's rule may have kept alive, through the seventeenth century, the more complex notion of "piety" as a term to describe how people navigated duties both supernatural and earthly.[15] Others, however, including John Dryden, question the decline of the broader sense of the word "piety." "Piety alone," Dryden notes, "comprehends the whole Duty of Man towards the Gods; towards his Country, and towards his Relations."[16] Dryden offers this reminder in the preface to his translation of the *Aeneid* (1697), published the same year that Cotton Mather's *Pietas in Patriam* was first issued in London, a text deeply invested in bringing the notions of piety as service to God and piety as service to the state into relation.[17] Still, it seems that by the eighteenth century, as today, it was unusual to write of one's devotion to family or to the state as "pious."

It has been argued that piety's decline as a broad cultural ideal was a function of its slipping solely into the domain of personal religious transformations, an Augustinian subjection only to God: "For piety," writes Augustine, "is the true cult of the true God."[18] The pre-Christian colonial connotations of the term would seem to have disappeared with this transition. Yet it could be argued that colonization, as well as religion's axial role in it, throughout the sixteenth and seventeenth centuries was integral to both the specialization of the term and the decline in its ability to speak to a form of commitment that would bridge kinship, the civic, and the supernatural. Certainly some seventeenth- and eighteenth-century critics of the role of piety in colonialism implied that a more complex grappling with the relationship of personal to national commitments might result in at least a different sort of colonialism. Consider Leiden separatist pastor John Robinson's reaction to news of the Pilgrims' killing of Wituwamat and his Algonquian allies in 1622—"How happy a thing had it been," he writes, "if you had converted some, before you had killed any"—or the well-known passage from Swift's *Gulliver's Travels*:[19]

> Here commences a new Dominion acquired with a Title by Divine Right. Ships are sent with the first Opportunity: the Natives driven out or destroyed... a free License given to all Acts of Inhumanity and Lust.... And this execrable Crew of Butchers employed in so pious an Expedition, is a modern Colony sent to convert and civilize an idolatrous and barbarous People.[20]

Here the Black Legend resonates, to be sure, in English deprecation of Spanish colonial cruelty, but piety and plantation are nonetheless linked in a way that criticizes colonization across all imperial settings.

The imagination of affiliation offered by the term "piety" has thus long had implications for the establishment of cultural boundaries even as its precise meanings varied. One of the reasons for this may be that ever since at least Plato's dialogue *Euthyphro,* there has been a tendency to define "piety" in ways that transcend space and time, which can distract from the ways the term divides groups of people. For Perry Miller, avatar of American Puritan studies, piety exhibits itself in intricate ways, including through social frameworks, as "a recurrent spiritual answer to interrogations eternally posed by human existence." Yet its appearance is almost biologically encoded. "Puritanism was," Miller writes, "yet another manifestation of a piety to which some men are probably always inclined and which in certain conjunctions appeals irresistibly to large numbers of exceptionally vigorous spirits." This definition of the "exceptional" is not limited to America; indeed, is implicitly non-Western. Yet for Miller, the point of studying New England's piety is to describe a broader Western orientation toward the divine because he sees the American Puritans as "spokesmen for what we call the Renaissance."[21] This is a transatlantic intellectual history, with a touch of universalism in its definition of "piety," but it is about some people and not others. Walter Mignolo's "darker side of the Renaissance" is missing from Miller's formulation, and one wonders if Miller would have included New England's Indigenous people among his "some men."[22] Janice Knight has elucidated the multiple pieties within the mainstream American Puritan world, and Matthew Brown and Lisa Brooks have underscored the irony that the archive on which Miller's argument is built was in part printed by Natives and also in many cases directed at a Native audience. These arguments, however, still imply that understandings of cultural difference and of piety are interdependent. As Jordan Stein and Justine Murison put it, at times it "becomes difficult to imagine what 'religion' could mean, besides something like 'culture.'"[23]

According to the *Oxford English Dictionary,* piety's meanings in English have come to be "godliness," or, in Calvin's formulation, "fervent attachment to the service of God and to the duties and practices of religion." But compare this to the use of the term in Saba Mahmood's influential book *Politics of Piety,* a feminist analysis of Islam in contemporary North Africa; the Arabic equivalents of "piety," such as *taqwa,* involve fear no less than duty. Mahmood's analysis respects the particular instantiation of fear—both as outward display and internal feeling—that characterizes the women of the Egyptian mosque movement.[24] The Quran here is not the source of a timeless definition of "piety" but a plank for historically specific interpretations and behaviors, not unlike the popular piety explored by New England historians. That region's ethnohistorians have also argued that a set of broadly held beliefs about people's relation to the invisible world—there being little distinction between "natural" and "supernatural" matters—existed among Algonquians of the northeastern woodlands, and that Native popular or everyday practices coexisted with more formal rituals and enactments of particular communities' cosmologic commitments. If the ontologies of religious feeling may differ, so too may the disciplinary uses of the term "piety," which develop an analytical patina that might obscure alternative histories, or that simply make it hard for us to imagine another phenomenon as the axis of analyzing a time and place like early colonial New England.

Piety's historiographic entanglement also has to do with the way in which the term "piety" contained multivalent senses that put it at the nexus of sociopolitical disagreements in the Anglophone world. It is not that one can't figure out whether or not a given Puritan writer is using the word in one or another way that is historically accurate. Rather, it is difficult to describe how piety cannot function within a theological context alone, or the context of private worship or the conscience. The same goes for the connotations of piety that have to do with governance—that is, with civic piety. The Puritans made piety a matter of worship and conscience, but they disagreed with each other and with other Englishmen about how much its civic version was necessary. Roger Williams criticized the Massachusetts Bay settlers and their governors for putting too much emphasis on civic piety, rather than achieving a true separation from a state he regarded as still aligned with the Antichrist. Such disagreements signal the degree to which, when we talk about piety, even in the most radically conscience-oriented of cases such as Williams's, the word entails a context. In that context, the uses of the term or discussions of it as labels for a certain kind of activity, orientation, or emphasis on the part of a historical actor are necessarily tied to other formations, forcing us to take into account the resonances of piety beyond its ability to name a feeling or performance of affection for, or fear of, a deity.

Knowing how a term like "piety" has shifted in meaning over time introduces us to the problematic of its use in the historiographic imagination. Historicizing the term "piety," however, presents other unique difficulties, in part because by doing so, one risks raising readers' theological hackles or threatening their profoundly emotional senses of connection to a deity. To introduce one's own religious sensibility openly into a scholarly analysis seems to risk undermining the very historicity whose aura would ground a scholar's belief. That is as true in English as it is in history departments. "From Emerson and Matthew Arnold to Robert Scholes and Gerald Graff," Tracy Fessenden observes, "the story told of literary studies' emergence as a discipline is a supersessionary tale, in which religion cedes authority to forms of truth and suasion that no longer require its grounding."[25] Academic disciplinary authority and the authority to write about piety as other are mutually constitutive within the terms of secular modernity.

Whether it is a jeremiad against the sins of Puritan self-conception or an earnest investigation of the spiritual dynamics of their theology, the premise that we can either judge the people of God out of time or embrace the historical sympathy that they would ask us to impose on an analysis of their beliefs seems indefensible from the standpoint of the history of piety itself. The term has always implicitly dragged with it a series of contexts of power and judgment whose design is to hierarchize, separate, distinguish the "in" from the "out"—in short, to sort the world and make boundaries. This is not to say we haven't learned from the jeremiads or from the believers' accounts of the extraordinary self-manipulation and sense of uncertainty that the Puritans invented in order to instantiate their version of piety: manipulations of language, of law, of whole mental orientations, households, iconography, and so on. The tendency of those studies, however, has often been to exclude sociohistorical contexts in a way that furthers the depletion of context that Puritan piety itself was trying to manage. It is not as if the contents of Puritan piety are being reproduced or expressed in studies of the Puritans' beliefs. Rather, it is an attitude toward the relationship between the human and accounts of the human and what those things can produce in the way of the world that is the unacknowledged gift of an ancient regime of piety linked profoundly to the maintenance of social hierarchies. Our narratives are sometimes believing in piety when they claim to be studying it.

Pious Resistance

Departing from previous scholarship's focus on settler piety, students of early colonial North America during the past two decades have taken a range of approaches to centering Indigenous religious experience. Some of these approaches have been shaped by a desire to transform scholarly or popular preconceptions about Natives and Christianity, while others aim, explicitly or implicitly, at legal definitions of forms of belonging or performances of community that underpin the U.S. federal recognition process for American Indian tribes. A few of them are attentive to the contemporary spiritual landscape of the groups whose history they explore, adding a rich but potentially contentious historiographic texture. As for Posey's "pious members of his clan," for some traditionalists, what Scott Richard Lyons calls the "policing of traditional knowledge" involves gatekeeping the historical reputations of ancestors who were early adopters of non-Native religious ways.[26] Taken together, however, from the standpoint of the study of colonial New England, this body of work suggests a provocative new range of meanings for the term "piety."

In a collection of essays by influential scholars in this movement, *Native Americans, Christianity, and the Reshaping of the American Religious Landscape*, editors Joel Martin and Mark Nicholas situate their approach as informed by religious historians who focus on lived practice and popular religion as well as by Latin American historians interested in the relations between political movements and popular religion in Indigenous contexts. Such a strategy, they argue, "enables scholars of contact and colonialism to demonstrate how Native American individuals and communities could appropriate Christianity without necessarily agreeing with what missionaries and other professional Christians said about Christianity." This approach has been pivotal to telling stories long hidden, and it would be hard to find a better example than David Silverman's study of the Wampanoag of Martha's Vineyard and their complex relationship with Christianity, *Faith and Boundaries*.[27] Silverman uses the term "religious translation" to describe the spiritual transformations of Martha's Vineyard, borrowing from but in some ways setting aside the arsenal of terms precipitated from the previous few decades of anthropological and cultural studies, from assimilation through syncretism to interculturality. Religious translation in this context, Silverman argues, moved in two directions. First, the Mayhew family, the lords of Martha's Vineyard, used Wampanoag concepts to convey Christian ones to their converts. Second, Native listeners adopted and pushed back according to the needs of their community.

Silverman's analysis is sensitive to the ways in which Christian and Wampanoag traditional ways shared conceptual common ground.[28] In this approach, historical piety, understood either as a kind of internal code or way of judging a performance of faith, is tuned down as a factor both in the daily lives of New England's denizens and in the larger picture of supernatural beliefs or practices in history. Other studies keep that sort of piety more central but shift the center of value for studying religion in Indian Country. Rachel Wheeler's *To Live upon Hope: Mohicans and Missionaries in the Eighteenth-Century Northeast* thinks flexibly about the factors that deserve attention in considering the entry of missionaries to Mohican communities. Some Native groups, for example, understood themselves as intercultural brokers, and missionary work could be elegantly adapted to their purposes; others, even when members of related groups, found less value in missionary efforts supernaturally or politically, and pushed back. Wheeler argues that in some cases, "Moravian missionaries did not serve as agents of colonial power." Given this heterogeneity, the uptake of Christianity must be studied as both a political and a spiritual phenomenon. "The question is not simply what Mohicans hoped to gain by admitting missionaries to their villages," Wheeler insists, "but what Congregational and Moravian Christianity became as practiced by the Mohicans of Stockbridge and Shekomeko."[29]

Not infrequently, as we have seen in the case of Olaudah Equiano and the Miskito prince George, Christian proselytizers were Indigenous or African. In his study of Atlantic-world Native and Black missionaries, Edward Andrews shows that such representatives of the Christian faith were integral to missionary efforts across the British colonial world, both as symbols and as actual laborers in the spiritual field. Such efforts shaped and were shaped by arguments about the most effective ways to spread the gospel; about the theology of race and of missionizing; and about the relationship between religious and other forms of colonialism.[30] "This complexity," Andrews argues, "underscores the point that missionaries, especially native ones, cannot simply be lumped into the binary categories of compassionate martyr versus avaricious imperialist," echoing Wheeler's valorization of both church and secular interpretive frames. By implication, such an approach posits that present-day claims that agents of the faith were either complicit with Native dispossession or heroes of adaptive resistance are not just oversimplified but ahistorical.

For the most part, Andrews's book, like the others discussed here, upholds its commitment to noncategorization. In this, these scholars respond to Fessenden's reminder that a "particularly resilient trick of the secular sphere's emergence is to cast religion as *itself* otherworldly, atemporal, purely spiritual." These writers all unsettle the analytical tendency of previous scholarship to center settler struggles over religion, even as their work suggests the rich potential of such an approach if brought together with analyses of everyday settler religious feeling.[31] Douglas Winiarski has done just that, compellingly putting Native and settler lay convictions into the same frame of comparison.[32] Winiarski agrees that New England witnessed overlapping domains of religious belief, but he goes further to suggest that Natives, settlers, and African servants and enslaved people all took a kind of modular approach to piety. They maintained a "repertoire" of practices and rationales to deploy or not, at will, in their minds or in the world, rather than a set of codes to obey in public or catechistic vigilance to internalize. Crucial for Winiarski's argument, and indeed enabling all of those described above, is David Hall's notion of popular piety. "Popular religion," Hall writes, "encompassed an ideal of piety that people may have reverenced even when they did not wholly follow its prescriptions."[33] Constitutively inconsistent and interlaced with beliefs in the occult, fortune, or competing interpretations of Scripture, popular piety reconceives the study of religion as the description of a field of tensions. Winiarski tries to set aside cultural difference and colonizer–colonized status in his account. "Acknowledging the cross-pollination of Native American and European occult traditions," he concludes, "blurs beyond recognition the thin line segregating English religion from Indian superstition."[34]

What emerges across all of the work discussed here is a picture of supernatural relations as a patchwork of practices, specific beliefs, and modes of worship. In this outlook, piety is to some extent what piety does: it is pragmatic, often political, seldom orthodox. This analytical inclination, however, also raises questions. Some of these questions have to do with the relationship between individual and collective belief, and the structures of collective conviction in differently organized communities. How does the modular spirituality referred to as popular piety, with its hint of liberal-individualist thinking, relate to communal commitments to supernatural relations, such as thanksgiving feasts or fasts, mass public mourning, or public executions? Did those activities' collective dynamics parallel, overlap with, draw from, or open a path between settler modes of group feeling and those of Native people? If kinship influenced religious commitments but these too were crosscut by private appeals to Abbomocho or Satan, when does piety begin to register unmistakably? If "the majority of the Old Colony's Indian denizens inhabited the untidy cultural space between ... rapidly converging conceptual worlds," should accounts of historical agency focus on the untidy majority or on the piety inscribed by the original "conceptual worlds" still rigorously maintained by leaders in Native, African American, and settler colonial communities? What is an established religious tradition if these new descriptions of belief are true?

There is also the persistent question, inevitably political in the present, of cultural distinctiveness. It is not clear how deeply the blurring on which Winiarski insists runs into the analytical architecture of these studies. For Winiarski, beliefs are still held at a slight distance from each other: Native popular piety "closely mirrored" the English one; "language barriers and racial stereotypes ... promoted acts of religious exchange," but the imagining of exchange entails thinking of two previously existing, differentiable agencies.[35] Although Martin and Nicholas say that the essays in their collection move beyond "authenticity" or cultural reification, one gets a sense from time to time, even in essays by visionaries in the field, that cultural particularity has not so much been displaced by hybridity or practice-based appropriation as it has moved elsewhere. This is evidenced in, for example, Daniel Mandell's description of Massachusetts Natives' "distinctive regional subculture," or Joanna Brooks's identification of Northeastern Natives' "distinctive rituals."[36] Inside a shared resistance to describing cultural boundaries as fixed or clear (either at the historical moment under analysis or today), disagreements gestate about how to locate or describe particularity.

To an extent, the need to find that particularity is a basic analytical problem, because without a vocabulary of differences, it is difficult to make any kind of argument. That need is also an artifact of the analysts' different historiographic intentions and assumptions—about the process of secularization, about the historical quality of subjectivity, and about what historical scholarship on this topic and era might produce in the present, beyond new information from the archives. The point of clear agreement among most scholars in this field today is also the vanishing point of the broad-scale significance they claim. As Andrews phrases it, Native people "drew from Christianity to frame new identities, amass spiritual power, preserve their cultures, and protect their peoples during a period of unprecedented change. In doing so, they became pivotal players in Protestant missionary activity and cultural exchange in the early modern Atlantic world."[37] This guiding idea for a religious studies methodology can promote a more or less similar understanding of any given colonial religious situation, wherever it might be, with respect to the agency of the colonized. In other words, "resistance" or "co-optation" might become the new "authenticity"—which is to say, a new piety. Andrews's list constitutes the categories—not identity categories but rather categories of contemporary critical regard, or perhaps of activist relations to their social historical contexts—that function just as powerfully as any previous categories did to organize today's reception of these early colonial figures and groups. That isn't necessarily bad, but we should recognize how hard it is not to be pious in new ways, even as we complicate the notion of the uses of piety and theology in the colonial era or the past scholarly pieties through which they have been narrated. Such an approach, despite its healthy focus on Indigenous cosmologies, might forestall asking a larger question of the study of colonial religious history: what was Christianity becoming as a result of colonization? What was it as a result of sustained contact with others who, while having motives, did not necessarily regard those motives as godly, worldly, social, economic, and so on, but in different terms?

In offering various ways to imagine religion's relationship with group identity, a multilayered politics weaves the concerns of Native groups struggling for self-determination or survival into a larger, long-standing debate about culture and agency in the humanities. Ideas of collectivity are historically specific and evolving; the shifting definitions of "nation," "church," "tribe," and "race" have all been studied in depth, and each of those studies takes aim at what it regards as the shortcomings of applications of these terms in its time. The resonances of this historiographic condition extend beyond the limited frame of "getting the story right" from the standpoint of history. In the Native American case, tribe-to-U.S. sovereignty has often depended on an accounting of the external dimensions of tribal belonging, according to ideas about nations as being constituted by continuous existence. Such accounting is a legal convenience for the United States rather than a historically rigorous framework for judgment. Still, that standard for recognition has produced benefits for many tribes; further, recognizably Christian forms of belonging—the outward if not the inward forms of piety—have frequently been crucial to making the case for continuous tribal existence.

We stand in relation to the religious transformations of the past as both inheritors and others. Can the imagination of piety in New England expand to bridge human groups? Can it extend an invitation to Native American audiences today who are rejecting, reimagining, reviving, or creating new forms of what has gone by the name of piety? More is at stake here than the description of vernacular theology or an interrogation of the role of codes in the evidentiary regime by which piety was inculcated, asserted, and evaluated. Involved is how we imagine the relationship between feeling selves and the world—what we, informed by the sometimes repulsive historical specificities of previous pieties, might be able to sense as agency in a past world felt both as an heirloom and as a refraction through the archives.

Spiritual Parasites

Kevin McBride, an archaeologist and ethnohistorian, was working for the Mashantucket Pequot tribe on its reservation inside Connecticut when he found a ritual bundle in the burial site of a young Algonquian girl, probably Pequot. The bundle included a bear's left paw and a fragment of finely woven cloth containing a piece of a page of a small-format, Dutch-printed Bible, featuring part of the text of Psalm 98. The date of the burial is estimated at between 1660 and 1720. This object has attracted interdisciplinary attention. Hugh Amory, a book historian and bibliographer, emphasizes that the Bible from which the text fragment came was a "hand piety" object. Such books were personal copies whose format and structure aided the "religious socialization of readers" through habitual consultation of a sacred text and a performance of godly inclinations.[38] But could this child or her parents have read the Bible, much less accessed it with the kind of sophisticated referential system that Christians of the time and region did? Amory suggests that the Bible from which the fragment in the Pequot bundle was taken might have been a war prize rather than an anchor of Christian godliness.

Perhaps, however, it was given as a gift or token in, or stolen from, a household in which a Pequot enslaved person worked. Many such "servants" allocated to English settlers in the wake of the Pequot War of 1637 eventually ran away from their masters. A group of Pequots led by Robin Cassacinamon cohabited with John Winthrop Jr.'s settlers at Nameaug, a plantation Winthrop established in 1645 and that would come to be known as New London.[39] As for the use of an English-language Bible among Pequots (and setting aside the possibility of a fully English-language-literate Pequot, which some translators probably were), Amory suggests that "both cultures recognized its decorative, talismanic function," and that "it matters little whether we describe small-format Bibles as European medicine bundles, or this medicine bundle as an Indian Bible. The two are culturally congruent, in their respective cultures." Amory's assertion that there is "cultural congruency" to guide us implies isomorphic pieties, but can we be sure? This statement echoes familiar assertions about the universality of pious rituals in an assertion of boundaries—"respective cultures." We certainly have here what Nicholas Thomas calls "entangled objects," literally and analytically, but do we have entangled pieties?[40]

McBride disagrees about congruency even as he relies on an assertion of definite cultural boundaries structurally similar to Amory's. "The inclusion of the page in the bundle," McBride argues, "transforms the symbolic system of the printed word to another communicative system—that of the Pequot mortuary ritual." In that context, he continues, "Native and European objects represented links with the community, the individual, and the afterlife and were considered highly symbolic of Pequot beliefs and practices in the physical and spiritual worlds."[41] This seems true, but it is equally so of the Puritan mortuary rituals that, for example, involved writing anagrams using the letters of the deceased's name, or attaching written elegies to coffins as they were carried to burial. Of course, were we to speak of English practices more broadly, we would find differences in the ritual, and in what people were willing to bury with the dead, by locale, time, and sect. Those differences often spoke to varying ideas about the afterlife and the person being interred, whether political or theological (say, in the case of traitors, or of Quakers unlucky enough to be put to death in Massachusetts).[42] The Pequots appear as a unified group in these analyses, but we know that they were, and remain, one of the most spectacularly contentious groups in New England, woven by kinship relations into the fabric of both surrounding and distant communities.[43]

Rather than insist on the unity of Pequot piety, we might speculate more aggressively across the conceptions of the invisible world in a New England both shared and divided. The concepts of "community mortuary ritual" and "piety," linking the worlds of humans, other-than-human persons, and spirits, are both useful, but they can impede more flexible ways of thinking about a shared past and future, keeping us from certain interpretive insights. The bear paw, for example, McBride tells us, is unusual in sites like this. The bear was considered "capable of transitioning between the physical and spiritual realms of the sky and the terrestrial world and between the terrestrial and underwater worlds." The paw, though, reminds us of the bear's power to deal shredding, mortal blows; its presence in conjunction with a page torn from a Bible might suggest a less rosy interpretation of the kind of power being sent along with this child to Cautantowwit's house. Moreover, among the bear's distinctive behavioral properties is hibernation: a state between life and death, a survival habit based on renewal and reemergence—or, as Ralph Ellison puts it, "covert preparation for a more overt action."[44] If such was part of the message, then present-day interpreters are participants in the reawakening of this Pequot spirit both heralded and brought about by the choice of burial arrangements. Finally, if it is true that, as McBride argues, "children were perceived to be in a state of liminality, existing on the threshold or boundary between the physical and spiritual worlds," the same might be said of Puritan children.[45] The Salem witch trials serve as an excellent example of that. Further, seeing across the rituals and pieties of these two groups reminds us that children were also importantly, and troublingly, on the threshold between the Native and English worlds as denizens of the region imagined their futures.

The in-between use of the page has a kind of parasitical quality. I mean this in a positive sense. The Bible buried represents a means of opening a path or window to another world, a cosmos from which power might be drawn. As is often the case with real parasites, however, there is more than one potential host. A practice might draw power from more than one cosmology: bear, Algonquian traditions, Pequot kinship, English piety, European technology, and earth are all potentially contributing domains in this instance. The burial and its objects constitute a technology of mediation between the visible and the invisible, but simultaneously between the long-standing and the newcomers. These dimensions of that mediation may offer potential resonances or value for the ongoing recovery of Pequot history and the forms of renewal or creation in their new age of self-determination. Amory was probably wrong to say that the function of the Bible is the same. The formal context of burial matters, not least because of the well-documented foundational significance of spatial orientation in Indigenous North American ways. Psalm 98, in which the sea, rivers, and mountains join humans in singing a new song to the creator, may sing from this grave in ways that link past and present cultural needs, in another era of intense change for tribal members.

A different set of objects in a different site also suggests an environment saturated with attempts to open otherworldly connections that do not quite fit what we have taken to be either Native or nonconformist modes of divine mediation. Behind the original walls of Benjamin Horton's Long Island house, first erected in 1649, were found three cloth poppets, with stick legs, now held at the restored Old House in Cutchogue (Figure 2). In an article describing the restoration of the house in 1940, Frank Brown speculates that the poppets were preserved by chance, dragged into the walls by rats. Robert St. George, perhaps doubtful of Brown's interpretation owing to the comparatively undamaged quality of the poppets, suggests that these may be similar to poppets found in 1685 when the Salem house where Bridget Bishop lived when she was

Figure 2. Photograph of cloth and stick poppets, Cutchogue, Long Island, and other items discovered in the mid-twentieth century during the renovation of a seventeenth-century house now known as the Old House. Photograph by Dorothea Jordan. Courtesy of the Cutchogue–New Suffolk Historical Council.

accused of witchcraft was torn down—dolls found "w'th headles pins in Them, w'th the points out ward."[46] Magical and countermagical items were buried in and around Christian houses as a means of circumventing the powerful pull of providence. Such practices were constitutive of the vernacular world of spirituality, which drew on both magic and Christian worship.

As St. George vividly illustrates, houses were contested spaces, both between men and women and between earthly needs and divine authority. But the differences between the public and the intimate also shaped the power of magical mediations like those offered by poppets. Buried under a stoop or built in the wall of the house, an invisible third power could lurk, contending with those of men and gods. Given Puritan ideas about predestination, it is not merely spatial propriety that was being transgressed with such objects. Time was also being mastered, in the old, magical mode, against Calvinist logics of divine temporality and inevitable judgment. For St. George, such practices indicate a syncretism within settler Protestantism, but not one that involves Indigenous divine forces or rituals. Native Americans are, in his analysis, mere projections. The Puritans' denial of Indigenous subjectivity, for St. George, robs real Natives of cultural agency. This is a pity, not least because we know from both ethnohistorical and archaeological evidence that lodgings, in their construction, orientation, size, allocation of interior space to individuals, and decoration, were also sacred mediators for Natives of the region.

Perhaps it is true that these poppets owe less to the presence of Native American modes of communication than to the traditional European magical world Keith Thomas describes, or that they were no more sacred than as unexpected beneficences to the house's furry parasites, the rats. But then again, these poppets were found in a house in Cutchogue, just across the Long Island Sound from Pequot territory (indeed, a number of Horton's relatives had come from Connecticut) and near one of the prime wampum-manufacturing areas that the tribe had controlled on the eve of the Pequot War.[47] In the settlers' understandings, the degenerate sons of Adam roaming the wilderness did not lack for magical power. In a land still ringing with the chants of the *pawwaw* and the mourning songs of bereaved Pequot women, a land still laced with the memory holes and rock-and-stick piles created by Native hunters and travelers, would not Old World magic have a better chance of working? The imagination of agency that attached to the risky practice of trying to work around divine providence might have been enhanced by the near presence of people with different ways, accessing alternative, invisible powers.[48]

As in the case of Benjamin Horton's rodents, there are more parasitic or transferential agents here than just Pequots and English settlers or their divine forces. The text in the Pequot bundle was illegally printed in Holland and smuggled into England for sale, eventually reaching the colonies and the Pequots. There is a temporal transference as well: the page fragment in the bundle "was preserved by contact with an iron ladle," Amory reports, "which converted the cloth and paper to a lump of iron salt known as a pseudomorph, because it exactly reproduces the form and structure of the original in a different material."[49] An English form and a Native structure, then, are preserved for us today only because of a third material transaction with no "culture" associated with it. This structure was subsequently resurrected for analysis by the Pequots themselves, who some non-Natives in Connecticut today consider to be not only parasites but also posers because the restoration of the tribe happened through the agency of nonlocal, non-Native-identified descendants—"Indians" in legal form and economic structure, but not "material."[50]

Neither the poppets nor the bundle clearly indicates piety, broadly speaking, as we tend to think of it today, either for settler nonconformists or Algonquians. Either could be supernaturally additive, syncretic, or simply traditional (in the sense of pronouncing, "I have taken the other's spiritual power and carried it with me to the invisible world"). Neither quite proves a synthesis of beliefs, either, if that was what was sought. These are parasitical objects, mediators of agency, placed in between both immaterially and materially: between the earth world and the human world in the Pequot case, and between the public and the intimate in the Protestant one. Here cohabitation seems to be a mode of transformation, a practice acknowledging and drawing power from difference. Amory and McBride's disagreement boils down to a conflict of epistemological schemes that have been given their current conformation in part by colonial activity: a prioritization of the universal for Amory, a prioritization of difference for McBride.

Crucially, in the contexts in which these objects reside today, they continue to perform this porous work. Neither the bundle nor the poppets have strayed far from the places of their creation; both link past and present in the context of historical preservation and education. Their interest lies perhaps more in their capacity to inspire wonder than in their potential to fuel historical judgment. Their talismanic quality, now in the context of a research center or historical museum, is retained as a residue of the sacred even as they function politically. Their political function, as emblems of Pequotness or Long Island settlerness, is difficult to distinguish from their more arcane powers, as parts of collections, to defend the existence of the Old House museum at Cutchogue or the Mashantucket Pequot Museum and Research Center. Our work of scholarly analysis consequently proceeds under the rule of a diachronic parasitism in the critical act, experimenting with a conception of time and evidence that might make a virtue of the unknown by embracing the unknowable in an act of intuition or imagination.

The experience of North America for many of its denizens has been, Joanna Brooks observes, "a story of catastrophe, chance, and radical disruption." A narrative of personal revelation, of a path to wholeness outside of dominant discourse and under the eye of God, helped redress this experience, Brooks claims. It "worked for so many Americans in the eighteenth century, and . . . might work as the conceptual engine for one new way of telling of American religious-literary history: it is a narrative formula that summons meaning from randomness and disaster and uses this meaning as the basis for new, if temporary, forms of intimacy and relationship."[51] This elegantly reformulates the story of American religion on a more inclusive basis than many previous narratives, routing it through seeming discontinuities and surprising personalities, such as Samson Occom, John Marrant, and James Baldwin. I would not deny the importance of healing, intimacy, or reliable relationships. Yet that same deeply felt experience underwrote some of the more violent instantiations and narrations of piety—heterodox and orthodox—whose relationships were built on exclusion, not extension, and were comforting precisely for that reason.

I began this chapter by describing how as a student I was drawn to the Puritans' systematic doubting of human knowledge and power. Another dimension of nonconformist ways of looking at the world attracted me as I considered the alternatives of atheism or agnosticism, the religions of so-called reason. "The genius of the Puritan movement," as Stephen Foster puts it, was always "to invest transcendent, numinous meaning in happenstance and particularity."[52] Foster calls this the "motor force" of Puritanism and labels it as one of the few transcendent qualities of the movement itself. It seems particularly generative and nurturing to me, and it is shared by many believers across the world. When I began to learn about Native America, it struck me that this everyday ethics of finding worlds of wonder must have been one of the things that made even basic communication possible between Indigenous Americans and this group of European settlers. The study of Native ways and histories from the early colonial era, however, seemed to have more immediate bearing on the lives of people descended from those groups and places. This led to a more difficult question than whether Native people became Christian, or to what ends. Surely the Northeastern Indigenous cultures and the land in which they grew influenced Puritan ways, not just the other way around. One big question is surely how history can be told in a way that nurtures life and self-determination for people dispossessed by colonialism. Another, related one asks how it can be told in a way that helps settlers face and come to terms with what happened to the foundations of their systems of conscience, morals, and ethics in a way that will promote a more collaborative attitude toward building the future of the United States and Indian Country.

It is all too easy to become like Momaday's dog when we begin to study piety. Perhaps, as he suggests—because for writers like Momaday and Deloria the telling of history itself is a key act in generating, elaborating, and preserving the sacred—it is merely a matter of whether we are the stuff of martyrs to the gods of history. My hope is that the objects discussed above and the trickiness of piety outlined here call attention to the difficult position scholars are in, writing across time and parasitizing evidence to try to shape our futures—whether a future we can *believe in* or a future in which we *can believe*. "Historical knowledge," Carlo Ginzburg writes, "is indirect, presumptive, conjectural."[53] The logics of spirituality in a colonial condition are multiple, transformative, emergent, and even resurgent (as the United States' current religious awakening, with its depressing moral vagaries, suggests), calling for a different sort of narrative about history, even a different narration of history. Making poppets or the bear paw and Bible-page bundle and then removing them from human circulation may be regarded as attempts to master time, to refold it according to the desires of the individual or small groups that crafted and buried these things. These uncanonical objects and their users' attempts to disrupt the temporalities of their moment hold lessons for our narratives—lessons about the knowable and the unknowable, about the persistence of the not-modern or the already presentness of the future, as we attempt to change the asymmetries of power in the present.[54]

3 Waiting for the Beginning

> In many areas whites are regarded as a temporary aspect of tribal life and there is unshakeable belief that the tribe will survive the domination of the white man and once again rule the continent. Indians soak up the world like a blotter and continue almost untouched by events. The more that happens, the better the tribe seems to function and the stronger it appears to get. Of all the groups in the modern world Indians are best able to cope with the modern situation.
> —Vine Deloria Jr., *We Talk, You Listen*

> Nay *Roger* thou must be punctual if thou wilt be a Christian.
> —William Edmundson, quoted in *George Fox Digg'd Out of His Burrowes*

In the fall of 1652, at the Native Christian town of Natick in Massachusetts Bay, a group of Algonquian converts underwent the local ritual of a public description of their experience of coming to faith. Area divines were invited, and the fervent missionary John Eliot translated, with the help of a Native, the declarations of the converts. The process took so long, however, that only a few of the speakers were able to finish, and the discomfort among audience members with the length of the proceedings was palpable during this cold and dark time of year. Here is one of the uncomfortable moments, described in Eliot's book *Tears of Repentance*, published in London the following year:

> Thus far he [Monequassun] went in his confession; but they being slow of speech, time was far spent, and a great assembly of English understanding nothing he said, only waiting for my [Eliot's] interpretation, many of them went forth, others whispered, and a great

confusion was in the house and abroad. And I perceived that the graver sort thought the time long, therefore knowing he had spoken enough unto satisfaction (at least as I judged) I here took him off. Then one of the elders asked if I took him off, or whether had he finished? I answered that I took him off. So after my reading what he had said, we called another.[1]

One wonders what Monequassun thought of all of this whispering and interruption, accustomed as he was, if we may believe European descriptions of Algonquian public meetings, to quiet and profoundly attentive audiences.

Over two hundred years later, in Buffalo, New York, another drama of patience unfolded at an 1884 ceremony memorializing the reburial of the Seneca leader Red Jacket. The ceremony included Native leaders from a range of nations, as well as non-Native speakers of both local and national importance (many of them adopted Senecas). "After musical selections rendered by Wahle's orchestra," the Buffalo Historical Society's publication about the event tells us, "Chief John Jacket addressed the audience in the Seneca language, expressing the thanks of the family and people for their generous reception by their white brethren; and said that but for the lateness of the hour several of the Indian chiefs present would have been pleased to deliver addresses appropriate to the occasion. . . . General Parker then spoke, without notes."[2] Ely Parker, the Seneca hero of the Civil War, started his speech with a diplomatic acknowledgment of the time constraints of the situation. He noted that the sense of urgency thus caused might inhibit his audience's grasp of the complexity of the Indigenous situation. "I regret the lateness of the hour at which I am called to speak to you," Parker began, "as the Indian question is an almost inexhaustible one. . . . I also realize that you are exhausted from your long sitting, hence I promise you to be as brief as possible in what I say, a task, however, that I may find difficult to accomplish."[3] Parker's speech, as reported, was indeed about a third the length of George W. Clinton's, which had occupied much of the early part of the program that evening.

These moments, emblems from a vast archive of similar episodes, seem to indicate a historical constant: an unrelenting urgency on the part of the colonizers of North America. Patience seems to have been short as a matter of course, even in such crucial moments as joining a regenerate congregation or mending historical relations across nations. Why were the white folks in these moments—to say nothing of more horrific ones—in such a hurry? As cultural historical analysts, we can supply any number of answers to this question that suit us. We could point to a history of punctuality in colonists' cultures; we could claim that economic motives were supreme; we could argue that heaven beckoned to the faithful that they hasten to the embrace of the Lord. Yet to resort to answers such as these would be to take patience for granted as a timeless virtue—one that we readers today might appear, through the illusion of historiographic time, to share with Native Americans of the past.

Thinking and Feeling Time

Claiming patience as a path to mending cultural misunderstanding has a colonial history. Attending to that history might spur reflections on the intersection of time and language. Patience is, after all, part of a humanistic tool kit that, many of us hope, will help make human relations better—whether by better we mean more just, more equal, or more happy. Patience with others, and with ourselves, seems fundamental to the improvement of human relations at which much work in the humanities aims. It is hard to be patient. That alone, to say nothing of its often good results, tends to make one think patience has great powers. When we accomplish patience, it can feel like we have mastered time.[4]

Academic studies of temporality—the feeling of time, the measurement of time, and cultural or religious ideas about time's progression—have tended to focus on extremes of its sensibility. In the study of a work of literature or art, time as a formal property (duration, detail, rhythm, and so on) has long been a basic tool for interpretation. Such interpretation often involves the smallest units of representation, such as words, phrases, brushstrokes, beats, or units of measure like a foot. In broad-scale theorizations of religion, ideology, and literary and historical change, an attention to temporality's big picture has been fundamental. It has engaged broadly recognizable concepts: progress, the ages of man, the

Christian millennium, manifest destiny, the collapse of civilizations, the course of empire. Some of the most powerful expressions of temporality, however, happen in everyday interactions, such as the quiet but consequential breaking point expressed in the stillness of Rosa Parks or the fidgety urgency of someone behind you in line at the grocery store. The former we might regard as a decolonizing act, the latter something of a colonizing one—at attempt, without dialogue, to get you to share impatience and hurry up. In either case, although they might be characterized within a larger framework, these actions emerge from complex senses of pressure that transcend their immediate moment. There are elements in each that are framed by being considered part of a group, or by personality, or by religious affiliation (or lack thereof), or by a sense of pressure induced by a competitive economy that monetizes time.

Knowing this, we often think of a person's temporality as conditioned by culture. Vine Deloria Jr. once wrote that if American Indians were in control, "the tempo would be much slower."[5] Serious or not, such assertions have a long historical context in Western theories about the four elements, the bodily "humors," and national "temperaments," dating back at least to Aristotle. In this interpretation, different kinds of bodies, in different contexts, sense and enact the passage of time differently. We intuit what we mean when we tell ourselves to "slow down," but it is hard to nail down in describable actions or thoughts. Some larger forces are at work even when we try to master our own minds and movements. Religious traditions across the world have produced a range of techniques for such mastery, with strategies so different (from, say, St. Ignatius's "spiritual exercises" to Zen master Dogen's *u-ji,* or "being time") that it would be hard to deny some kind of group-based specificity involved in the feeling of time.

That said, it turns out that managing the experience of time can help extend your life, whomever and wherever you are. Nobel Prize–winning studies by Elizabeth Blackburn, Carol W. Greider, and Jack W. Szostak on chromosome health (awarded in 2009) and by the trio of Jeffrey C. Hall, Michael Rosbash, and Michael W. Young on circadian rhythms (awarded in 2017) have uncovered some of the chemical processes that link humans' internal tempos to external ones. While curbing impatience and stress certainly helps lengthen life-spans (by maintaining telomerase, an enzyme that preserves telomere length on chromosomes), recent studies have shown that it is less simple relaxation and more a reflection on the relationship between one's feelings and one's thoughts about them that produces results. Certain kinds of meditation, such as that practiced by Zen Buddhists, are more effective than other kinds at maintaining telomere length, scientists speculate, because their immersive quality connects reactive emotional states to cognitive ones; over time, this creates a habit of such rerouting. We might say that the intense emphasis of religious groups like the Sufis, the Puritans, or Zen Buddhists on an inward turn to reconnect with the infinite might well be among the most effective ways of postponing the divine union they seek.[6]

"There is no inherent good or bad to an individual tempo," Robert Levine writes; "what we make of time is a very personal matter."[7] Collective impatience, however, urges us to attend to its potential for historical injustice. In the study of early colonial America, differences between ideas about time and history held by Indigenous people and Europeans have been characterized by decades of scholarship as a key element of the colonialist hierarchies of power that positioned Native people as incapable of knowing their own histories, because they were argued to be tied to rhythms of nature and lacked the recording power of alphabetic literacy. The role of cosmologic and historical concepts of time had been intensely analyzed in the seventeenth-century Northeast. Yet patience is a more quotidian, seemingly less theorized concept; it is historically and culturally specific in many cases but is difficult to study as a system. It tends not to receive the degree of intellectual or sociohistorical treatment we are accustomed to in discussions of ideas of history, eschatology, or economics. It is also difficult to trace in terms of evidence. What is the fossil record of patience? There is much theorization of patience, much prescription of it, but when we assert its actual practice in history, we often have to do so indirectly.

Patience, I propose as a starting point, functions at four analytical levels. First, it has a historically situated, philologically specific sense. Patience, in all its linguistic concreteness, means specific things in certain times and places. It may even, in different moments and situations, be said to have an aesthetic. It can mean different things in different semantic contexts, of course; consider Christian patience versus the patience of a plantation investor. These meanings are conditioned by time and culture. Second, patience is a cultural problematic. Within any given encounter or negotiation, does the time of interaction, or the time between interactions, measure the same to all parties? To what extent is such a sense an individual one, on the part of one of the people or groups involved, and to what extent do groups or individuals have different kinds of patience, with their own historical dynamics? Third, patience is a lived value or experience within the framework of the present day, in all of its contingencies and particularities. Some people feel that having patience is a good thing; some find it annoying or an impediment. Finally, patience is a critical value for historical and Indigenous studies in particular and for the humanities broadly. As a consequence, to consider academically the question of the history of patience as an ideal and its ethical potential means turning a critical lens on academics' feelings of and about time.

These four levels are rooted in the notion of patience as something valued in social communication in the West. The presence or absence of patience, a sense of a need to maintain it, a sense of someone else having it—all seem to function socially in relation to a broader sense of time, to circumstantially specific notions about responsibility or role, and to a comparative framework with a tendency to treat patience and impatience as recognizable, if not definable, phenomena—something one knows when one experiences or witnesses them. The term links together feelings, temporalities, and social institutions (such as religion, economics, and the family) in suggesting a positive model of how a person or group might relate to them.

That positive model is often contentious, however, for a host of reasons. A politics attaches to patience, but it does so in a way that resides both within a moment of historical interaction and across time in its subsequent recounting—including those of our analyses here.[8] How much, after all, can we put ourselves into the mind-sets of the "graver sort" that Eliot mentioned—folks used to sitting through, and in some cases going home and transcribing, hours-long sermons? People accustomed to the pace of communication in the early age of print, who lived on the slower side of transatlantic information transmission? Among Indigenous Americans, similar questions resonate. There is good evidence that Walter Ong's insistence that oral cultures require repetition and long performance times is not always true; certainly English culture was still largely oral at the time of, say, Eliot's conversion attempts.[9] The stage for the reading of patience or impatience might well have been set similarly, but it might also have been uneven, particularly given the substantial variance among the languages, practices, and protocols of Native kinship and affiliative groups. The protraction of Native American public events had a function at least as cosmological as it was technical—that is to say, it was simultaneously a spiritual and political form—which was no less true of the Christian virtue of patience and its display.

Patience and Early Colonization

The problem of translating concepts like patience may be helpful for thinking differently about how colonial relations unfolded and what that unfolding means to us today. In the scene Eliot describes, for example, we see both the failure and success of patience. Different parties to this scene exhibited patience or impatience along a spectrum inscribed not just by personal character but also by larger cultural tendencies, as Eliot's phrase "at least as I judged" signals. For European Christians, patience was one of seven virtues that could, with the right discipline, be used in an almost Galenic way to displace the seven deadly sins. Patience was an antidote to wrath in particular, and to certain other maladies of the mind less familiar to us today, such as acedia. The world's evil and boredom could be borne, and good things wrought both within the soul and in one's material sphere, if the words of James could be obeyed: "let patience haue her perfect worke, that ye may be perfect and entier, lacking nothing."[10] Treatises by Henry Scudder, Cotton Clement, and Richard Younge, all of which engage Christian patience as a central theme, were reprinted frequently during the seventeenth century. (Scudder's book is about eight hundred pages long, thus exemplifying its lessons about patience in its very form—truly a brick for a spiritual edifice.) Job is the great model of patience for Christians, though the steady sellers just mentioned engage deeply with a range of biblical patterns. Sexuality and marriage were other domains in which patience had a popular, ancient, and multinational history—women waiting for good men; men waiting for virtuous women; and so on. Puritans named their girls "Patience" and their boys "Wait," gendering even this supreme quality, as girls and women embodied the virtue and boys and men the command. Such patience was an investment in futurity, to be sure, but it was a kind of performance as well, tied to other domains and models of patience; in this case, their temporal framework is the steady, multigenerational work of family and reproduction.[11]

Patience has always been an economic strategy too, of course; the capacity for it functions in many ways to stratify economic power. In the seventeenth century, colonial ventures were signature sites of the relationship among risk, earning, and patience. Often, in New England and elsewhere, commentators drew on biblical notions of patience in speaking of the investment temporality of plantations. "Planting is a work of time, it requires vast expense," writes Governor Thomas Lynch of investment in Jamaican sugar growing, "wherefore who will plant, must (like the builders in the Gospel) take their measures beforehand, and furnish themselves with money and patience."[12] In the language of the enslaver, we find a claim on patience. What are we to do, looking back, with this claim? The challenge to patience as a humanistic method is palpable in the patient enslaved person who quietly cultivates kinship and prays for freedom; in the patient master who, by controlling time, cash, and the self, dominates another human being; in the patient Monequassun who is interrupted in his confession; and in the patient English listener who demands an explanation despite the hour. It is evident in both Olaudah Equiano's teaching of Miskito prince George and in the latter's subsequent silence. Patience was a virtue at the core of colonization's unfolding.

It is not simply that Europeans lacked patience and Indigenous people had it, whether it was rooted in oral temporality or whether it was just an irreducibly "different" cosmology. Instead, we might regard patience as a shared value emerging across cultures, but unevenly and with different gestures, feelings, vocabularies, and political and economic valences attached to it. What was shared might not be a concrete mutual understanding of the "forbearance or long-suffering under provocation" that the *Oxford English Dictionary* defines as patience. It seems rather more like a shimmering sense that everyone involved in a particular conversation was experiencing meaningful differences in the perception of time. As such, the evidence we are left with of such moments can open historiographic paths off the beaten ones. Might the elder who asked Eliot to call another convert have been trying to save face, aware of Algonquian protocols for public speech? Why not otherwise call Monequassun back to finish his confession, especially given the importance of the confessional form to evidencing God's grace? While on the whole this incident shows English impatience, within it is nested a contest of judgments about time, translation, and belief.

Perhaps, on the Native side, the tempo of American Indian discourse was a form of resistance not just to the European regime of making modernity that Johannes Fabian famously describes in *Time and the Other* but also to any outsiders' different temporalities.[13] The Red Jacket memorialization saw two different navigations of the feeling of time by Indigenous leaders: one by Chief Jacket and one by Parker. Chief Jacket spoke in Seneca, dividing the audience and signaling to Seneca speakers that a different rhetorical frame would attend the conclusion of the ceremonies, for better or worse. We don't know whether his words were translated at the time for the Anglophone members of the audience, but it seems possible that they were not, given how attentive the rest of the report was to such details. Parker, in English and without notes, delivered a promised short speech, but he demanded of his audience a tolerance in return—a tolerance for the complexity of Native politics on which his speech insisted. The Indian question is "inexhaustibly" complex; Parker acknowledges the audience as "exhausted." We might imagine different purposes for the protocols of patience exhibited across these documents, even as we acknowledge that the Europeans reporting the events were filtering them according to the cosmologic and economic considerations described above. At times there are significant convergences across different kinds of group boundaries, or at least recognitions of the manipulations of concepts like patience across them. To illustrate the unstable landscape of patience in colonial New England, as well as the uneven results of patience as a culture-bridging method in both a historical moment and in historiography, I will retell the story of an extraordinary episode in colonial religious history, and the context of Algonquian time in which it unfolded.

Thou Must Be Punctual if Thou Wilt Be a Christian

Late seventeenth-century New England witnessed a war of patience among the Quakers, the region's Natives, and Roger Williams.

Williams, who had been exiled from Massachusetts Bay and shunned from Plymouth Colony, helped found Providence Plantations under the banner of freedom of conscience and a policy of fair dealing with the local Narragansett people. Over decades, Williams became a key node in relations between the settlers and the many Indigenous groups in the region. The same frankness and inquisitiveness that led in part to his banishment created trust with the area's Native leaders, who were wrestling with a complex, unpredictable political landscape. Ironically, once put into law in Providence, the same rigorous insistence on the primacy of conscience that had made Williams declare his thoughts so vocally to orthodox authorities opened the door to an influx of believers whose doctrines Williams found dangerous: the Quakers.

It is difficult to characterize Williams's radical protestantism succinctly, but he certainly shared many points of belief with the followers of George Fox. Both emphasized the equality of persons in the church; the distinction between civil and scriptural authority, along with a concomitant refusal to swear oaths to earthly authorities; and the rejection of what Williams termed the "hireling ministry" characteristic of Anglican church order, with its salaried clergy. Moreover, the danger to civil order that Williams anticipated from the Quakers—a fear he shared with his nemeses in Massachusetts Bay—was not of violence, since the Society of Friends' peace testimony precluded the use of physical force. It was less Quakerism's planks than its foundations that troubled Williams. A committed biblicist, Williams found the Friends' belief in the "inner light"—a direct communication with God—to be a dangerous tenet, allowing any worshipper to supersede the laws of Scripture and obey only a personal notion of the divine will.[14]

Of course the Friends were a social community as well as a religious one, so the civic implications of their theological positions were more complex (and in historical hindsight patently less disruptive) than their opponents claimed. However appealing the inner light may have been as a way of relating to the divine, it took a lot of patience. One had to wait to hear that real voice, so Quaker meetings became notorious for their slow tempos and silent quorums. The operational dimensions of the Friends' patience were manifold, as they borrowed from the history of spectacular Christian patience no less than they innovated with respect to the personal management of one's voice. In the contested theocratic landscape of New England, the results were notorious, as in the cases of Puritan executions and public tortures of Friends in Massachusetts Bay. The more tolerant authorities of Providence Plantations nonetheless warned their neighbors that Quaker patience, as they saw it, was a tactical spectacle. "Surely we find," they wrote to the Commissioners of the United Colonies in 1658, that the Friends among them "delight to be persecuted by civill powers, and when they are soe, they are like to gain more adherents by the conseyte [conceit] of their patient sufferings, than by consent to their pernicious sayings."[15] Patience brought Friends closer to God; it also brought them converts.

Conceit or not, by 1672, the Friends' movement in New England was strong. The progenitor of Quakerism, George Fox, made the transatlantic journey and toured the region, causing a stir and making new Friends. Roger Williams had had enough; it was time for the Cambridge-trained theologian to try to stem the tide. He wrote up his cardinal accusations, fourteen in all, against the sect and its political consequences. Then he challenged the Quakers to defend themselves in a public debate. After a series of back-and-forth claims of public misrepresentation and attempting to rig the system of the debates, the parties agreed on a two-part event. The first encounter, to be held at Newport, would concern Williams's first seven accusations; the second encounter, to be held up Narragansett Bay at Providence, would concern the remainder.

In the accounts of the dispute, a surprising amount of prose is taken up with mutual indictments about the use of time—indictments of the other side's impatience, prolixity, or tendency to interrupt. The obsession with time could be seen in the way the participants structured the events as well as in rhetorical exchanges in the heat of the contest. As reported in his book *George Fox Digg'd Out of His Burrowes,* Williams's first demands in his letter summoning the Friends to "conference" involved structuring the debate explicitly to ensure "free uninterrupted liberty to speak" and to facilitate the discussion of all of his fourteen points. With this gesture, Williams attempted to operationalize patience with "*Ingenuity* and *Humanity,*" he insisted, thus counteracting the spontaneity protocol of the Friends' inner light by organizing the debate in what Williams described as a "civil" manner.[16] Yet Williams himself had decades before described the humane scene he seems to have imagined for his declarations in the "uncivilized" world of his neighbors, the Narragansetts. He described local Native oratorical procedures in his translation manual, *A Key into the Language of America,* published in 1643:

> Their manner is upon any tidings to sit round double or treble or more, as their numbers be; I have seene neer a thousand in a round, where *English* could not well neere halfe so many have sitten: Every man hath his pipe of their *Tobacco,* and a deepe silence they make, and attention give to him that speaketh; and many of them will deliver themselves either in a relation of news, or in a consultation with very emphaticall speech and great action, commonly an hour, and sometimes two houres together.[17]

Williams had appealed to this use of secular patience to engender Christian debate many times before, in his battles both printed and legal with a range of authorities. In the context of this debate, his insistence on respect for procedure took both concrete and emotional forms. Williams structured the debate as having two main branches. The first branch, fundamental but politically unpractical, concerned the legitimacy of Quakerism as a religion. The other branch involved the question of earthly, political sovereignty. Would the Friends submit to the rule of Rhode Island, or would they follow their own consciences and undermine it? "We have a People here amongst us," Williams is reported to have asked, "which will not Act in our *Government* with us; What Course shall we take with them?"[18] In the context of economic and military environments that were far from under English control, Quaker civic unpredictability and refusal to bear arms against others were worrying.

Before the debates began, Williams heralded his concerns about the Quaker threat to the fledgling colony's sovereignty in a vitriolic exchange of letters with his neighbor, John Throckmorton, a recent convert. He offered as evidence the Quaker sympathy for William Harris, who had played a key role against the colony in a boundary dispute with Connecticut despite being a substantial Providence Plantations landowner. "I think you have been an *Officer* your self in a *Corporation* in *England*," Williams challenged Throckmorton; "I question how you durst then (or durst now) omit to take *Cognizance* of such Actings, against your *Corporations* safety, and the Honour and royall supream *Authority* of his *Majesty*."[19] Early in the first stage of the public conference at Newport, Williams declared his intention of clearing his conscience for having tolerated the Quaker presence by "vindicating this *Colony* for receiving of such persons whome others would not," because "we suffer for their sakes, and are accounted their *Abettors*."[20] It was not just Christian conscience that was on the line in tolerating such potentially heretical theology, but also the trustworthiness of the fledgling colony among its English peers.

Unlike the orderly Indigenous conferences Williams had described in his *Key*, the debate with the Friends of Newport and Providence depicted in *George Fox Digg'd* was a welter of interruptions. William Edmundson, one of his opponents, was full of "Boisterousness": "he would speak first and all" and "frequently and insolently interrupt me."[21] Having by the second day set time limits on speaking turns in order to speed up debate, Williams found even these allowances cramped. Edmundson "was often remembring me saying *Is this thy Quarter of an hour?* for I believe they stood there upon *Coals* and were not willing that I should insist upon it my full *Quarter*."[22] Even before the formal meeting, Williams had encountered the power of Quaker protocols to derail opponents. At one of their public assemblies in Newport, the Friends, led by John Burnet, had issued a volley of prayer and dismissed the meeting the instant that Williams proclaimed his objection to Quaker women speaking in public. As a consequence, Williams tells us, he had "resolved (with Gods help) to be *Patient* and *Civill*."[23] But civility, the history of colonization teaches us, is in the eye of the beholder. Appeals to patience, read across the accounts of the tumultuous debates that Williams initiated, appear as a rhetorical pivot, woven into their writers' formal techniques.

Williams, for example, asks for his readers' patience only a dozen or so pages into his hefty tome, in the middle of detailing his debate with Throckmorton. "The Ingenious and upright *Reader* might now well suppose that the Contest were over," Williams writes, anticipating a reasonable reaction of exhaustion with his tale: "But it is not the *Light* of *Truth* or *Reason* or *Scripture* or *Experience,* or the *Testimony* of the *Prudent* or their own *Consciences* that will satisfie this *white Devill* of this pretended *Light* and *Spirit* within them, and therefore must I crave the Readers *Patience* while I produce J.T. his third and last Letter to me and my Answer to it."[24] The prolixity and the sheer heft of Williams's book weigh in, and on, passages like this, begging to be read as a material example of its author's patience. Yet one could just as easily interpret Williams's attempts to draw readers into his brotherhood of patience as patience's negative extremity: obstinacy. *George Fox Digg'd* addresses the reader twenty times, and many of these moments solicit readerly patience. Williams's very impatience with the reader's imagined impatience highlights this passage's droning insistence that trying to convince Quakers of their theological blindness is a fool's errand.

Might that inner voice not convey "the wild and foolish notions of the Devils whisperings," Williams asked his English readers?[25] The Quakers, he was sure, had a demonic "*black Familiar*" rather than a true Inner Light. The root of the problem, as he saw it, was once again the absence of patience. The inner light implied the immediacy of revelation and its transmission into words or action. Here "immediate" connotes rapidity in time, as it does today, but it also carries an earlier sense of a lack of mediation—by, say, signs, angels, or other divine "means," as it was often put. "Why should not this Argument be good for mee and for others as well as the *Quakers*?" Williams demanded in his opening salvo in the debate: "They say their commands are immediate (for *Interpretations* are *immediate*) but I say they herein suffer *Satan* to cheat them; for they say they pray, they fast, they wait, they listen, they judge of the motions that arise within them, and so I have done. The great maker and searcher of all hearts knowes, that none but his holy *Majesty* was privy to the *Conception* of this business."[26] Williams was unconvinced that judgment was involved in the Friends' response to divinity's immediate commands. Having warned man "against *false Gods, false Worships, false Christs, false Spirits, false Prophets*: He Commands us in Scripture not to believe them, &c. but to try them, to try all things." Williams hypothesized that, for example, God might permit the "*black Familiar*" through an "immediate revelation to employ some malicious soul to *Murther* me."[27] While such a demonizing assertion about a people who had committed to nonviolence was both illogical and insulting, the Friends' response focused on the pivotal nature of divine revelation in defining Christian purpose rather than the rational dynamics of contemplation that Williams would have preferred. The Friends implied, too, that a responsiveness to immediate inspiration defined the polity—a sophisticated end run on orthodox fears of Quaker civic unreliability. "And how dost thou *differ* from *Mahomet* or the *Papists*, and the *Powhows*," they asked, "that hast *No* Voice *or* Motion *within in Heavenly things in matters of Supernatural* Light?"[28] An irresolvable disagreement about the role of latency in Christian revelation smoldered at the core of the debate.

The Friends' response to *George Fox Digg'd*, titled *A New-England Fire-Brand Quenched*, though just as lengthy, took the more energetic and alluring form of a dialogue. In place of Williams's long disquisitions and qualifications are short assertions by each side, taken from notes made during the conferences; quotations from Williams's account; and correspondence. Unsurprisingly, the Friends' responses get most of the airtime, and the interruptions that Williams complains about are not reflected in the dialogic form. (At one point, the authors acknowledge in passing that Williams was interrupted—but only to ask in turn why, when he had the leisure to write *George Fox Digg'd* without such disruptions, he still failed to make a convincing case.[29]) The Friends' riposte concludes with "A Catalogue of *R.W.'s* Envious, Malitious, Scornful Railing Stuff," as well as Quaker testimonies, as counterevidence.[30] Despite the deprecatory language on both sides, the impression given overall by the formal choices in *A New-England Fire-Brand* is of a more balanced back-and-forth, as well as a fuller representation of the stances of both parties in the dispute. The reader is constantly addressed in *A New-England Fire-Brand,* hailed as an authority (as "Gentle") and a "sober," reasonable fellow traveler.[31] "*Reader* did'st thou ever hear, how he hath jumbled things together here?" we are asked, with a playful touch of homonymy.[32] Williams's style is impugned as sharply as his readings of George Fox's work: "Let the Reader observe, what Railing Expressions he giveth in the Front of his Reply!" To be sure, the Friends claimed the same moral heights of patience to which Williams had requested title. "And was not our *patience* manifest, in bearing thy *Cankcred Spirit,* which utter'd forth all these *railing words* against us, let the people Judge?"[33] But not once does *A New-England Fire-Brand* request the reader's patience.

The Quakers also protested against Williams's assertion that they were "a dangerous People to *Nations* and *Kingdomes* & *Common-weales.*"[34] In their account of the debates, they turned Williams's claims of patience against him in their denunciation of the use of state force both to convert unbelievers (including, by association with Catholic colonization, Indigenous Americans) and to punish the Friends for nonconformity.

> And we have and do deny outward, *Carnal Weapons* to convert people to *Religion* by, but those are your *Weapons* of *New-England,* their Fruits have declared it, whose *Souls cry under God's Altar*; How long, O *LORD!* &c. And therefore let thee and them Dread *God's Vengeance* from Heaven. So with your *Carnal Sword* ye are like *Mahomet* and the *Papists*; for thou say'st, thou would'st have us Punish'd: and that must be by such, as have the Sword.
>
> And so thine and your *Pretences* are *Opposite to the Meek and Patient* Spirit *of true* Purity *and* Holiness.[35]

At times, Williams's "Pretences" argued against him even in the space of his own book, in a way that shows how little power patience had to effect a reconciliation between him and his adversaries. When, at Providence, one of the assembly called for "the Choice of a *Moderator* between us," the boisterous Edmundson answered, "*Roger Williams* had himself provided a *Moderator,* and he produced and Read my *Paper of Position.*" "I knew with whom I had to deal," Williams tells us in response, "and therefore purposely waved, what ever I thought they would bogle at, & purposely gave them all *possible Advantages,* &c. and I humbly waited on God for patience for his sake to bear with all Inconveniences, Insultings, Interruptions, &c. and then, *I knew there would be no great need of a Moderator.*"[36] Ironically, here Williams places the moderator within himself, his own inner light of patience functioning as the dispute's regulator. Yet to wait on God for patience was surely no less mystical a feat than to wait for immediate revelation.[37]

They Would Live Upon Us, and Dear

While the war of words was kindled in Rhode Island, a war of deeds was raging all around Williams and his fellow settlers.

As the debates in Rhode Island and Providence Plantations rattled on in 1672, the settlers' Native neighbors watched—and waited. They watched from the hill at Montaup, the fortified community of the Wampanoag sachem Metacom, also known as King Philip. From Pocasset, on the opposite shore from Rhode Island, the *saunkskwa* Weetamoo followed the comings and goings of their European allies in the estuary. The management of patience—of time—for the Wampanoag and Narragansett people who surrounded this English settlement was only one dimension of a deep relationship to place that was threatened by the expansion of settler territorialism. The Native communities around Rhode Island had for a decade been under land extraction pressure by Massachusetts, Connecticut, and especially Plymouth. The tactics included incarceration of Natives for debt or drunkenness, leveraging personal or tribal differences to obtain favorable outcomes in property acquisitions, and using the relations of Native leaders to pry away land through agreements that had not undergone the proper processes of authentication.

Williams's concern to establish the legitimacy of the colony he had founded had multiple audiences. These included the English crown and colonies, to be sure, but also other nations, and most crucially, the Indigenous nations with which he had labored more than most settlers to establish right relations. At one level, his debate with the Friends was an instance of interpolity conversation that might seem extraordinary today because so few such spirited civic contests, with such great stakes for souls and states, happen in public lately. Regarded from a Native standpoint, however, this conference was one of many discussions made possible by an Indigenous context, citing comparisons on both sides with Indigenous ways, perhaps even using Indigenous protocols—but to the end of weakening Native sovereignty. When King Philip's War broke out, Williams would find himself once again in the position of experiencing "grievous *Interruption*."[38]

The Wampanoag leader Metacom's dissatisfaction with English settlement dated back years before the dispute between Williams and the Quakers. While the main line of the controversy had been between Metacom and the Plymouth Colony over land and legal jurisdiction, Natives across New England always kept careful track of the affairs of the colonists. Their religious differences, like their economic competitions and their charter controversies, were part of an integrated political landscape, which even this late in the seventeenth century still principally comprised Native interests and networks of relations. For the most part, good diplomacy between Rhode Island and the surrounding communities had been maintained despite the deed war.

Weetamoo and her husband, Petonowowet (also known as Benjamin), met with Rhode Island governor John Easton about English encroachment in May 1675, a month before the war began. "In the meeting with Easton," Lisa Brooks tells us, "Weetamoo sought to maintain the still considerable expanse of territory at Pocasset, including her town at the falls of Quequechand, where no Englishman had yet dared to plant. The town was seated near the ferrying place from Portsmouth, a likely site for the meeting."[39] Easton's response, a request made to Plymouth for arbitration in the case, "was not entered into the court records." Easton tried again to mediate the conflict a few weeks later. Meeting with Philip and many of his men at the south end of Montaup (just across the bay from Patience Island), Easton once more suggested arbitration. "They told him that it was by supposed 'arbitration they had had much wrong, many miles square of land so taken from them.'"[40] Even as Plymouth fomented the perception that Philip had engineered a widespread and unstoppable "insurrection," Philip was still negotiating formally with Rhode Island's leadership.

These conferences were part of a decades-long, slowly unfolding diplomatic effort by Weetamoo and many other leaders to slow the pace of English expansion and to transform its terms into ones of coexistence rather than alienation. Grounding this effort were the annual cycles of planting, harvesting, hunting, and fishing as well as of the ritual celebration of all these activities that the Wampanoags, Narragansetts, and Nipmucs surrounding Williams's plantation not only valued but also understood as pillars of time. Such events upheld the future bounty of nature. These frameworks for participating in time and history are woven into the very names of the people of this area. "Long before it was reinscribed as 'New England,'" Brooks writes, "this place was named Wôpanaak or Wabanaki, 'the land where the sun is born every day.'"[41] Even the English name, New England, looked forward but summoned the past—indeed, it looked eastward. Its yoking of time and place unknowingly inherited a spirit from the names that preceded it. Those names linked the diurnal responsibility to welcome and thank the life-giving sun to the place in which the people lived.

The struggle over Quaker legitimacy in which patience played such a starring role unfolded inside a much larger conflict of temporalities. Native people repeatedly waited for English settlers to be true to their word, then persistently appeared in court to complain or to renegotiate against increasingly long odds and ever more elaborate English work-arounds designed to acquire land. Williams's concern that Quakers were weakening Rhode Island's sovereignty seems distinctly out of proportion compared to the many attempts, by way of deed manipulation, on the part of Plymouth, Connecticut, and Massachusetts to chip away at Rhode Island's stability by manipulating Indigenous people with whom it had maintained comparative peace. Williams, the Quakers, and their Native neighbors were all in one sense acting in 1675 in ways that attended to long scales of time, whether Christian millennialism or the ancient cycles of earth, air, and water that kept the Wampanoag and Narragansett worlds in harmony. In other ways, they could not have felt the passing of time more differently. For Indigenous residents of the land where the sun is born every day, the time had come to restore balance. For English settlers, balance seemed to be just around the corner, in little need of force. However patient Williams was for the beginning of Christ's new reign, and however patient the Quakers were for the end of all war, neither could imagine the long outwaiting their wronged hosts were undertaking.

Williams's career as a mediator put him, despite his "old bones and Eye," at one of the crucial junctions of these networks as the conflict ramped up in June 1675 with the burning of Swansea.[42] For a time, the town Williams had founded was spared. Eventually, at the end of March 1676, Native warriors came to burn Providence. Like Abraham trying to dissuade God from hastily razing Sodom and Gomorrah, the aged Williams, against the warnings of his neighbors, walked to a point of the river at the town's edge to parlay with the attackers. Time was on both sides' minds:

> I asked them Whither they were bound. They Said to all the Tows [Towns] about Plimoath. They would Stay about two dayes more with us (which they Did not but [went?] away yestrday afternoon the day after their coming). I asked them Why they assaulted us With burning and Killing who ever were. . . . Neighbours to them (and looking back) said I this Hous of mine now burning before mine Eyes hath Lodged kindly Some Thousands of You these Ten Years.[43]

As his own house was consumed by flames, a scene played out that repeated in miniature the structure of Williams's earlier conference with the Quakers. Having admitted that "they were in A Strang Way," the Indigenous leaders "desired me to come ovr the River to them and Debate matters at larg."[44] They nonetheless put Williams to a test that emphasized their superior negotiating position, encouraging him to return to the town to get a hostage, though the land between had already been occupied by Native warriors. Informed by runners of the danger, and having heard the raid's leaders' disavowal of control over the warriors destroying Providence, Williams consented to talks with the commanders.

Just as in his debate with the Friends, Williams both displayed and requested patience. He was met with a clear response:

> We had much repetition of the former particulars Which were debated at the Poynt. Nawwhun Said that we broke Articles and not

they (as I alleadged).... He said You have driven us out of our own Countrie and then pursued us to our Great Miserie, and Your own, and we are Forced to live upon you. I told them there were Wayes of peas [peace].... I told them planting time was a coming for them and Us. Cuttaqueen Said they cared not for Planting these Ten Years. They Would live upon us, and Dear.[45]

Williams, increasingly agitated, warned that the English king would send a flood of soldiers into the conflict if the Natives continued to resist. In reply, it appears that Kutquen—a leader of the raid—told Williams they could talk again "a moneth Hence after we have been on the Plimoth side," presumably wreaking havoc there. In short, Kutquen had said, we have waited long enough; it's your turn.[46]

Kutquen was a Kwinitekw leader, from a people who lived, in Brooks's words, in "a middle ground between territories, cultivating alliances from the inland" and who worked with the Narragansetts and Wampanoags both to prosecute and to mediate the conflict.[47] His mere presence must have signaled to Williams the wide-ranging alliance that had been formed—and consequently the potential resilience of the Native force. Kutquen would, the following month, play a key role in the negotiation for the release of Mary Rowlandson. The stance that he articulated to Williams, however, had been uttered earlier, in a famous handwritten note left after the Indigenous devastation of Medfield. Thought to have been authored by James Printer, it was posted on the remains of a bridge burned by the Native warriors. It declared, "Thou English man hath provoked us to anger & wrath & we care not though we have war with thee this 21 years."[48] "It seemed that Kutquen's statement was not his personal opinion," Brooks writes, "but a common belief held among the alliance at Wachusett, interpreting the political landscape through a syncretic lens, wherein divine will was directed toward rebalancing the scales of justice toward Indigenous continuance."[49] But if it took imbalance—whether for ten years or twenty-one—to find a way back, the protectors insisted they would persist. Patience was an implicit part of Native military strategy as well as an explicit rhetorical stance.

No Englishman should have known better than Williams that a

reckoning was coming. None knew better, or had described with more care, the senses of time and justice that guided local Algonquians' lives and politics. In *A Key into the Language of America,* he had been careful to note his neighbors' different forms of both patience and precision. "They are punctuall in measuring their Day by the Sunne, and their Night by the Moon and the Starres," he wrote, sensing the ways in which, no less than the landscape, changes of season and weather profoundly shaped the lifeways of the region's people. He found Narragansetts relentless "in their promises of keeping time; and sometimes have charged mee with a lye for not punctually keeping time, though hindred"—a fact he would have done well to recall when William Edmundson was insisting that his dilatory tendencies made him un-Christian.[50] At the same time, Williams emphasized patience's other edge: that the Natives would test English patience in turn, writing, "Who ever deale or trade with them, had need of Wisedome, Patience, and Faithfulnesse in dealing: for they frequently say *Cuppànnauem,* you lye, *Cuttassokakómme,* you deceive me."[51] Yet how much advice about this connection between patience and truthfulness could convince Williams's audience, or even Williams himself, to enact the virtues Christian civilization already prescribed?

At one juncture of an earlier colonial war (against the Pequot tribe), the English and Narragansett allies were gathered outside a Pequot settlement when one of the tribe's elders came out to negotiate. He asked the English many questions and elaborately answered their queries in return, buying time for the village's residents to escape quietly. Strategically, the English "were patient, and bore with them, in expectation to have the greater blow upon them," as Captain John Underhill put it in his account of the war.[52] After all, did not Scripture assure them that "he that is slowe to wrath, is of great wisdome: but he that is of an hastie minde, exalteth follie"?[53] Messengers were then sent to and from the Pequot settlements; after hours of this delay, and the "greater blow" obviated, the Pequots "did laugh at us," Underhill reports, "for our patience" instead of engaging with arms.[54]

Scenes like this help us explore the notion of patience as historically specific, as a cross-cultural problematic, as a lived experience, and as a critical value. Such episodes distance us from the immediacy of patience, within which patience is often posited as a key to cross-cultural understanding—a conceit that may come with risks both methodological and strategic. Patience may be regarded as a function of desire in some times and contexts, and as a function of culture in others. What we wait for is what we want, be it spiritual or material redemption, an individualist cosmos, the fulfillment of a group way of being, or an epic historical pattern. In this chapter, we have seen both it and its claiming as a material means of obtaining power and an instrumental moral imperative.

These lessons may be brought to bear not just on the historical concepts but also on the intellectual-institutional politics within which the historiography of early America is enacted today. The academy has famously long timelines compared to other industries, but today's researchers and writers of colonial history are, in reality, under increasing time pressures: the usual six years to tenure evaluation; increasingly frequent demands for workplace assessment; thickening bureaucratic requirements; growing classroom sizes and shrinking faculty rosters; a sense borne of social media that there must always be a new product, a new post, a new argument. The open-ended calendar of collaboration across the bounds of disciplines, cultural groups, or political orientation demands courage, imagination, or a Roger Williams–like level of self-confidence, which few of us have. It's still unusual to find graduate programs whose structure accommodates training that would ground a wide range of cross-cultural collaborations and prepare a scholar for decades of such work. The measuring sticks of the humanities tenure process have only slowly begun to adapt to collaborative practices in cultural studies, critical race studies, and other areas like the digital humanities. The pressures of scholarly relevance, of applicability to a career or argument, of rapid downloadability for rapid digestion—all inflect the feeling of reading for many academic readers and shape what answers can be given to the question, to what can an academic essay speak? This state of things is where the colonial meets the study of the colonial. As Brooks reminds us, there are other ways to imagine the activity of scholarly recounting of the past. "The work of history" itself "in the Abenaki language is called *ômjowôgan,* a cyclical activity of recalling and relaying in which we are collectively engaged."[55]

Patience is surely essential in such a context, but just as surely, it is not enough. What N. Scott Momaday has called the Indigenous "long outwaiting" of colonial invasion, or what James Clifford calls "the indigenous longue durée" cannot be turned into rules to live by. Sometimes the short run matters; sometimes the peace will be broken. "If there has been any progress in securing our rights to land and life," writes Yellowknives political theorist Glen Coulthard, "this progress is owed to the courageous activists practicing their obligations to the land and to each other in these diverse networks and communities of struggle"—networks and communities reminiscent of those built in seventeenth-century New England.[56] The patience and perspective summoned and attested by Indigenous persistence was not and will not be only rhetorical.

4. Rethinking Reciprocity

> Another of the attributes of power is, in effect, the notion of reciprocity. The chief has power, but he must be generous. He has duties, but he can also have several wives. Between himself and the group there is a constantly adjusted equilibrium of oaths and privileges, services and responsibilities.
>
> —Claude Lévi-Strauss, *Tristes Tropiques*

> But what violation soever they make of the Laws, they are forward to put the King in mind of His Duty; and therefore to tell Him, That He is sworn to maintain the Laws, as they are sworn in their Allegiance to Him, these Obligations being reciprocal.... That the Subjects Allegiance is no longer due than the King performs His Duty, nay, no longer than He in their opinion observes His Duty, whereof they themselves must be Judges; and if He fail in His Duty, they may take up Arms against Him: A Principle which as it is utterly destructive to all Government, so, we believe, they themselves dare not plainly avow it.
>
> —"A Declaration of the Lords and Commons Assembled at Oxford"

In the midst of King Philip's War, in the late seventeenth century, an imaginative Algonquian warrior cut open the English settler Goodman Wright's body and stuffed in a Bible. Something important was communicated, however gruesomely, in this act. Predictably, scholars have emphasized different parts of that message. To godly New English people of the late seventeenth century, we are told by generations of research on dissenting Protestant religious feeling, Indigenous acts like this one signaled a horrifying, demonic blasphemy, even as they evidenced how rapidly settler religious ways were attended to by Native people. Those who specialize in the study of Native North America, on the other hand, have stressed that warfare was sacred to Algonquians, through a widely held, foundational ethics of reciprocity that European colonists did not share or understand. In that context of reciprocity, the killing of Goodman Wright balanced a loss in a Native kinship network. The interpolated Bible perhaps indicated that the New England settlers' piety was perceived as a source of that imbalance, or that the warrior wanted to demonstrate that his supernatural partners were superior to those of the colonizers. It appears that two opposed systems of value could be enacted around the same gesture: Protestant horror at Indigenous ways reinforced Englishness and was made to justify anti-Native violence, even as violence against the Bible and a settler body enacted the reciprocity of Algonquian societies. This striking act of bravado in an ancient warrior tradition, in the common sense of those studying cross-cultural interactions in early colonial North America, may serve as an emblem of the collision of two radically different cosmologies, whether one sympathizes with Goodman Wright or with the Algonquian.[1]

Scholars of North American colonialism and Indigenous studies often position the concept of reciprocity on one side of a cultural divide. Reciprocity is argued to be the basis of Indigenous North American and certain African American communities' ethics. As early as 1947, this concept played an important role not just in thinking about Native history and culture, but in U.S. government policy: John Collier, who served as commissioner for the Bureau of Indian Affairs from 1933 to 1945, described Native American culture in the singular, as

> a way of life which realizes the individual and his society as wholly reciprocal and both of them as drawing value and power from the racial and cosmic past and transmitting value and power to the racial and cosmic future, and past and future are not only that which in linear time-sequence has been or is yet to be, but are propulsive, efficient, living reality here and now.[2]

Reciprocity is set outside of, at times in opposition to, the individualism and market capitalism of Westerners. Indigenous Americans—for this term has been used to describe a wide range of different peoples, across the hemisphere—do not operate according to unitary totalities, monadic forms of self-realization, accumulative economies, or linear causal conceptions.[3] Reciprocity used as a cultural analytic has held a promise of producing intergroup understanding both in scholarly analysis and in practical reality. It is envisioned not just as a way of describing an orientation to the cosmos that some Indigenous people might have or have had, but as some greater vision of a better way for humans to be. The term appears in academic discourse as well as in the statements of Indigenous activists, tribal governments, and spiritual leaders. There it serves as part of an internal conversation about cultural continuity or revival and as part of intergroup negotiation and self-determination efforts. It seems therefore to function at the nexus of the politics of culture and the sociointellectual world of the academy, to move between simple description and a kind of draft mission statement for the work the university can facilitate.

Scenes like the killing of Goodman Wright—and there are many like it—complicate that vision, for what has been called Indigenous reciprocity, at least in the early colonial era, entailed violent forms of balancing, not just benevolent ones. However justified, such acts may not exemplify ideal reciprocity for everyone. The epigraphs to this chapter suggest further complications. As Claude Lévi-Strauss points out, pure benevolence might not function as a concept in a cosmology dominated by reciprocity, and the concept was compatible with, and may even have grown out of, hierarchical, gendered distributions of power. We might also ask if it was the case that the English had no notions of reciprocity that would have made Native forms of it perceptible to them. The concept of reciprocity takes as its subject the core moment and conception of cultural transmission—even a culturalized notion of transmission. The appearance of the term in the domains of Western anthropology and political thought signals an entangledness that calls for digging deeper into its pasts and into its implicit logics.

This chapter considers the complex inheritances of the term "reciprocity" and the way it links the political visions it is made to articulate across a range of contexts today with those of the past. Why, I ask, is "reciprocity" so frequently the term used to describe early colonial North American Indigenous societies? Does that practice of description offer a more complex or a more limiting analysis of power, identity, and affiliation, or the persistence of settler colonialism? Finally, what other articulations of human give-and-take with other humans and other worlds, natural and supernatural, might qualify, specify, or recast reciprocity?[4]

A Golden Rule

"Is there any one word that can serve as a principle for the conduct of life?" Confucius was once asked, according to *The Analects*. "Perhaps the word 'reciprocity,'" replied the sage. "Do not do to others what you would not want others to do to you." This too, without the "perhaps," is the most basic charge to Christians, their Scriptures say time and again.[5] The logic is simple, turning an internal, natural feeling outward to produce a social ethos. In the American Indigenous context, this outward world often includes not just humans but all that is other than human, including spirits. Western notions of this ethical reciprocity rely on the notion of subjectivity, on clearly defined boundaries that delineate "others" in a way that Indigenous notions do not always demand.

Perhaps it is not surprising, given the reach of spiritual reciprocity, that almost everywhere one turns in the sciences, too, the concept appears as a crucial plank, either of methodology or ethics. "Reciprocity" is a key term in disciplines across the academy and the professions, including economics, environmental ecology, sociology, behavioral science, political science, marketing, game and risk studies, and medical ethics. In those fields, it tends to be (but is not exclusively) pivotal for studies of altruistic behavior, including unrewarded participation or sharing in any number of contexts. Reciprocity is also still fundamental in the fields from which it originated as a technical term, mathematics and physics. As a consequence of this widespread use of the term, an analysis of the concept of reciprocity as it functions in the study of the relations between Indigenous people and the natural world or other social groups, including colonizers, takes place within a complex semantic landscape in which the term is controversial in some areas, de rigueur in others.

Reciprocity is a key concept in three domains of Western thought and praxis that particularly bear on the use of this term in discussions of cross-cultural relations in early America. In the domain of philosophy, and in particular those strains of thought grappling with questions of recognition, multiculturalism, and globalization in democratic societies, it descends principally from Hegel's discussion of recognition and its basis in reciprocity in *The Phenomenology of Spirit*.[6] In anthropology, scholars like Lévi-Strauss and Marcel Mauss in the last century invoked reciprocity as a way of understanding everything in Indigenous societies, from wealth distribution to spiritual behaviors. In the political sphere, the term took on particular weight at the imaginative core of geopolitics in the wake of the treaty leading to the Peace of Westphalia, in which it was the ideal, if circumscribed, relation at the heart of treaties, whether to end war or to begin commerce between nations that, by virtue of such agreements, mutually constituted each others' sovereignty. Of course these domains do not exhaust its discursive landscape, but already this is a heavy heritage for the word to bear. The uses of this term in Native American and American colonial studies today draw on all three of these genealogies, sometimes in conflicting ways.

The *Oxford English Dictionary* records the first use of this form of the word "reciprocity" in 1753, but there are instances of it earlier. It is a small but significant semantic shift from reciprocation or the idea of the reciprocal to "reciprocity," and the areas of political and commercial treaty making catalyzed the connotations of the nominal form. Reciprocity was a technical term in English mercantile endeavors, to describe, in the words of one early seventeenth-century treatise, "Reciprocal and Double Exchanges, made betweene Merchants for several places, without disturbing of any money on either side where the said Exchanges are made, but being meerely depending upon the paiments to be made in forreine parts."[7] The Peace of Westphalia is perhaps the best-known example of the application of the reciprocity concept to political agreements. The documents and proceedings associated with this negotiation brought an end to the Thirty Years' War in October 1648. Article 3 of the agreement declares a "Riciprocal Amity between" the warring sides, which other articles more particularly name a "Reciprocal Obligation" to prevent hostilities and to render unto "Oblivion" the grudges both preceding and produced by the war.[8] Reciprocity also forms the architecture for the settlement of material differences across the treaty, each concession and each "Restitution of possess'd Places" by one sovereign being mirrored by another in the language of reciprocation.[9] This treaty played a role in crystallizing the nation-state as the framework of justice and sovereignty; it did so by codifying specific mutual expectations such as noninterference and respect for territorial borders. As this chapter's second epigraph suggests, the notion was being used prior to the Peace of Westphalia in English arguments about both the internal obligations between subjects and leaders and the external responsibilities of states. In short, the concept of political reciprocity, rooted in the mutual recognition of states, was foundational to the conception of sovereignty in the West and beyond today.[10]

In the eighteenth-century Anglophone world, the term was increasingly used in reference to treaties or other agreements; it also began to take on a philosophical dimension. In such agreements (in the case of trade, in the nineteenth century often known as reciprocity treaties, and today still sometimes referred to as reciprocity agreements), the term made reference to specific rights that would be allowed to each party by the other. For example, nations might agree to allow each others' ships access to ports or to trade in specific goods. Reciprocity in these instances was and is usually in kind: the objects, privileges, or punishments on either side are agreed on in advance and have an explicit equivalence, rather than being dynamically defined in ongoing acts of interpretation or negotiation.[11]

Robert Keohane suggests a distinction between this kind of relation, which he calls "specific reciprocity," and "diffuse reciprocity," in which an agreement gestures to a broader basis of trust and equality of exchange.[12] This distinction is key to an analysis of the evolution of the term "reciprocity" and its entry into writing about Indigenous-to-European colonial relations because the more diffuse version of reciprocity was linked to a philosophical or theoretical discussion of the concept. An early moment in the intertwining of these discourses occurs in John Locke's second treatise on civil government. A state "of equality, wherein all the power and jurisdiction is reciprocal, no one having more than another," is the "state of nature," Locke claims. In this sense, it was Locke who first posited Native American reciprocity as a social foundation because he had also famously declared that in the beginning, all was America—and thus America was definitively a state of natural equality.[13] Thomas Hobbes, in *Leviathan*, suggests a transactionalist bent of reciprocity in the maintenance of the unequal social relations attendant on man's entry into the unideal world of governance: "to receive benefits, though from an equall, or inferiour, so long as there is hope of requitall, disposeth to love," he writes. Without hope of such reciprocation, depression or even hatred would be the natural consequence.[14]

Similarly, in Hegel's *The Phenomenology of Spirit*, reciprocity is for the most part not a moral principle, spiritual duty, or political necessity. It describes relational mechanisms, both internal to the mind and between minds—a term not distant from its mathematical sense of describing equal and opposite or equal and parallel effects, such as consciousness of the self, or one person recognizing another in the relation of marriage, or, notoriously, in the struggle of master and slave. The nuances of recognition that resulted from reciprocal identification were more Hegel's concern. For Hegel and the seventeenth-century English philosophers, however, the term describes the basis for an ethical community.[15] This sense of reciprocity has come crucially to influence anthropological analyses of Indigenous groups (to which we will return in a moment) no less than contemporary discussions of Western democratic principles of social belonging.

"Reciprocity is widely recognized as a core principle of democracy in its many moral variations—liberal, constitutional, procedural, and deliberative," the political philosophers Amy Gutmann and Dennis Thompson write. That claim might raise eyebrows among some Native studies scholars, for whom it is precisely the absence of reciprocity as a binding democratic principle that characterizes the republican colonialism of the United States.[16] For Gutmann and some other advocates of deliberative democracy, reciprocity is less a spiritual principle or something that determines policy in any direct way, and more a moral and procedural regulator. "Reciprocity holds that citizens owe one another justifications for the mutually binding laws and public policies they collectively enact," Gutmann and Thompson argue.[17] This moral commitment means members of a polity must, for the laws or policies they advocate, offer reasons sufficient to justify such regulations to any person or group in that society potentially affected by them. Such a stance entails cultivating other principles in order to provide that common basis for judgment of the reasonableness of a proposition—basic liberty, for example, and a public sphere, along with accountability and equal opportunity. As a spur to the development and evolution of such principles, reciprocity for the deliberative democrat is a regulatory principle as well as a moral one, but not a fundamental and unalterable plank of social justice and governance. Compared to its description in Native North American contexts, then, this sort of reciprocity is limited in its scope of operation, functioning as an individual moral stance that in turn requires its operation as a regulatory mechanism in the establishment of other sociogovernmental principles. It is also profoundly individualist and human focused in its conception, requiring reason-bearing individuals as its most basic unit of agency, rather than collectives, and excluding other-than-human agents except as objects to be regulated.[18]

Beginning in the early twentieth century, anthropologists would put post-Westphalian and post-Hegelian conceptions of reciprocity to their own uses. Reciprocity was vectored into conversations about the history of Native–European relations by Mauss, Lévi-Strauss, Bronisław Malinowski, and other European and non-Native scholars reflecting on the general condition of human society through study of Indigenous ones in the Americas and elsewhere. One way to describe the result is that a profoundly diverse and multimodal set of Native attitudes toward exchange, obligation, and balance—operating in spiritual, political, economic, and other modes—became contained within the explanatory logic of Western economics, in which there is no such thing as free giving.[19]

For Malinowski, free gifts—love—within the Indigenous family constituted the model and engine of social reproduction. Mauss agreed that social solidarity depended on exchange and on an ethos of reciprocity, but he disagreed about altruism: there was no such thing as a free gift (Mauss tended to use the term "obligation" rather than "reciprocity"). "Reciprocity" is an explicit but nuanced descriptive term in Lévi-Strauss's analyses in his influential *Tristes Tropiques*. It is not holistic there; nor is it a system generalizable to all Indigenous groups. Still, his use of it to analyze the cultural "style" of Native Brazilian societies has shaped many subsequent anthropological readings of cultural systems. In these societies, Lévi-Strauss writes, contradictions in social structure are resolved by "a double antithesis": "Social mechanisms based on reciprocity are opposed to social mechanisms based on hierarchy. In the effort to remain faithful to these contradictory principles the social group divides and subdivides itself into allied and opposed sub-groups."[20] Here reciprocity is described as governing activity within the community, not between it and other-than-tribal entities. Lévi-Strauss concludes that it is all part of a grand illusion:

> For the moralist, Bororo society has one particular lesson. Let him listen to his native informers: they will describe to him, as they described to me, the ballet in which the two halves of the village set themselves to live and breathe in and for one another; exchanging women, goods, and service in a kind of shared passion for reciprocity.... Try as the Bororo may to bring their system to full flowering with the aid of a deceptive prosopopoeia, they will be unable, as other societies have also been unable, to smother this truth: that the imagery with which a society pictures to itself the relations between the dead and the living can always be broken down in terms of an attempt to hide, embellish or justify, on the religious level, the relations prevailing ... in that society among the living.[21]

Here the purpose of the supernatural world is to maintain the inequalities of the material one. The "other societies" Lévi-Strauss mentions are of course not too far afield; Lévi-Strauss often positions himself as a Cassandra, denouncing his society's ways, yet with a tinge of doubt about his criticism's efficacy. At times, however, he also praises Western ways. "The relationship between Man and the soil," he writes of soil erosion on plantations in Brazil, "had never been marked by that reciprocity of attentions which, in the Old World, has existed for thousands of years and been the basis of our prosperity."[22] Reciprocity here modifies "attentions," but it leans toward a cultural-historical accusation: reciprocity as a function linking land and people is a thing that has failed to appear in Indigenous

Brazil. Whether as the window onto a universal indictment of human cultural illusions or as praise for Western agricultural tradition, reciprocity remains, for Lévi-Strauss, a European property.

When in 2009 a group of anthropologists asked themselves if the "anthropological fixation with reciprocity leaves no room for love," they described a panoply of culturally specific definitions of love, but they never defined "reciprocity."[23] Part of a long rethinking of basic anthropological terms (such as kinship, culture, and love) along with the positional bias of the observer, this debate exhibited cultural anthropology's now characteristic reflexivity—and in no small measure the influence of the debates about recognition and democracy mentioned earlier. Strategically or not, the debate did not make clear what reciprocity means or does. Rather, reciprocity as an analytical tool seems to have become part of the binding imaginary of the social-intellectual realm of anthropologists themselves. This fact ironically refracts how anthropologists once described Native societies. What is agreed on is that to anthropologists, reciprocity matters, as a term used to frame largely but not exclusively human transactions, exchanges of information, money, goods, and so on, and the rules that govern them or the patterns of expectation or evaluation that these exchanges create.

The term "reciprocity" by this path—and before the flowering of cultural anthropology—made its way into the mainstream of Native American studies, where it is now commonly used by theorists, linguists, literary scholars, and historians. Among the early influential uses of reciprocity in North American Native studies after John Collier's discussion of it was David Aberle's, in his 1966 book *The Peyote Religion among the Navaho*. Barre Toelken made the term the axis of an essay in an important 1976 collection on Native religion, *Seeing with a Native Eye*. Citing Toelken, Kenneth Lincoln used the term in his field-shaping book, *Native American Renaissance*.[24] In recent scholarship, the word is used in a range of ways. Some scholars refer to reciprocity as the foundation of all Native American religions, usually to distinguish Indigenous beliefs from those of European settlers and their descendants. Others use it more cautiously in reference to the specific ethics of a tribe—in David Silverman's case, for example, the seventeenth-century Wampanoag, among whom he finds kinship to have been a more crucial framework than reciprocity for understanding both individual commitments and broader historical transformations in the group. Abenaki historian Lisa Brooks uses it in her book *The Common Pot,* usually in its nineteenth-century political sense, of equal obligations between nations. In her essay "Locating an Ethical Native Criticism," Brooks focuses on the term "relationality" as a basis for ethical critical work, rather than "reciprocity."[25] Legal historian Robert Williams argues that reciprocity is the basis of Indigenous approaches to treaty making both over a long spread of time and across tribes, and as Ned Blackhawk, Daniel Richter, Neal Salisbury, and many others argue, Indigenous diplomatic protocols based in reciprocity were first learned and later neglected or deliberately ignored by North American colonizers.[26]

Given the term's history, however, the use of "reciprocity" to describe Native cultures of the early settlement era is attended by at least two problems, one historical and one philosophical. The first involves the question of what forms of reciprocity European cultures brought with them—that is to say, whether reciprocity can in fact name a basic difference between human groups, or translate without distortion across contexts. The second, on which the entailments of the first can help us reflect, is philosophical: what do we, or could we, want of reciprocity as an idea?

A Doing One for Another

Whether regarded as an infracultural or intercultural phenomenon, what scholars of colonialism seem to be talking about when they invoke reciprocity as a social principle could be found equally in Native and European settler communities. While the settler religious world featured some of the most important articulations of an attentiveness to mutual giving and to achieving a balance of duties that involved both the visible and the invisible worlds, other realms of English colonial activity could also be described as guided by an ethos of reciprocity.

The English conception of "sympathy," for example, and particularly that brought over by the nonconformist settlers of New England, was rooted in a notion of reciprocity. This vision was of mutual bonds among

Christians, premised on biblical injunctions such as Romans 12:15, to "rejoice with them that rejoice, and weep with them that weep." "Scripture," Abram Van Engen summarizes, "commanded the godly to unite and cohere, and many Puritans understood that concord and harmony to require an imaginative reciprocation of affections that involved putting oneself in another's place and feeling as that person felt."[27] The golden rule not only asks Christians to put reciprocity first in their thoughts and deeds, but also, like Confucius's saying, embeds reciprocity formally through its chiasmus: do unto others as you would have others do unto you. Such commands had complex implications, including the temptation, often indulged by English settler Christians, to judge and at times condemn the outward evidence or lack of evidence of complicity with these reciprocal bonds. For a community premised on Christian unity, the violation of the reciprocity requirement could spell disaster, especially given the immediate presence, in the early years of settlement, of a whole population of Indigenous people, imagined by many colonists to be unassimilable to that regime of reciprocity. Because the people of God also owed reciprocal attention to the Almighty for his provisions, however scanty, a greater disaster loomed should they fail in their obligations: eternal damnation. The regulation of reciprocity involved attention not just to the heart and to the flow of charity but also to the signs and wonders emanating from the natural and invisible worlds.[28]

The most important loophole in this theory was the matter of the gift of grace. An unreciprocable grant from God, through Christ's sacrifice, to humans (or, in most sects of the time, to a select few humans), the gift of grace introduced a remainder, an irreducible fraction on the supernatural side, outside of reciprocity's emotional or spiritual economy. From the debates over the veracity of Algonquian "Praying Indian" conversions to Christianity recorded by John Eliot to the Antinomian controversy and beyond, the question of whether a subject had been demonstrably granted this exception was debated—or, probably more commonly, quietly suppressed by communities seeking concord. This gap between what could be owed to the human and what could be owed to the divine also ultimately placed the regulation of reciprocity in the hands of God. As

John Cotton put it, in a characteristic passage discussing the concept of the covenant between God and his people:

> And there is also a Covenant of Friendship between God and us, *A covenant of Salt,* 2 Chron. 13.5. A covenant of Salt is to be fed with the same salt, as it were, to eate many a bushel of salt together, that is a covenant of friendship; *Didst not thou give the Land to the seed of* Abraham *thy friend for ever?* 2 Chron. 20.7. therein he fitly expresseth the nature of a covenant of salt, by friendship for ever; salt eaten together expresses familiarity, and durablenesse, now God expresseth himselfe thus, to enter into a covenant with his people; he takes *Abraham* as a friend for ever, and *Abraham* takes God as his friend for ever; and this league of friendship implyes not only preservation of affection, but it requires a kinde of secret communication one to another, and a doing one for another. God he grants our Petitions for us as a friend, and we doe his Commandements as a friend out of the integrity of our hearts; *John* 15.14. *Ye are my friends if ye doe whatsoever I command you.*[29]

Reminiscent of the Algonquian "common pot" (or what John Smith called the "common Kettell") as this sharing of salt may be, Cotton's insistence that the covenant "implyes" and "requires . . . a doing one for another," no less than that fulfilling "whatsoever I command you" proves such reciprocity, demonstrate the element of necessity, governed by a hierarchy.[30] What at first implies ultimately requires. At the heart of Christian discussions of reciprocity is the element of benevolently proffered surrender, of a willingness to hand over the reins to a higher power—a willingness so deep that it cannot appear as coercion. Preserving the mystery of Christianity, its potentially humane sense of the limitedness of our knowledge of God, meant hedging the spiritual economy of reciprocity. Reciprocity functioned, then, both within and among English communities, but in ways limited by the imagined community of Christian souls, by cosmologic constraints on man's knowledge, and—it would come as no surprise to Lévi-Strauss—by a deep-seated hierarchicalism.

In addition to religious forms of reciprocity, settlers also thought their world governed by the natural relations among the elements and humors and the Aristotelian great chain of being. As Ann Bradstreet writes in her quatrain "Of the foure Humours in Mans constitution":

> Unlesse we 'gree, all fals into confusion.
> Let Sanguine, Choler, with her hot hand hold,
> To take her moyst, my moistnesse wil be bold;
> My cold, cold Melanchollies hand shal clasp,
> Her dry, dry Cholers other hand shal grasp;
> Two hot, two moist, two cold, two dry here be,
> A golden Ring, the Posey, *Unity*:
> Nor jars, nor scoffs, let none hereafter see,
> But all admire our perfect amity;
> Nor be discern'd, here's water, earth, aire, fire,
> But here's a compact body, whole, entire.[31]

One settler who mastered these amicable logics of physical interdependence was John Winthop Jr., governor of the Connecticut Colony and one of the better negotiators of his place and time. He may have been so successfully diplomatic in part because of his studies in alchemy. A Paracelsian, Winthrop pursued his experiments with minerals and medicines through a dazzling (and sometimes dangerous) combination of intellectual methods, bringing Baconian experimentalism, mystical traditions, astrology, magic, and alchemy to bear on his work. Far from contradicting his godliness, all of these labors proceeded under a divine plan. "The mission of the Paracelsian," writes Walter Woodward, "was to bring purity to a world enveloped in 'a darkness that strives for light'; mankind was divinely charged with obtaining 'the understanding and the fulfillment of the world.' Such fulfillment would come about as the result of careful experimentation and firsthand observation of the natural world."[32] Such understanding and fulfillment could be achieved by tracing sympathetic correspondences between the inanimate world and celestial objects. Animism was fundamental to the Paracelsian logic of correspondences, a notion not unfamiliar to Indigenous Algonquians: the *spiritus mundi,* a living force that infused every part of the universe, was reminiscent of the Algonquian manitou. Understanding was the mission of the Paracelsian, and reciprocity was the secret key to obtaining it. An alchemist like Winthrop was, perhaps as a consequence, more open to Indigenous people, working from a rational platform broad enough to inspire hard negotiating with Puritan leadership on behalf of his Pequot neighbors.

Yet one could not make gold out of lead without the approval of the Christian god. The subtle mysteries of alchemical thinking created in- and out-groups, relied on a Christian eschatology at odds with Indigenous modes of spiritualism, and were founded on a mystical kind of reciprocity that was hard for many people to comprehend. This reciprocity was not just social and religious, like that of the nonconformists more generally, but theoretical and philosophical. As in the case of God's command to live in reciprocity (and embedded in the hierarchicalism of the great chain of being), balance was an ideal in these domains, yet there was always what Georges Bataille, reflecting on the Indigenous North American potlatch ceremony, calls the "accursed share"—an unresolved fraction owed, whether this be the unpayable debt of Christ's sacrifice, the invisible bottom of the great chain of being, or the endlessness of the alchemical quest to turn dross into gold.[33]

Rethinking Reciprocity

The social history of settler reciprocity and the genealogy of the word since the seventeenth century suggest incommensurate conceptual vocabularies at work. Could we agree on how the boundaries of reciprocity-bearing entities are defined if reciprocity is to be both a moral principle, as in Gutmann's vision of democracy, and a broader one embracing the invisible world and other-than-human persons, as among Native peoples? Who would be the "we" to do so? Do state or tribal forms of obligation take precedence over individual or familial ones? Does reciprocity operate differently at different scales? Is a nation only sovereign once it has been accorded reciprocity by an entity of equal status—and what, given competing ideas of reciprocity's structure and agents, would guarantee such an arrangement? To fail in reciprocal duties to a squirrel or to a stone—is this the same order of moral failure as to violate a treaty? The answer may seem obvious, yet if we take seriously a wide-ranging set of definitions of reciprocity, we must be prepared to address these questions—to follow the squirrel to its nest, if you will. Four difficulties with reciprocity, moving from the concrete to the abstract, help outline the limitations of the concept for analysis, and perhaps more broadly: the dilemmas presented by violent forms of reciprocity and by hierarchicalism; the difficulty of defining frameworks or boundaries within which reciprocity operates; and the conceptual limitation presented by the ideal of balance.

The history of intertribal relations in the early colonial period was, after all, not one of unbroken harmonious coexistence under the starlight rule of reciprocity and mutual respect. Protocols for violent reciprocity were established among Native people long before the arrival of Europeans.[34] The northeastern woodlands of the 1670s, however, bore witness to an unusually massive settling of accounts, the killing of Goodman Wright among them. King Philip's War, a conflict that caught up communities from Long Island to Wabanaki country and beyond, sprang from a range of causes, but the actions of many Native people during it were guided by an attempt to restore balance both between peoples and with the land and the ancestors. In one of those events, John Wakely and two of his children were killed in a raid in Casco Bay. Wakely was among several settlers who had recently encroached on Wabanaki lands in violation of earlier agreements, and the resulting series of raids destroyed both lives and the sawmills that had led to deforestation in the region. "Protectors," Lisa Brooks writes of these warriors, "strove for rebalancing at the falls by targeting traders."[35] Viewing the history of European depredations, deceptions, and mortal violence against the People of the Dawnland, it is hard not to feel that such actions were justified. "Europeans and Algonquians followed strikingly different rules regarding exchange, which frequently altered overall intercultural relations," Seth Mallios writes, expressing a sense common in the scholarly field. When Native protocols were repeatedly violated by Europeans, "the resulting Indian attacks against the European settlers were culturally justified and effective."[36] Effective they were. But does not adopting this position, while establishing cultural relativism in one area of judgment, call for a balancing sense of what would have been "culturally justified" actions from the standpoint of the Europeans?[37] Even in asking such a question, we may be depending on a kind of internalized methodological reciprocity that we have not adequately interrogated.

For scholars writing these histories, the old and hard question remains: where is the line between hagiographic presentation and culturally sensitive depiction when it comes to violence? Can deeper understanding of war and its causes, or its enacters' motivations, lead us past the point of deadlocked claims about what was right or wrong in colonial history? One group's balance is another group's terminated future; one group's hand of God is the death of another's beautiful creation. It is surely a good thing in this latest moment of surging resistance, from antifa to #MeToo to the Water Protectors of Standing Rock, to regard warriors as protectors, and Brooks meticulously depicts the mixed motives of most of the individuals whose stories are woven into her account of King Philip's War. Yet that question concerning the inheritance of violence in which we all share remains on the table. The achievement of balance through war is a limit case of reciprocity's ethics. How are we to know how that balance is achieved—from both sides? Whose terms, whose weights, whose scales?

A related difficulty is the degree to which reciprocity as it has been described in seventeenth-century Native communities functioned in relationship to human authority hierarchies, such as sachemships, matrilineage, and *pawwaw*-ing. Lévi-Strauss, as we have seen, warns that social systems "can express, not only mechanisms of reciprocity but also relations of subordination."[38] Just such a system among the English is perfectly witnessed in the now-famous sermon known as "A Modell of Christian Charity," which begins from the Pauline premise that some people are ordained superior and they should be generous to their underlings even as underlings toil quietly to their benefit. But such was the case in Native communities too. "While there is no question that sachems assumed some responsibility to provide for the needy," David Silverman writes of the tribes of southern colonial New England, "the main purpose of tribute was to fund the sachem's political activities.... Eyewitness observations and the archaeological record agree that Indians of sachem status enjoyed better nutrition, less physical stress, and greater material comfort than their people."[39] Jenny Pulsipher points out that hierarchy and inequality were sometimes the very goals of an ethics of sharing, as leaders gave gifts in Maussian ways, in order to bind other leaders or to induce commitments among their own people. In addition to signifying relationships using kinship terms, Algonquians had core status conceptions as well. The word for "under" in Massachusett, *agwa,* "is at the root of the words for 'subject' and 'subjection'" and distinguishes these relationships as "vertical, rather than equal."[40] There were nested relationships of inequality, signaled by tribute patterns among communities and perhaps more importantly by the ways in which alliances rapidly coalesced in times of armed conflict. There were also layered or contested relations, emergent situations in which ties of family or proximity and those of trade, tribute, or respect could be at odds.[41] Multiple coexisting structures characterized Indigenous governance in the Dawnland. What goes by the name of reciprocity could describe both mutual exchanges that we value today and violent forms of social regeneration, such as redemptive warfare or adoption. Reciprocity can be a bit like family in *The Sopranos*: we like it, but it sometimes comes with grim obligations. Or, as evolutionary anthropologist Joan Silk puts it, "Mutualism does not necessarily make you nice."[42]

Even if one accepts not-niceness as a consequence of reciprocity as an ethos—indeed, even if not-niceness is embraced as a sometimes necessary trait—there are more abstract difficulties with reciprocity. The logic of reciprocity as ethical governor does not have a natural or inherent limit, either in time or in space. That is to say, both its component interdependencies and the time frame within which exchange could happen are conceivably infinite. A society has to define reciprocity's reasonable boundaries, either explicitly or implicitly. Those boundaries in Indigenous culture vary from group to group, though there are some common threads of convention. Among the entities to be considered are the people, the sky, the land, the water, the animals, the spirits; among the things to be exchanged are love, time, food, drink, human-made objects, songs, speeches, writings. These components are also subject to creative manipulation; indeed, the figures of coyote, Iktomi, the spider, crows, ravens, and many others in Native storying all remind us that manipulability and transformability must also be considered in satisfying mutual obligations. The question of what obligations must be met and how to meet them are often subject to interpretation—as for example in the case of the dream soul's encounters with manitou in the lives of Algonquian people.[43]

Yet what counts as a thing to be valued, as the foundation of reciprocity, is not just a matter of convention. It can also come into being in the very act of exchange. The implications of this dynamic value generation are crucial for thinking about the possibility of reciprocity as a political ethics because the role of economy in such an ethics becomes hitched to potentially radically divergent notions of time as history and of time's impact on exchange. Scholars emphasize the distinction between commodity-based exchange in European society and gift exchanges among Native peoples. On the one hand, can reciprocity be based in commodity exchange at all, in its indigenist elaboration as a community ethics? On the other hand, is commodity exchange utterly unsusceptible to a foundational ethos of reciprocity? Arjun Appadurai wryly suggests that the anthropologist's fetishization of reciprocity as an analytical model obscures "the common spirit that underlies both gift and commodity circulation" when these are understood as emergent, as the result of moments of transfer, and consequently as transformable into each other in both prospect and retrospect.[44] What seemed a gift may in retrospect not be best interpreted as such; what one intended to trade under the banner of commodity exchange might turn out, in the moment, to be better presented as a gift. Sociality is key to exchange of any kind, and its modes and specificities are an important analytical lever against the tendency to describe—or prescribe—societies in economic terms.

The question of time in the economy of reciprocity, too, is unavoidable, because the effect on human beings of regimes of reciprocity depends on it. To put it starkly: are you willing to wait a thousand years for your people finally to get their due? Some might say yes; others might say there is no redeeming past sins that resulted in irrecoverable lives lived in misery. In any case, equality does not happen in a temporal vacuum. There is an assumption or fantasy, in even the more technical invocations of human reciprocity, that the moment or condition of exchange will not affect the value of the thing exchanged. Yet consider one of the most storied examples of a Native people's insisting that a moment of exchange can remain open as long as necessary to bring the other side into its logic of reciprocity: the Oceti Sakowin and their refusal of payment for the loss of the Black Hills. The United States, rich though it be, cannot seem to afford to return the Black Hills, and a monetary exchange falls short of balancing the scales, in part because such a payment would redefine what is perceived as balance, what counts, in relating to the land. Perhaps in exchange, equivalence is neither possible nor ideal; reciprocity functions in a mixed-up economy, but more fundamentally is a mixed economics. The deal well sealed is never independent of an imagination of the future.

This future-oriented quality of reciprocity means that balance is never quite achieved and indeed is never even really desirable. Yet "balance," both in and out of the academy, is one of the most common ways people think about what reciprocity can help humans accomplish. Consider one of the West's foundational allegories of retributive justice, the *Oresteia* of Aeschylus. In the contest between Clytaemnestra and her son, Orestes, over the murder of Agamemnon, justice and pure reciprocity are at odds. In order to end the cycle of retributive violence, the gods transform the bloodthirsty Furies' supernatural remit from revenge to fertility. Even when all humans in the dispute have made their sacrifices to the sustaining gods, human customs and desires leave a remainder that must be tamed arbitrarily. The people of Athens split on the question of whether Orestes should be put to death for killing his mother, and Athena casts the deciding vote to leave Clytaemnestra's claim unfulfilled. The *Oresteia* asks its audiences to consider the impossibility of balance without divine intervention.

The Haudenosaunee diplomatic metaphor of "polishing the chain" captures this temporal open-endedness in a different way, thinking of a treaty as not merely a document or an event but rather as the beginning or the maintenance of a relationship. The Irish GoFundMe campaign for the Hopi and Navajo nations in 2020, which has raised millions of dollars in relief aid as an act of reciprocation for Choctaw assistance to the Irish during the famine of 1845, was not meant to settle a debt but to create a bond between "brothers and sisters" in "solidarity," as organizers and contributors describe it.[45] Imbalance is a spur to an ongoing exchange, a relationship that must be curated, renegotiated at times, and interpreted by the community. Even an ideal act of altruism between two individuals may be understood differently when regarded at the scale of the relations between their families, communities, or nations. Nicholas Thomas expresses the consensus scholarly position: colonialism has always been simultaneously an economic, political, and cultural process, and "even what would seem its purest moments of profit and violence have been mediated and enframed by structures of meaning," such that cultural mediations are "constitutive of colonial relationships in themselves."[46] Rather a process than a system, in this account, reciprocity upsets an intelligibility based on balance, and it privileges attentiveness to inequality and endless, open incommensurability—not justice, but always trying to do justice.[47]

Other Words, Other Worlds

"It's easy to talk about sovereignty because I look at it as a state of mind," says Mohawk political scientist Taiaiake Alfred. "It means you think like a nation, like a sovereign people, or a sovereign person." Because the term has its roots in European law, however, Alfred says it is also "an exclusionary concept rooted in an adversarial and coercive Western notion of power."[48] So it is with "reciprocity"—easy as a state of mind, difficult as a colonial semantic and political inheritance. What other concepts or terms might help us talk about the past while opening new paths in the present?

Vine Deloria Jr., reflecting after twenty years on the influence of his book *God Is Red,* lamented that his predictions about the religious roots of global conflict had come true, but he also noted that a larger framework of failed mutual care had risen to international visibility in the meantime. With chagrin, he wrote that he did not "look forward to paying the penalties that Mother Earth must now levy against us in order for Her to survive." Deloria did not use the term "reciprocity" in his introduction to *God Is Red;* he writes of having "as a structure a set of relationships in which all entities participate" and "a recognition of the sacredness of places."[49] In this formulation, recognition is shifted from the Hegelian domain of human relations into a mode that links humans and the earth, such that the form of universal participation Deloria describes includes nonhuman agents.

Back in 1970, in his book *We Talk, You Listen,* Deloria had described the ethos governing such a shift in this way:

> The Indian lived with his land. He feared to destroy it by changing its natural shape because he realized that it was more than a useful tool for exploitation. It sustained all life, and without other forms of life, man himself could not survive. People used to laugh at the Indian respect for smaller animals. Indians called them little brother. The Plains Indians appeased the buffalo after they had slain them for food. They well understood that without all life respecting itself and each other no society could indefinitely maintain itself. All of this understanding was ruthlessly wiped out to make room for the white man so that civilization could progress according to God's divine plan.[50]

Not reciprocity but respect and relationality, as in Brooks's arguments about ethical Native criticism, are privileged here. Each creature's or landscape's economy, after all, might function differently, but sustained relations are indispensable, whether to maintain an information loop about changes in the environment or to grasp the chance to combine forces. The emergent quality of exchange and its values, the situatedness in time of any act of giving or returning, is accommodated by this stance.

Paula Gunn Allen did not use the term "reciprocity" in her influential book *Off the Reservation,* but respect is a key term in her thinking too. In writing of the enactment of democracy, which Allen insists cannot be merely a concept, she posits these values, taken from Indigenous ways: "It is a matter of the way persons go about being in the world—both interiorly and exteriorly—and a matter of social and institutional interactions that *cannot but mirror* this way of being. These behaviors are characterized by a sense of harmony, respect (or reverence), balance, and kinship (relationship)—which qualities are the basic values that govern (underlie) democratic life."[51] The parentheticals here enclose alternative vocabularies for key concepts in Allen's vision, a rhetorical approach that opens up a dialogue about the basic elements of an ethics of mutuality. Whether or not her demand for balance and that a person irresistibly "mirror" a particular way of being is achievable, the sensibility Allen describes would, through its emphasis on respect and relationship, encourage a dialogic stance with one's fellow beings and the earth, as well as with the past and future.

Consider another example, this one from the work of First Nations political theorist Glen Coulthard. In Coulthard's thinking, reciprocity is not an exclusive cultural property, but its entanglements offer a spur for the instantiation of a new politics. One of his fundamental warnings is that settler states do not mean by "reciprocity" the same thing Indigenous people mean. Coulthard defends an Indigenous "unwillingness to reconcile" with settler governments such as Canada's. For justification, he draws on the ethics of reciprocity he finds at the heart of his Yellowknives Dene people's cosmology. "Humans held certain obligations to the land, animals, plants, and lakes in much the same way that we hold obligations to other people. And if these obligations were met, then the land, animals, plants, and lakes would reciprocate and meet their obligations to humans, thus ensuring the survival and well-being of all over time."[52] Such a relation "ought to teach us about living our lives in relation to one another and our surroundings in a respectful, nondominating and nonexploitative way."[53] Here, as for Deloria and Allen, respect emerges through a sense of mutual responsibility incumbent on appreciating the complex spiritual and physical relationships that inform the imagination of survival, and broader well-being, into the future.

Simultaneously concerned with the political and economic architectures of Canada–First Nations relations and with their cultural and psychological effects, Coulthard leverages reciprocity not just to highlight how irresponsible and exploitative Canada has been in its material relations with Indigenous people but also to insist on the need for a more fundamental transformation in the logic—not just protocols—of nation-to-nation responsibility. It is a tricky line to walk. The engine of colonialism must be transformed, yet at the same time, the Western ethics that ground the stories settlers tell about their pasts, their versions of reciprocity, cannot be completely ignored in the process. Reciprocity as a principle of liberal governance is inadequate to what Coulthard proposes because ultimately the framework of cultural valuation and political representability would still be determined by a settler colonial state. The reciprocal recognition proposed by the theorists of multiculturalism, which would yield acknowledgment of cultural specificity and place in the national identity, can only function as reciprocal within the limited terms required by a capitalistic, individualistic, settler-controlled government. Coulthard emphasizes political modes of "honoring ... interconnection," modes that do not necessarily prescribe civic reciprocity but rather speak to the more basic means of accomplishing broader material and psychological well-being. Coulthard, drawing on Frantz Fanon, crucially adds "respectful coexistence" to reciprocity as a principle to guide our lives.[54]

Scott Richard Lyons pursues a similar interrogation of cultural recognition within Native communities. In one part of a kaleidoscopic reflection on moments of public contest over Native cultural authenticity, Lyons responds to Eva Garroutte's arguments for what she calls radical indigenism in her book *Real Indians: Identity and the Survival of Native America*.[55] Lyons, in the spirit of Garroutte's insistence that her work is an invitation to more dialogue, admires attempts to reinstill traditional tribal values, but he questions their prescriptive tendencies: "Garroutte's second criterion for indigenous identity is 'responsible behavior,' which means adhering to certain principles like reciprocity and caring for others. One gets the sense that what Garroutte calls responsible behavior is in fact a universal human longing for functional communities, and the particular behaviors she discusses (caring, sharing, helping, being honest, etc.) are certainly worthy of esteem."[56] Lyons's question for us is "not whether the criterion is valuable" but "whether it is traditional," and he concludes that responsible behavior constructed as mandatory reciprocity is not traditional, at least among the Ojibwe. "Ojibwe identity words *describe* certain behaviors but they do not *prescribe* them," he points out. "They do not speak of *ethics*. They speak of *ethnics*." This point about the translatability of reciprocity could be made of other Native North American languages. Lyons argues that among the Ojibwe, there is little evidence that "people would lose their identity because of bad behavior," at least until today's "age of banishment" for transgressions of authenticity. Lyons, by examining both Ojibwe history and language as history to think traditionalism through a material linguistic basis, sifts out presentist or anthropologically derived terminologies from Ojibwe ones and reconsiders the bases of community belonging. "Defining our identities in ways that promote tradition," he argues, rather than "using tradition to define identities," promotes a creative two-way path between past and present, between roots in language and contemporary conditions and ideas.[57] This is an agonistic yet mildly messianic relation to the past, one deeply contingent on cultural context, and one that Lyons argues can guide definitions of tribal citizenship for the future.

All stories about what gifts mean, all interpretations of the act of exchange, are themselves part of the overall politics of exchange in any given moment. This fact looms each time one is tempted to use the term "reciprocity" to talk about Indigenous ways and the potential for building an analytical community at the nexus of the cultures wrought under colonialism. It is true for the stories we tell about what happened in the events associated with Don Luis de Velasco and the Jesuits in Ajacán, with John Smith, Pocahontas, and Powhatan, or the "first Thanksgiving," no less than it is true for describing or enacting exchanges happening in our daily lives. The act of theorizing about reciprocity participates in the potential for people to live imaginatively within its ideal manifestations, in part by asserting that a debt from the past is still payable, or that it is not, or that it was never a debt at all.

What is the economics of reciprocity if its matrix must include the idealism—or the skepticism—of the scholar? As surely as responsibility does not come without a past, openness does not come with a set of instructions. If the full historical relation between past and present must be factored into reciprocity's descriptive function, perhaps economy malfunctions as a way of thinking about responsibility. Instead, the unknowability, temporal suspension, and heterogeneity of domains of exchange (human, world, gods, society) become primary. Whether another vocabulary is called for, or whether a strategic redefinition of reciprocity might be the path, the history of the term may be of use for considering whether it is working to elicit or to constrain not just the imagination but also actual conversation among us—whether or not it promotes an entanglement, a potentiality, however idealistic or agonistic, that moves us toward creativity, happiness, freedom, and justice.

128   RETHINKING RECIPROCITY

In a 2015 interview, Gerald Vizenor used the term "reciprocity" as a way of breaking down the centrality of sovereignty in debates about Indigenous self determination. In the Native past, Vizenor asserts,

> you see trade items all the way from Canada and the Canadian plains, trade from Mexico and Central America. Even from—possibly—some things from South America. There were extensive trade networks. That's a dynamic, reciprocal system carried out by trade. That is transmotion, that's not sovereignty. It was complicated; warfare existed just about everywhere and maybe almost all the time—but there's warfare now, and there always has been, all the time. . . . But it's about resources and it's about trade, and in fact the same kinds of principles that are fraught with disagreement and misunderstanding are present today, and they were present earlier on.[58]

"So I challenge you, as I've challenged myself," Vizenor concludes, "to find a new language that's more emotive, that allows history to include theory and emotive possibilities for which there are no documents and that are critical in understanding a people."[59] In giving some deeper sense of the history of the word "reciprocity," I have hoped to offer a stimulant for that more emotive and creative way of thinking about mutuality and the imaginations of relation among people and with the other-than-human world.

5 Beyond Understanding

> But Abel was gone. Father Olguin shivered with cold and peered out into the darkness. "I can understand," he said. "I understand, do you hear?" And he began to shout. "I understand! *Oh God! I understand—I understand!*"
> —N. Scott Momaday, *House Made of Dawn*

> Their misunderstanding of me was not the same as my misunderstanding them.
> —Roy Wagner, of the Daribi, in *The Invention of Culture*

My argument in this chapter seems simple, perhaps even so obvious as not to require argument: we humans must be able to do right by each other in this world without having to understand each other.

That avatar of early American studies, Perry Miller, would have found my assertion appalling, on its face. In it he might have seen an expression of a long anti-intellectual arc, perhaps with its distant roots partly in the attitudes of the separatists who settled Plymouth and whom he displaced with the Puritans at the origins of "American" thinking. As Miller famously described his purpose as an intellectual historian, "the essence of the challenge" was to present the terms of Puritan doctrine, "just these and no others, as being comprehensible. I have never entertained the slightest ambition of making these ideas palatable to my contemporaries in any other sense than the historical one. There they are—those with which American thought began."[1] At the end of Miller's historical reconstruction, Puritan ideas would be self-evidently the origin of "American thought"—there they are!—and by virtue of that self-evidence, "American thought" will be recognizable as such. Comprehension, or understanding, as a goal, clarifies, and it does so in relation to something that we can by an imagined consensus name "American thought." Miller's stated goal is merely to induce comprehensibility, explicitly divorced from the notion of conveying belief, or indeed interpretation. This is the Western intellectual charge of the modern era, and Miller himself doesn't quite stick to it. He has moments of puritanical doubt, though even these are depressingly high-handed; like God, for example, Jonathan Edwards "is a mysterious being, and any effort to interpret the Awakening through his view of it comes to a dead stop before his reticence."[2]

Miller's desire for comprehension, however, is grounded in only one of the many definitions of "understanding." The myriad meanings of this term are important because they are so slippery in themselves, and so quick to overlap in our habits of reading and speaking. Understanding can mean, as in Miller's "comprehension," a general conceptual alignment among many people about a topic. But that in turn is rooted in at least two other uses of the word. One is a more technical sense, describing the processes by which the physical brain creates the immaterial mind. The other use is the one I trace and think about here: the idea of intersubjective agreement about something. Most of us reading this chapter might agree that Miller's sleight of hand in presenting as a given the notion that Puritan theology represented the beginnings of "American" thought is no longer tenable. Not only did many Puritans fetishize nonknowing, as Miller himself shows, but the People of the Dawnland were thinking long before the English arrived, as were the people of Africa whose descendants were brought to America against their will. Miller may well seem like Momaday's Father Olguin, shouting that he understands into the echoing night of the colonized, in whose ideas he could never have imagined roots.

Yet among the ideas many today share with Miller is the notion that scholarship can induce the kind of agreement that grounded Miller's claims for his work's transformative potential. Surely if only we understood each other, or the Puritans, or the Indigenous people of the historical Northeast better, then this world could be a better place. Indeed, the notion is codified in no less significant a global educational sponsor than UNESCO, in its constitution's first article. To effect its contribution to "peace and security by promoting collaboration among the nations through education, science and culture," the organization vows to "collaborate in the work of advancing the mutual knowledge and understanding of peoples, through all means of mass communication and to that end recommend such international agreements as may be necessary to promote the free flow of ideas by word and image."[3]

As the world witnessed with the rise of social media—had we not learned before?—the free flow of ideas by mass communication guarantees nothing in the way of peace and harmony. Sometimes people hate each other more the more they learn about each other. Is the Israeli–Palestinian conflict fundamentally a matter of a lack of understanding? Recent research into racial conflict has taken a skeptical turn, seeing relationships between social proximity and empathy development that trouble simple formulas about desegregation's chances of increasing cross-racial understanding. Political scientist Ryan Enos observes that violence and distrust increase in urban border communities, where neighborhoods that differ by class or race adjoin. Enos's central claim is that human geography is an underanalyzed factor in social and political fragmentation, but along the way, it becomes clear that histories, both personal and collective, are equally crucial psychological factors in places like Chicago's South Side or the Israeli border, where groups that interact every day nonetheless maintain deep social and political distance.[4] "Combating hate requires understanding it," insists writer and editor Seward Darby; "Not what it seems to be, but what it actually *is*." Yet having spent extensive, intimate time studying white supremacists, she concludes that "people don't leave the hate movement because a veil lifts and they are suddenly able to see hate for what it is. The truth is more disappointing. They leave because it makes sense to them and for them, because the value hate once gave them has diminished or evaporated."[5] This is all to say that understanding hate is unlikely, in any single individual, to prevent that individual from becoming hateful. Nor does understanding hate offer a road map for peeling people in the white supremacist universe away from that place, where they feel wanted.

Long ago, Standing Rock Sioux intellectual Vine Deloria Jr. wryly insisted that "understanding" is a Western colonial project—indeed, that misunderstanding Native Americans was integral to that project. "Easy knowledge about Indians is a historical tradition," he wrote in 1969. "We need fewer and fewer 'experts' on Indians. What we need is a cultural leave-us-alone agreement, in spirit and in fact."[6] Yet "understanding" has been a significant keyword for Indigenous intellectuals, including Deloria. "Generalizations about how we are all alike—all people—are useless today," Deloria wrote in 1970. "Definite points of view, new logic, and different goals define us. All we can do is try to communicate what we feel our group means to itself and how we relate to other groups. Understanding each other as distinct peoples is the most important thing."[7] Here understanding is defined not as intersubjective community but as open acknowledgment of difference. One vision of understanding, based in a knowledge of the properties of different cultures under the banner of universal humankind, is set aside here as secondary in significance to the establishment of group sovereignty as self-meaning.

Donald Fixico, in a 1999 essay, takes a stance that seems to differ from Deloria's Red Power–era one, arguing that "the moral ethics of properly working in American Indian history include deliberate removal of ethnocentrism."[8] Taking up the Western vision of understanding that Deloria criticized, Fixico asserts that "understanding both the internalness and externalness of tribal communities—even if the assignment is to study or teach the relations of that tribe at war with the United States—is critically important in presenting a balanced history. Unfortunately, this balanced history has been lacking in the practice of American history."[9] We have already seen, in rethinking reciprocity, the potential drawbacks of imagining "balance" as a historiographic goal, given its rootedness in economic or mechanistic thinking. Despite its emphasis on the concepts of "understanding" and "balance" as goals of American Indian historiography, Fixico's methodological requirement is more complex, as his mention of "moral ethics" suggests. Historians' "proper attitude," Fixico insists, "is ethically to subvert racist analysis and subconscious thought about Indians. Respect toward Indian people and their heritage is ethically important."[10] Respect precedes understanding, and it even precedes trying to gain "a tribal viewpoint, a Native feeling"—themselves two non-scientific modes of analysis. As we saw in the case of reciprocity, "respect" has long been the name for a stance toward others that, for many Native thinkers, properly grounds sustainable communities, psychologies, and environments.

Fixico and Deloria may differ in their sense of the possibility of bridging human groups, but like many Indigenous intellectuals, they agree on the problematic relationship between understanding and knowledge. Historiographic ethics pertain—respect is demonstrated—at the level of the outlining of a historical project, not just in its finished contents or claims. Establishing a chronology or other temporal conceptualization, selecting evidence, coordinating with interested collectives both tribal and other than tribal, and, crucially, phrasing the main research problem as a decolonial matter—all of these activities of retelling the past are beholden not to a professional discipline but to the people whose struggle to survive has been made necessary by the "racist analysis and subconscious thought about Indians" Fixico names. As Saidiya Hartman puts it, we are left in the subjunctive mode by the difficult terrain of narrating histories of Indigenous people, the enslaved, and the formerly enslaved. The challenge is to respect Black and Native utterance and opacity toward "imagining what cannot be verified, a realm of experience which is situated between two zones of death—social and corporeal death"—and reckon with "the precarious lives which are visible only in the moment of their disappearance," showing how their times and lives are linked to ours.[11] The attempt to create in historical writing the intersubjective agreement that would count as "understanding" under colonization cannot rely on the traditional association of knowledge with authority.

In addition to, or perhaps as a result of, its colonial dimensions, there are technical problems internal to the project of understanding. The difficulty of judging mutual understanding in history comes back time and again not just to the ambiguities of the historical record or the desires of its recorders but also to the impossibility of being certain of human motives. "Understanding" in this sense serves as a kind of utopian nexus, an imaginary category to be filled with historical content when the analyst wants to assert a foothold in time, a moment when relations between people can be described as having reached an ethical mutuality. That, however, is a risky business—business of the same sort that early explorers and settlers engaged in, sometimes fatally. Subjectivity as an idea relies as much on a faith in ineffable, insuperable difference as on a dream of understanding. To live in a world that valorizes individuality is to require a demos of those who believe in individuality and its requirements, distinguished from those who do not. At the same time, even among those within the fold, the idea of individuality utilizes misunderstandings because they are evidence of that irreducibly different something that makes us each a unique self, something that no one but we, and maybe not even we, can know. To understand ourselves *as* selves means that we may never quite know even ourselves. In this way, intersubjective understanding is paradoxically rooted in a larger imagination of subjectivity in which self-knowledge always requires an other, and in which human identity can never be fully communal.

An insistence on understanding as a key to intercultural peace and justice works against its own intentions by positing an alignment of recognitions that, across cultures, may be both impossible and unnecessary. That sounds pessimistic, but it need not imply either giving up on learning about people and the past or rejecting the idea of communion. I like to believe that humans in general resist understanding's individualist pull in many ways, not least emotionally—in the rush of communal feeling we get in crowds, listening to music, or reading certain poems or novels, and in love; at those moments when we genuinely so feel happy and beloved that it doesn't matter whether or not someone fully comprehends us, and the pursuit of understanding simply fades from concern. "*To understand each other is profound beyond human words,*" writes Creek poet Joy Harjo.[12] Taking that "beyond" deeply to heart, in what follows, I trace some of the history of that human word "understanding" and its significance in early American scholarship. Returning to the scene with which this book began—the missionary encounter at sea between Olaudah Equiano and Miskito prince George—I locate a nexus of that troubled history and the desire to effect understanding across cultures.

Misunderstandings

Did Europeans and Indigenous Americans understand each other in those early encounters—or ever? Trying to answer versions of that question has brought colonial studies into wide-ranging theoretical debates about the nature of communication and its place in cultural studies. Richard White, in his influential book *The Middle Ground,* crystallizes an insight that troubles intercultural analysis: even those moments in colonial history that we might today identify as the most ethically promising for intercultural relations unfolded as much through misunderstandings between Natives and Europeans as through understanding. "The middle ground," White says, is "a process of mutual and creative misunderstanding."[13] Nancy Shoemaker's *A Strange Likeness* takes a related tack, suggesting that the perception of similarity could, seemingly paradoxically, exacerbate cultural difference. "Indian and European similarities," Shoemaker argues, "enabled them to see their differences in sharper relief and, over the course of the eighteenth century, construct new identities that exaggerated the contrasts between them while ignoring what they had in common."[14] The better they understood each other, the further apart they grew.

In a hemispheric study of French and Indigenous colonial interactions, Céline Carayon argues not only that these two groups had much in common but that they could communicate effectively across language barriers, even from the earliest days of encounter. "In early French–Indigenous America, communication consisted of much more than words, and there were no insurmountable linguistic barriers," Carayon claims.[15] Despite linguistic differences, French explorers, traders, and men of the cloth navigated the Indigenous Americas, built trading posts, negotiated political alliances, and established missions. In turn, Native communities encountering the French quickly deciphered newcomers' designs and maneuvered them into positions physical, emotional, and political that served the needs of the people. Much of this was accomplished through nonverbal communication rather than rapid or widespread mutual language acquisition. Against the image of either a chaotic or happily tolerant landscape rife with misunderstandings, Carayon posits a French colonial realm in which real and at times long-standing relationships— alongside a distinctly French sense of cultural mastery—were generated more through gestural signs, touch, dance, and other physical demonstrations than through language. "Moreover," she reminds us, "mutual linguistic fluency has never precluded misinterpretations."[16]

Just as importantly, however, violent conflicts emerged from mutual understanding. These conflicts cannot be reduced to signaling problems, whether nonverbal or linguistic; if minor conflicts and accidents were a function sometimes of a failure to communicate, then the major ones were rooted for the most part in European cupidity and religious prejudice. "Regional and cross-regional patterns or similarities formed connecting threads," Carayon writes, "which Europeans were often all too happy to seize upon to develop generalizations about 'Indian ways.'"[17] Those functional generalizations often evolved into "understandings" with fatal consequences for Native communities. Recall Columbus, describing an interaction with the people of Guanahaní during his first voyage: "I had taken some Indians by force from the first island that I came to, in order that they might learn our language, and communicate to us what they knew respecting the country; which plan succeeded excellently, and was a great advantage to us, for in a short time, either by gestures and signs, or by words, we were enabled to understand each other."[18] For the admiral and subsequent invaders, mastery could always be enforced by violence, should knowledge or understanding fail to produce it. Recounting an incident during his third Canadian voyage, Jacques Cartier wrote of the seemingly welcoming Native people that "one must not trust all these fair manifestations and signs of joy, for if they had thought they were the strongest, they would have done their best to kill us."[19] Was Cartier's reading right or wrong? Whatever the case, his skeptical bearing seems to have been perceived by his interlocutors and to have affected their actions. One's attitude toward understanding shapes the set of potentially interpretable interactions that would constitute evidence of understanding. Cartier's insistence that "trust" was at stake is premised on the notion that, had the situation been different, trust would have been impossible too; only force would have ruled the day. Why not trust the other's signs of joy when you think you are in the superior military position?

If understanding can bring rejection or historical violence, and misunderstanding produce harmony, then perhaps we might demote the historian's attempt to define past intentions and the notion of a determining, underlying cultural sensibility when we approach these interactions from the past. That is, we might bring to our historiography the lessons that seem only to pertain to history. Whether with Stephen Greenblatt we believe that European records only ventriloquize or project their authors' own idea-worlds, or with Carayon that embodied experiences are legible in them, it is unclear that trying to produce "understanding" from these methodologies is the only path. Is an embodied gesture, after all, any less a projection, any less rhetorical, than a narrative? Will "knowing" the past in this way heal or absolve in the present, and if so, how? To recover as much as we can of the lifeways of Indigenous people through the ages is surely a good thing. Can we inscribe this recovery with the same question mark we wish the colonizers had tended to put after their own "knowledge"? On the one hand, it seems reasonable to suggest that understanding solved few long-term conflicts in colonization. On the other hand, it seems a bit much to say that "understanding" was even an option. The problem here has less to do with the evidence about or the outcomes of colonization than with the conceptualization of understanding itself as a measure of such things. "Understanding" is the core of the humanistic quest, a form of desire, and the structural mainstay of a cultural stance, and it has a long history as such. Here is one version of that history.

Understanding Understanding

In the early modern era in the West, "understanding" was an element of what is known as faculty psychology, part of a set of supposedly inborn attributes of mind and body that also included the passions, the will, the memory, and the imagination. "In general," writes Abram Van Engen, "faculty psychology moved down a hierarchy from the understanding through the will to the affections, and it identified disorders as, in part, a rebellion of the passions."[20] In the Northeastern American woodlands, however, Indigenous people often encountered English notions of understanding filtered through a theological lens, in which the understanding was a more equal faculty. Puritan divine Isaac Ambrose offered a guide to the use of the faculty of understanding for those seeking godliness in a 1649 treatise, *Media: The Middle Things, in Reference to the First and Last Things*. The faculties were to be put to work to prepare or "quicken" the heart to receive God. "Work we upon our own hearts, by our understandings," he wrote, for "as the striking of the Flint and Steel together begetteth fire, so the meeting of these two faculties, having an internal life in them, do quicken the soul."[21] True to his book's title, Ambrose steered a middle course between enthusiasm and intellectual preparation, warning that theological debate "may clear the understanding" but not, perforce, excite us "to duty, to the love, and life of Christ." Their duties properly apportioned in the mental army of godliness, each of the faculties, being God-given, could become delighted in piety: "There joys the understanding, by a perfect knowledge and vision of God; there joys the memory, by a perfect remembrance of all things past; there joys the will, by enjoying all maner of good, without all fear of evil."[22]

In the hands of American ministers, this Protestant psychology became more distinctly about the heart, and understanding sank still lower. "God is not to be understood but to be adored," as Perry Miller put it.[23] Minister Thomas Shepard's *The Sincere Convert,* for example, insists that "the understanding, although it may literally, yet it never savingly, entertains any truth, until the affections be herewith smitten and wrought upon."[24] One might, for example, be perfectly aware of one's sinfulness, yet without the emotional commitment to change, the understanding might live with sin. Shepard indicts the understanding for a host of negative tendencies—he calls them "drunken distempers"—from craven rationalization to a constitutive incapacity to picture God's beauty.[25]

This insistence on a particular relationship among invisible faculties as a qualification for godliness meant that Indigenous Americans at the outset posed a test for psychotheological theories. One of translator and missionary John Eliot's early Native converts gave a sense of the challenge, worrying

> that hee prayed in vaine, because Jesus Christ understood not what *Indians* speake in prayer[.] He had bin used to heare *English* man pray and so could well enough understand them, but Indian language in prayer . . . he was not acquainted with it, but was a stranger to it and therefore could not understand them. His question therefore was, whether Jesus Christ did understand, or God did understand *Indian* prayers.[26]

In part the difficulty here is that in prayer, speaking in tongues was frowned on (because the supplicant knows not what he or she says), and praying while unconvinced was also frowned on (as a superficial act rather than one born of subjection). Problems like this one, in which "understanding" as cognition of a text and "understanding" as a predicate of prayer collide, were exacerbated by conceptual gaps that manifested not just in cosmologic dispositions but in everyday English and Algonquian syntaxes.

To the transitivity, explicit in the verb form and implicit, as we will see in a moment, in the nominal form of "understanding" in English, was added the highly situational nuance of Algonquian word forms. Take the Massachusett tongue, for example, into which Eliot (presumably with assistance from Native partners) translated Shepard's *Sincere Convert*.[27] Massachusett is heavily inflected, its words commonly compounds of noun or verb stems with prefixes and suffixes—but also sometimes stem modifications—governed by common temporal and modal concepts, a sophisticated differentiation by animateness, and by the situation of the speaker or the discourse. Ives Goddard and Kathleen Bragdon note also that

> Massachusett word order is of a type often referred to as free word order.... The observed patterns suggest that word order often has a discourse function, that is, that it has to do with the presentation of the entities being talked about within the framework of a segment of text, consisting of several sentences, or of the whole document, or within the context of the real-world situation in which the document was created and intended to be used. Word order, then, may function to emphasize something or someone being mentioned, to bring something forward as a topic, to focus on something, perhaps in contrast to something else, or to perform some similar function.[28]

The term used to translate "understanding" in Shepard's tract, for example, is often *wohwohtám8onk*. Its root form, *wáw-*, indicates something like "that which is known"—a reasonable approximation of understanding in the dissenting theological sense of man's knowledge or the process of coming to knowledge. As a noun in Massachusett, though, "the understanding" as a faculty is not only gendered but marked as animate or inanimate.[29] And because phrases in Massachusett can be interrupted by words that are not part of a phrase, allowing a speaker to link different phrases together in intricate ways, interpretation of them requires an iterative or recursive act of comprehension, as successive sentences weigh in on the meaning that went before. In this way, "understanding" operates in Massachusett within a different constellation of comprehension and interpretation than it does in English.

There is evidence that Northeastern Algonquian speakers were aware of the distinctions among English uses of the faculties beyond the conversion fields. A Mashpee petition of 1752 to the New England magistrates pleads, "Oh! Oh!, gentlemen, hear us now, oh! ye, us poor Indians. We do not clearly have thorough understanding and wisdom. Therefore we now beseech you, Oh!, Boston gentlemen." Goddard and Bragdon observe that "the reference to 'understanding' and 'wisdom' echoes Biblical passages, notably 'And God gave Solomon wisdom and understanding' (waantamóonk kah wohwohtam8onk, 1 Kings 4:29; cf. Prov. 4:5)."[30] This kind of usage suggests, to paraphrase Roy Wagner, that the Mashpee understanding of the English was not the same as the English understanding of the Mashpee—that the "understanding" that missionaries hoped to inculcate was marked as English and Christian, rather than either referencing or creating a parallel concept in Algonquian.

For all its theological confidence, the ministry was only one voice in a wide-ranging seventeenth-century intellectual struggle over the role of the faculty of the understanding in human will, for how, precisely, did human beings process sensory information, or come to agreements across languages or religions? Could one draw a hard line between imagination and understanding? Thomas Hobbes was skeptical of university-based debates about such matters. "Nay for the cause of *Understanding* also," he writes in *Leviathan,* "They say the thing Understanding sendeth forth *intelligible species,* that is, an *intelligible being seen*; which comming into the Understanding, makes us Understand." Such beams of comprehension would have made for a convenient materialist explanation; Hobbes mocked the theory as "insignificant Speech."[31] Hobbes's own definition of the faculty was more mainstream: "The Imagination that is raysed in man . . . by words, or other Voluntary signes, is that we generally call *Understanding.* . . . That Understanding which is peculiar to man, is the Understanding not onely his will; but his conceptions and thoughts, by the sequell and contexture of the names of things into Affirmations, Negations, and other formes of Speech."[32] For Hobbes, understanding was a faculty linked to signifying, producing linguistic agreement or parsing. "When a man upon the hearing of any Speech," he explains, "hath those thoughts which the words of that Speech, and their connexion, were ordained and constituted to signifie; Then he is said to understand it: *Understanding* being nothing else, but conception caused by Speech."[33] Yet that last clause betrays the contingencies of those before it, whose predicates have dogged theologians and philosophers for millennia. Who does the ordaining, in this vision of understanding?

The problem of the will shaped the development of influential philosophical approaches to understanding in the eighteenth century. In Kant, for example, understanding is a faculty (or, as he put it, a mental power) that provides form or unity for signals coming from the senses and from the imagination. It has the power of combining signals and images, but it does not operate completely on its own. Consequently, it is not the means by which intersubjective unity of mind between individuals could be induced. Kant is skeptical about the possibility of obtaining direct evidence from the mind, and his model of judgment features an intense interdependence of the faculties.[34] Although the German philosopher shared Ambrose's and Shepard's belief that they lived in a God-afforded world, for Kant, understanding prepared the way not for the Puritan divine's "heart" but for the exercise of Reason.

The pressure of scientific method on philosophers—recounted elegantly and rigorously by Hans-Georg Gadamer in *Truth and Method*—forced an evolution in debates about understanding. Philosophers came to center their claims about understanding around questions of alterity—of self and other. Those questions weigh heavily on the study of relations across social groups. For philosophers thinking about the implications of physical understanding—the fact that perception of any kind, perhaps even reflection, is conditioned by passing through the body—all forms of encounter are characterized by radical alterity. Understanding is a fraught concept because it is possible that there is no built-in set of concept generators we all share. It is possible that what we call the "world" is reconstituted in each person each time communication happens; on the other end of the spectrum, it is possible that we are all linked by a shared machinery of perception, or linguistic sensibility, or atomic, cosmic commonality; and so on. "The world is indubitably one if you look at it one way," notes William James, "but as indubitably is it many, if you look at it in another." The fact that we sometimes seem to understand each other is a proof, both positive and negative, for those who think about the human condition through the lens of the individual.[35]

For philosophers, "understanding" is an unavoidable term because without it, there is no platform for discussing humanity as a generality. An analyst's model of "understanding" is a model of the human. It entails positing human capacities, a claim about what makes humans different from other beings, and a sense of the limits of and potential for human cooperation. The question of the "I" and the "Thou," or the Self and the Other, pivots on the concept whose name has been given as "understanding." For Gadamer, there is no "understanding" outside the three-part relation between two people and a thing, usually a text or utterance. Language makes coming to an understanding possible, as in Hobbes, but reaching understanding also requires an attitude, a stance of openness to change or convergence on the part of the interlocutors. Thus Gadamer modifies previous philosophers' attempts to identify a mechanism of understanding (most famously Kant's a priori cognitive categories), turning instead toward a version of understanding that focuses on emergence rather than origin and negotiation rather than the absolute.[36]

Gadamer asks how understanding is possible. This places "understanding" under a shifting sign. Gadamer agrees with Martin Heidegger that because human beings have to interpret before all other things, the problematic of understanding, rather than a predictable mechanism for it or universal condition of potential agreement, sits at the heart of all scholarly study—indeed, all that goes by the name of study. Understanding here unfolds within the determination of an unknowable history within which we are always catching up to the truth of our own perceptions and motives. "In understanding we are drawn into an event of truth and arrive, as it were, too late," Gadamer concludes, "if we want to know what we are supposed to believe." Understanding is the experience of meaning. It is not solving problems, deciphering, or thought alone, but rather a set of feelings and memories that cohere, as opposed to a mental chaos that makes us feel like we do not really exist. Consequently, "there is no understanding that is free of all prejudices" (or, as Édouard Glissant puts it more forcefully, "a generalizing universal is always ethnocentric").[37] This is a daunting definition for historians whose most common underlying claim is that human understanding, and thus happiness, can be advanced by the tales about to be told in their books.

Such a historian might be relieved to find that at the root of Gadamer's arguments are a host of assumptions and universal ideas common to Western thought with which Native American thinkers might disagree. Among the most fundamental of these is this: "Man is characterized by a break with the immediate and the natural that the intellectual, rational side of his nature demands of him."[38] Without this monadic, individualistic break, and the presumption of a definition of the "rational" or of what is "nature" and what is not, the notion that "understanding"—as opposed to direct revelation, or simple harmony, or a continuity between what are called the conscious and unconscious modes of mind—is necessary at all steps aside, and in its place rises the more limited sense of understanding as a kind of temporary, delimited, and not-quite-perfect agreement about something. Such a stance would qualify the habitual scholarly declaration of understanding as something a historical narrative can produce. Each act of historiography could only be one part of a set of social embodiments of history that extend well beyond the pages of the book that will outlive its author. Non-Natives often study Natives to find a truth about themselves outside of themselves—a root from which to fight exploitation perhaps, but also around which to form an identity. In Indigenous groups, however, this is the function of the tribal or the kinship philosophy—to find that truth from within a world not constituted of selves and others, humans and objects, a rigorous separation of the living from the nonliving. On that path, definition and understanding are not so much wrong as beside the point.

When we turn to the study of the early American colonial period, things get even more complicated. Most obviously, history writing itself has been a weapon of colonization since before the English began to arrive in North America.[39] History writing as a discipline and the profession of historian have both changed a great deal since the sixteenth century. The Western historical profession's commitment to engaging preceding historians—preserving if modifying the tribal knowledge, if you will—has meant that, as Gadamer would point out, a double veil has been cast around the subjects and objects of colonial studies, before one even confronts a historian's individual biases. The "knowledge" scholars have received as narrative has been profoundly shaped in every historical field by Western ideas of civilization, progress, justice, equality, and so on. To cut through these, or even to suspend their naturalness, might sacrifice the coherence of a historiographic project, and with it readerly attention. Thus a seemingly natural, professionally wise, disciplinary piety casts a further shadow over the telling of the already dark history of colonization. The second veil, familiar to all students of the Native past, is an evidentiary one. So much of colonization's success depended on *not* understanding Native life, or pretending that one did not, or pretending one did when one did not; and so much depended on erasure. Misunderstanding, often masquerading as or built into a larger model of understanding, was an engine of colonization. Language, material culture, song, dance—the evidentiary record of Native life in the colonial Northeast customarily consulted by historians is ragged compared to that of the colonists. The irony is, without the deadly historians of the past, we might not even have that much, for they were also preservers of a sort.

Understanding as a concept rests on the idea that individual consciousness must be the basis for the formation of the self and its interpretations. This conception sets aside—in some cases even derides as unscientific superstitions—non-consciousness-based forms of self-shaping, including, among many others, mystical inspiration, kinetically induced somatic knowledge, communication by smell or pheremones, or starvation- and disease-induced mental states. As Irving Hallowell observed long ago of the Ojibwe, "If, from the standpoint of the people being studied, the concept of person is not, in fact, synonymous with human beings but transcends it," then liberalism's parameterization of political personhood—indeed, its conception of society itself—as bounded by living *Homo sapiens* is at a loss to provide representation.[40] In the hands of phenomenologists or new materialists, the scope for potential understanding has been expanded, but in many cases, it continues to proceed with the "I" of the West as its implicit end, both subject and object. "Understanding" is a good liberal idea. But how badly do we need it?

Understanding the Miskito Prince

In late 1775, Olaudah Equiano, a formerly enslaved man, sailed for Central America from England as part of a plantation-establishing venture. The English planters were headed to the contested Mosquito Coast in what is now Nicaragua, and they brought with them four Miskito people who had journeyed to England a year before on a diplomatic mission, "during which," Equiano tells us, "they had learned to speak pretty good English."[41] Equiano, a recent convert to Methodism, befriended George, the son of a prominent Miskito leader and destined to become king, and began to instruct him in English reading and writing, and in the basics of Christianity. George began to exhibit signs of interest, but not long before the ship reached its first stop, Jamaica, some fellow seafarers began to mock his emerging belief. Equiano, in his now-canonical *Interesting Narrative* of 1789, tells us that these jibes "caused the prince to halt between two opinions."[42] Here is how he relates the tale:

> In our passage I took all the pains that I could to instruct the Indian prince in the doctrines of Christianity, of which he was entirely ignorant; and, to my great joy, he was quite attentive, and received with gladness the truths that the Lord enabled me to set forth to him. I taught him in the compas of eleven days all the letters, and he could put even two or three of them together, and spell them. I had Fox's Martyrology with cuts, and he used to be very fond of looking into it, and would ask many questions about the papal cruelties he saw depicted there which I explained to him. . . .
>
> Thus we went on nearly four-fifths of our passage, when Satan at

> last got the upper hand. Some of his messengers, seeing this poor heathen much advanced in piety, began to ask him whether I had converted him to Christianity, laughed and made their jest at him, for which I rebuked them as much as I could; but this treatment caused the prince to halt between two opinions. . . . Thus they teazed the poor innocent youth, so that he would not learn his book any more! He would not drink nor carouse with these ungodly actors, nor would he be with me even at prayers. . . . At last he asked me, "How comes it that all the white men on board who can read and write, and observe the sun, and know all things, yet swear, lie, and get drunk, only excepting yourself?"[43]

Equiano answers that it is because they do not fear God as they should, and he clarifies the tortures of hell that such an attitude will bring. This conversation "depressed his spirits much," Equiano reports, with the result that George "became ever after, during the passage, fond of being alone."[44] The phrase "halt between two opinions," echoing 1 Kings 18:21, may suggest that Equiano had hopes that the prince would, like the followers of Baal convinced by Elijah, come around to worshiping the Christian god. But no such conversion happens, and we hear little substantive of Prince George again in the *Interesting Narrative*.

Is this scene a drama of the failure of understanding, of a missed chance at cross-racial, international harmony? Certainly for Equiano, operating under the aegis of Protestantism, it was. But how do we read it from a great historical distance? Our desires to read or teach Equiano in a certain way are almost as powerful as his religious motivations may have been. Consider the ruling controversy about Equiano's life and narrative, which frames itself in a way that will be familiar to readers of Native American literature and criticism. If black writers joined the contractual system of European liberalism, religiosity, and capitalism, the thinking goes, then they pose for us a dilemma. Are we to conclude that they were making the best of a bad situation and trying to tweak that system from within its discourse and behavior? Or should we rather take them to have been coerced at best and collaborative at worst in the liberal individualist speculative capitalist system that would eventually deprecate slavery but leave the more persistent phenomenon of racial and class dispossession in its place? "By viewing Equiano through the optic of minority literature or making him represent an African American or black British slot in an ever-expanding canon," warned Srinivas Aravamudan, "the modern reader also edifies nation into imperium," for as we can see in this brief excerpt alone, his narrative cleaves to colonialism in no small measure.[45]

Ian Finseth has proposed a reading that steps outside this debate's terms. Finseth considers the role of irony in the representation of the linguistic foundations of contract by authors of early slave narratives. The use of irony expanded the category of the contract to include not just religious covenant or individual self-possession and economic responsibility but also ideals of friendship. "For narrators such as Brinch, White, and Equiano," Finseth writes,

> interpersonal duty, or the contract of feelings and words that weave together the social fabric, provides a measure of stability amid the vicissitudes of slave life. . . . Here and elsewhere, the basic social contract—a promise between emotionally linked individuals—is not some abstract concept or rhetorical device, but a way of stitching together black communities and forging a new black subjectivity in the Atlantic crucible.[46]

This notion of friendship, a bond with the reader or a familial commitment as equal groundings for an understanding of contract and thereby a revision of hegemonic modes of it (liberal, legal, financial, philosophical), is refreshing, and speaks to the three-way relationship Equiano attempts to establish between himself, the prince, and the reader (whom he is also attempting to convert, in a way). Yael Ben-Zvi goes so far as to suggest that Equiano

> mounts a diasporic indigenous critique of Eurocentric denials and subversions of the universal entitlement decreed by eighteenth-century conceptions of reason and Christian theology. . . . This inclusive perspective recasts the world's population as a community united by horizontal, nonhierarchic relations that Equiano offers as a challenge to Eurocentric commitments to a vertical, hierarchic global

order and to the idea that property and mastery are the foundations of civil society.[47]

For these critics, then, the scene of George's conversion would represent an attempt to reach out across racial or ethnic boundaries, exemplifying the ways Christianity or friendship could help build solidarity among minorities in the special space of the ship, a microcosm of a contested Atlantic world.

Certainly the revolutionary Atlantic of the eighteenth century, embodied by sailors and slaves—the "motley crew" whose histories Peter Linebaugh and Marcus Rediker dramatize in their book *The Many-Headed Hydra*—was one context for Equiano's representation of himself as orderly, legalistic, economical, and rational. That context also influences his depictions of coming to religious awakening. Equiano learned that terror "was the fate of both sailors and slaves," in Linebaugh and Rediker's words, and that cross-racial education and collaboration were important to achieving material and spiritual freedom.[48] Irishman Daniel Quin helped Equiano learn to read the Bible; Equiano makes his friendship with Richard Baker a central part of the narrative; and sailors and reformers from a range of backgrounds (including poverty and criminality) and countries aided him along his way. Equiano is studied and admired to this day for what Linebaugh and Rediker term his "miracles of social alliance . . . in the making of the United Irishmen, the English working class, and the Scottish convention movement."[49] For Finseth, Equiano weds friendship, commerce, and Christianity to build an alternative Enlightenment; for Ben-Zvi, that new universal vision is trans-Indigenous; and for Linebaugh and Rediker, Equiano's partnership with the Miskito tribe is one of many social miracles.

This Miskito emissary, however, was neither sailor nor slave. He was not a commoner or a criminal. He was one of a ruling Indigenous elite that shared the reins of colonial power, a people whose seafaring might and tributary networks were necessary to the success of English endeavors in Central America. Indeed, his father, King George, had recently promised the British government Miskito support against the colonial rebellion in North America. Although Equiano, like many Indigenous writers of his time and after, insisted that "the horizontal logic of human relations reflects Christian values better than prevalent European practices do," in Joanna Brooks's words, he did not take up the mutual covenant hinted at by George.[50] So let us take another look at this scene.

Equiano in this interaction was a good reading and writing teacher but a poor proselytizer.[51] He himself had been led to the fold in part by reading about the conversion of Native Americans in two books: Thomas Wilson's 1740 *An Essay towards an Instruction for the Indians* and the twenty-four-page *The Conversion of an Indian, in a Letter to a Friend*, first published in 1774.[52] The latter is in the voice of a Native from "the province of New-York" leaving on a diplomatic mission, written to his friend, Drurow, a fellow Native, and depicts the narrator as naturally prepared for Christianity (he fears loss of neither property nor life at sea, for example) and curious about religion.[53] The book is less a programmatic conversion text than a Methodist evangelical indictment of English impiety, a claim cemented in a passage that links the worlds of Equiano and Prince George: the English, "altho' they are distinguished by the name of Christians from many other nations, yet as far as I can learn, they have no more regard to the reality of this book [the Bible], than our poor slaves, who have never heard of its being in the world."[54]

Equiano's account of his shipmates' mockery of his conversion attempts mirrors that criticism. Yet it was perhaps from other experiences that Equiano got the idea of using John Foxe's *Acts and Monuments* to draw in a potential American convert, with its vivid illustrations of the tortures of Protestants by Catholics.[55] From George's perspective, Equiano tells us, these silent parts of the text spoke the most compellingly, counteracting the potential for linguistic misunderstanding. Foxe's *Acts* had been eloquent by this time for over two hundred years of Protestant education (it was first published in 1563), calculated as it was to head off direct competition for souls from Catholic imperialists, the ancestors of the colonizers against whom the English were competing in Central America.[56] Foxe's book of martyrs may have held an appeal for Equiano structurally similar to one it held for many in the English Atlantic multitude in that it speaks the history of a persecuted minority into the dimensions of a cosmologic struggle. The act of trying to convert George might be regarded as a return of the favor of help to Christianity that Equiano received from all of these texts. At the same time, that act was the fulfillment of the model of English, Christian behavior advocated in books like *An Essay* and *Conversion of an Indian*. (Many observers have pointed out that grammatically, at least, George's question implicitly makes Equiano white: "All the white men . . . only excepting yourself.") Equiano's description of the prince, and his later ethnography of the Miskito as a group, exhibits a rhetoric familiar from *Conversion of an Indian*—that these Natives are already prepared to receive the gospel, needing only literacy and (Protestant) Christian guidance to become eligible for grace.

Despite the help of these models, Equiano's evangelizing failed. The drunken cursing of the tempters did not seduce Prince George either. By publishing the story, however—by exposing the withdrawal of the Miskito prince and by wrapping his critique of English behavior in a Christian interpretation—Equiano may have succeeded in filling out the role of the proselytizer. George's self-imposed solitude calls us to think again about the history of attempts to cross cultures and the difficulties of telling that history. Those attempts had complex motives. Equiano had been formerly enslaved, but he was involved here in an extractive venture and an attempt to replace an Amerindian cultural way with Western Christianity. Yet the unruly seafarers who questioned the joys of Christian order seem themselves to have offered no friendly place, for this Native at least.

In their turn, elite Miskitos such as Prince George were important agents in enslaving members of their neighboring tribes through warfare. Their presence on this English ship was part of a complex power struggle with both local Indigenous groups and competing European empires. The Miskitos were supremely strategic in their negotiations with the English, as the English themselves noted. In their agreement to help the English expedition against the Spanish fort El Castillo de la Inmaculada Concepción, for example, the Miskitos made it clear that they would not be compelled to labor, and they required that the English "take every Step that the Soldiery have little connection with them in Order to avoid the possibility of Disgust on their Side."[57] That ethnic caution may have been at work in this scene too; it is precisely the silence of the Miskito prince, his refusal to make a transracial contract with Equiano, that gives particular weight to this episode.

The connection did not fail for lack of opportunity. For all that Equiano shows an awareness of Miskito–English power dynamics, and for all his evident efficiency at teaching reading and writing, he appears, or makes himself appear, somewhat inattentive to what George was asking by way of his question. That inattention is a function of a potential conflict over what the process of learning to read might afford beyond Christianization. George's question is about literacy and intellectual ability, and its role in creating a happy social world:

> At last he asked me, "How comes it that all the white men on board who can read and write, and observe the sun, and know all things, yet swear, lie, and get drunk, only excepting yourself?" I answered him, the reason was, that they did not fear God; and that if any one of them died so they could not go to, or be happy with God. He replied, that if these persons went to hell he would go to hell too. I was sorry to hear this; and, as he sometimes had the toothach, and also some other persons in the ship at the same time, I asked him if their toothach made his easy: he said, No. Then I told him if he and these people went to hell together, their pains would not make his any lighter. This answer had great weight with him: it depressed his spirits much; and he became ever after, during the passage, fond of being alone.[58]

Fellowship is the shared ground that the prince proposes: sinners all, we will be in hell together, and that at least will make our pains easier to bear. But *friendship* is the metatopic here—friendship between Equiano and the prince. Equiano has befriended George through learning how to read and looking at woodcuts of martyrs in books. George begins to spend his time alone when Equiano insists that, in effect, friendship does not survive the torments of hell. Equiano's gesture of "covenanting together" with the Miskito prince is interpreted in Prince George's response as a stage for thinking about the long-term entailments of friendship. The social space between the two that is opened by the jeers of the ship's company and the relaxing of institutional force at sea (force, that is, of church, state, or homeland) resonates with the themes of Christian brotherhood, and it offers an occasion for a sort of cross-cultural bonding under the rubric of friendship or fellowship.

"Friendship" is a key term for Equiano, frequently used in the *Interesting Narrative*. Having described a compact of love and friendship with his sister and then with Richard Baker, Equiano strangely does not come through in this case, and it ends the missionizing transaction, even if the prince has been given pause about fraternizing with the ship's rowdies. Prince George refuses to be remade into a Christian, but more important, he refuses to be made to fear the end of relationality (in the separation of souls after death into saved and unsaved) and its material implications for relations between living people. Even if Equiano's respect for the silence of the prince indicates that he includes the Miskitos in his universal human rights scheme—which is by no means on the surface of the narrative—his narration nonetheless enacts a Christian kind of colonialism, one Equiano desires to continue in Africa when the *Interesting Narrative* has done its work. The failed conversion comes as a result, the narrative implies, of his shipmates' unchristian static, a confusion of voices that renders subjective silence. Sublimated in that way of telling the story is that the silence may be a protest or criticism. In its failure, Equiano's conversion scene shows his potential to convert Africans under the right conditions. Viewed in the grand scheme of English conversion efforts to that historical moment, Equiano is actually at his most English when he fails to convert Prince George.

That failure in turn opens potential meanings of the prince's silence to Equiano's readers today. These potential meanings are not ethnographic. They are, rather, warnings about the limits of understanding as a rubric for what scholarship can achieve in the assessment of moments like this one and the texts that represent them. If Equiano's goal was to include all indigenous people, African and American and beyond, in a transformed scheme of human rights, then the price of the prince's universal rights is cultural silence—or even merely the silence of uneffected friendship. Not quite sovereign, and certainly not English, Prince George remains apart both in his moment and in literary historical, critical time. What George's specific alternative vision of friendship or fellowship might have been is made unavailable by the same mechanisms that Equiano hoped would enchant George with Christian piety: the book, the engraving, learning to read and write, spending time praying with a fellow former heathen, conversation. Indeed, it might have been rendered beyond understanding by Equiano's very attempt to depict his own scene of persuasion within the terms borrowed from those supposedly culture-crossing technologies.

Then again, what if precisely the opposite were the case? Why does Equiano let the prince walk away into silence? Perhaps Equiano, in depicting his failure to convert, was not just displaying martyrdom on the English model but was also suggesting he could handle a gap of understanding—its impossibility—in a way that did not parse according to the civilized–barbarian binary, the quantification of conversions, or the scholarly guides for converting the heathen. Might not Equiano have been hinting at that which cannot be understood as a means of any sort, withholding his own instrumentality in a way parallel to the prince's self-isolation? The prince, after all, also fails to convert Equiano, in his way.

I don't know. The feeling of immediacy in the passage about Prince George and Equiano is seductive. It feels teachable to me, dramatic, just rough enough to be reportage. That feeling, however, is partly a function of the media of our time, or of our generic and narrative lenses and habits, rather than those of the eighteenth century, whether the prince's or Equiano's. Wary of why it appeals to us, we need not become Equiano in the metaequation of historiographic encounter. George's silence as represented by Equiano makes it possible for his readers to regard it as an act of distancing sovereignty, imminent hybridity, autocritique, a more exoticizing mystification, and any number of unthought-of other possibilities. It is possible that colonial discourse has some inherent characteristics, or that it observes a poststructuralist order of endless differentiation, but it is important to the life of criticism for us to suspect sometimes that it does neither—that there may be multiple and coexisting practical ontologies of representation. Equiano and the Miskito prince warn us that imagining we understand the structure or parameters of a discourse has its limitations, even dangers. Equiano's text hints that depending on achieving understanding as the fulcrum or measure of our work may be the very thing that renders understanding as such impossible and unnecessary at the same time.

Beyond Understanding

"Can this being together in homelessness, this interplay of the refusal of what has been refused, this undercommon appositionality, be a place from which emerges neither self-consciousness nor knowledge of the other but an improvisation that proceeds from somewhere on the other side of an unasked question?" ask Stefano Harney and Fred Moten.[59] "Difference must not be merely tolerated, but seen as a fund of necessary polarities between which our creativity can spark," as Audre Lorde puts it. "Only then does the necessity for interdependence become unthreatening. Only within that interdependency of different strengths, acknowledged and equal, can the power to seek new ways of being in the world generate, as well as the courage and sustenance to act where there are no charters."[60] Equiano, fugitive product of the ship's hold, and the Miskito prince, held in an Atlantic imperial scheme, question each other, but they leave much unasked and unanswered. The silence between them might signal the collapse of an undercommons relationality on board the *Morning Star*, or it might signal a mutual accommodation to the colonial project in which they each shared in different ways—perhaps an act of resistance, perhaps an echo of solidarity in respecting each other's difference. As an event about which we write, it is both an apposition and an invitation to historiographic improvisation. "After all," says the narrator of David Treuer's *The Translation of Dr Apelles*, "when confronted with death we mourn the past, but when confronted with silence we mourn the present and the future as well."[61]

The Miskito prince's silence could be thought of as a form of what Marisol de la Cadena and Audra Simpson call Indigenous refusal—an engagement of an outside politics that resists and constitutes its own world by refusing its terms.[62] Understanding is deliberately set aside in the gesture of refusal. Such refusal is an intervention, but one that keeps its distance and refuses to reproduce the terms of engagement set by colonizing forces. Yet if George's silence is considered as such a refusal, it is also the case that what was refused was fellowship with a formerly enslaved subject, one of the Atlantic world's other others. It is also the case that what was refused was not just the Christian paradigm (the eighteenth-century version of which only uncomfortably maps onto what would be called "politics" today) but a political alliance that the Miskito people might benefit from forging. This is to say it was an individual act and an act of sovereignty on behalf of a community, but, crucially, only to the extent that the notions of "individual" and "community" function across the historical distance from which we observe Equiano recording this refusal.

This equivocality is daunting, but scholars of Indigenous politics in the Andes have embraced it, to productive ends. "Equivocations, if controlled," writes de la Cadena, can occasion productive disagreements that are based on "the understanding that the interlocutors both understand and do not understand the same thing by the same words."[63] The goal is not to "settle" on one definition in, say, a civic dispute—which would be settling in two senses of the word—but to draw out something of the difference that constitutes the equivocation from each side. That is, disagreeing about the uses of terms can create an occasion for agonistic exchange around world visions rather than seeking to have one world vision (and hence definition) supersede or graft the other. Even if, in successive linguistic interactions, these worlds do not become mutually "understood" to each other, the habit of embracing equivocation and opacity, and of the temporal dilation and sharing of space necessary to these, may and in some contexts already does—de la Cadena offers the example of successful collaborations between Indigenous Peruvians and ecological activists—transform the nature and to an extent the content of conversations among settler regimes and Indigenous peoples.

"If we examine the process of 'understanding' people and ideas from the perspective of Western thought, we discover that its basis is this requirement for transparency," writes Édouard Glissant. "In order to understand and thus accept you, I have to measure your solidity with the ideal scale providing me with grounds to make comparisons and, perhaps, judgments. I have to reduce."[64] To prevent the negative consequences of this demand—Glissant notes that hierarchy is not inevitable in this reaching across solidities, but that it is a colonial norm—he suggests that we have somehow to eliminate the scale. It is not merely that normalizing difference as a right is required; we must "agree also to the right to opacity that is not enclosure within an impenetrable autarchy but subsistence within an irreducible singularity. Opacities can coexist and converge, weaving fabrics."[65] Crucially for settlers engaging the history of colonialism, the opacity of which Glissant speaks is both a matter of public interactions and policies and a more intimate, psychological transformation: "It does not disturb me to accept that there are places where my identity is obscure to me."[66] If this were so with each of us, to accept the opacity of the other might be easier. Glissant implies that there is a reflexive reaction between being at ease with not seeking always to master ourselves and a politics that creates time and space for not knowing.

The scenes analyzed in this book offer occasions for an appositional, equivocal practice of historiography that both respects the right to opacity and models its value. Without understanding Equiano or George completely—either as individuals or representatives of affiliative communities—and without choosing Algonquian over nonconformist patience, without being certain what group might claim this or that practice of engaging the invisible world, we can narrate the past into a creative relation to the present. To enact study of what are called "cultures" as a poetics might give us new languages, concepts, or concerns around which to focus dialogue across differences. It might at times obviate the prince's felt necessity of silence on one side and Equiano's felt necessity of conversion on the other. Not a definitive accounting but "an aesthetics of turbulence whose corresponding ethics is not provided in advance" could be produced.[67]

Experiments in enacting this stance beyond understanding are happening in many places today. Consider another example from Peru. How can people who have lived through the intimate violence of a localized civil war, like the one Peruvians experienced during the Sendero Luminoso days, manage to live with each other in peace once more? Medical anthropologist Kimberly Theidon asked the people in Ayacucho, with whom she had been periodically living and working since before the conflict. Although her informants at times mention understanding as part of their healing process, it seems clear that something more complex was being generated through both Peru's Truth and Reconciliation Commission and local efforts for justice and accommodation. "We have laws now, to civilize us," one says, "to make us understand each other." The law is a point of mutual consent, however, a set of agreed-on behaviors rather than enforcement of mutual knowledge. There was far too much mutual knowledge in this environment: brothers were assassinating brothers, with small neighboring villages falling into cycles of revenge. The Truth and Reconciliation Commission and local groups forged official moments of confession, occasional public punishments, and a collective fiction of forgetting. The amelioration is constitutively dynamic and relational, at times improvisational, but it persists—for now. "This local moral idiom is one of condemnation and transformation," Theidon writes.[68] Justice neither guarantees nor depends on understanding, in the intersubjective sense. Hannah Arendt's admonition that retribution, not revenge, and forgiveness, beyond mere toleration, are required to put a stop to the cycle of violence was exemplified in Peruvian postwar rapprochements, in which communal rituals forged, in Theidon's words, "socially acceptable truths that involve a mnemonic readjustment both for those who confess and repent and for their audience."[69]

In the bright sunlight of May 21, 2017, I found myself on a trailer behind a tractor in Neligh, Nebraska, with a small party of activists. Art Tanderup, farmer, ex-schoolteacher, and charming representative of the Cowboy–Indian Alliance, was driving us out to his fields to plant sacred Ponca blue corn and trees in the projected path of the Keystone XL tar sands pipeline. Like many of the events organized by the Cowboy–Indian Alliance, a collaboration between Native people of the region and settler farmers and ranchers, the event featured Native rituals, shared meals, and a distinctly unhierarchical, relaxed feel. There were professional activists, families, farmers, goths, professors, and tribal leaders, all coming and going freely. There were Ponca rituals whose roots were (deliberately) only partly explained, as well as an invocation, distinctly historical but not naming particular settler names, of the deep past of Native presence and of colonial dispossession. The city folk present followed the farmers' rules for how properly to plant the corn and trees. This event offered a platform for comparing pasts and learning about different lifeways, without requiring complete mutual knowledge or harmony. It was action with *an* understanding, but not understanding. Native activists and farmers and ranchers do not need to mean precisely the same thing by the terms "land" or "water" (in both cases, these terms are always sacred for many Plains Native people but only on specific occasions for most settlers, especially Christian ones) in order to accomplish both political and spiritual ends. For such equivocation to work requires a shared set of goals and practices, however temporary or emergent. It also requires a mind-set, a stance of awareness of the other's world, and a forbearance with respect to mastering it or demanding that what is meant on one side by "land" is paramount.

How to interpret the expressions and ways of people with utterly different ideas about the cosmos, authority, humanity, and the natural world? To me, this task seems, or feels, benignly impossible—impossible because if there is anything the Puritans and the Indigenous people of America have to teach us, it is that you just never know, that it's good for body and soul to have a little habitual uncertainty, and benignly because there are so many other ways to study the past, and turn that study into the cultivation of Lorde's "fund of necessary polarities," or Harney and Moten's informed improvisation, or Glissant's sense that the opacities within each of us might guide our appreciation of difference outside of us. This book itself witnesses my belief that all of us today have inherited and enact in some way—whether as heritage, antagonism, anxiety, or something else—the ideas, concerns, conceptions, habits, and even gestures of all of these long-dead people. I hope that it also may serve as an instrument to help make that space that Joy Harjo describes, a place where "we will wind up back at the blues standing on the edge of the flatted fifth about to jump into a fierce understanding together."[70]

Notes

Introduction

1. Olaudah Equiano, *The Interesting Narrative of the Life of Olaudah Equiano, or Gustavus Vassa, the African,* 9th ed. (London: For the author, 1794), 306. Some contextual information here is taken from Vincent Carretta, *Equiano, the African: Biography of a Self-Made Man* (New York: Penguin, 2007).

2. James Brooks, "Continental Shifts," *William and Mary Quarterly,* 3rd ser., 74, no. 3 (2017): 534.

3. See also his later indictments of Western knowledge disciplines in Vine Deloria Jr., *Red Earth, White Lies: Native Americans and the Myth of Scientific Facts* (New York: Scribner's, 1995); and the discussion thereof in Scott Michaelson, *The Limits of Multiculturalism: Interrogating the Origins of American Anthropology* (Minneapolis: University of Minnesota Press, 1999), 3–15. There are also everyday attempts at cross-cultural understanding that can stand in the way of actual positive change; see, e.g., Jodi Melamed, *Represent and Destroy: Rationalizing Violence in the New Racial Capitalism* (Minneapolis: University of Minnesota Press, 2011), which shows how "racial-liberal reading practices" ultimately "made it possible for white Americans to comprehend the act of reading a novel as (and as a substitute for) an active politics of social transformation" (24). See also Sylvia Wynter, "Unsettling the Coloniality of Being/Power/Truth/Freedom," *CR: The New Centennial Review* 3, no. 3 (2003): 257–337; Jennifer L. Fleissner, "After the New Americanists: The Progress of Romance and the Romance of Progress in American Literary Studies," in *A Companion to American Literary Studies,* ed. Caroline F. Levander and Robert S. Levine (London: Wiley-Blackwell, 2011),

171–90; and Alan S. Rome, "Killing with Kindness: The Benevolent Roots of Violence in Early Virginia," *Itinerario* 38, no. 1 (2014): 57–80, which insists that the "true tragedy of colonial relations—as well as humanitarianism—is that it is precisely the genuineness of benevolence, and not its cynical exploitation or subordination to other ends, that is often the compelling force behind conflict and suffering" (58).

4. See Simon Harrison, "Identity as a Scarce Resource," *Social Anthropology* 7, no. 3 (1999): 239–51; and Aileen Moreton-Robinson, *The White Possessive: Property, Power, and Indigenous Sovereignty* (Minneapolis: University of Minnesota Press, 2015).

5. Édouard Glissant, *Caribbean Discourse: Selected Essays* (Charlottesville: University of Virginia Press, 1999), 64.

6. Kenneth M. Morrison, *The Solidarity of Kin: Ethnohistory, Religious Studies, and the Algonkian–French Religious Encounter* (Albany: State University of New York Press, 2002), 5. On the same problematic of reproducing the terms of domination in literary criticism, see Terry Eagleton, *Literary Theory: An Introduction* (Minneapolis: University of Minnesota Press, 2008), esp. 1–14 and 169–208.

7. For good examples of this, see Lisa Brooks's account of the land-related transactions and judicial maneuvers leading up to King Philip's War in *Our Beloved Kin: A New History of King Philip's War* (New Haven, Conn.: Yale University Press, 2018).

8. Jodi Byrd, *The Transit of Empire: Indigenous Critiques of Colonialism* (Minneapolis: University of Minnesota Press, 2011), xviii.

9. Stephanie Nohelai Teves, Andrea Smith, and Michelle H. Raheja, "Introduction and Acknowledgments," in *Native Studies Keywords,* ed. Teves, Smith, and Raheja (Tucson: University of Arizona Press, 2015), viii. The terms in this volume are "sovereignty," "land," "indigeneity," "tradition," "nation," "blood," "colonialism," and "indigenous epistemologies/knowledges." Each term is taken up in two short essays by scholars taking different approaches to the concept, a dialogic structure that departs from other keywords studies, including recent ones such as Roland Greene, *Five Words: Critical Semantics in the Age of Shakespeare and Cervantes* (Chicago: University of Chicago Press, 2013).

10. James H. Merrell, "Second Thoughts on Colonial Historians and American Indians," *William and Mary Quarterly,* 3rd ser., 69, no. 3 (2012): 457; see also Merrell, "Some Thoughts on Colonial Historians and American Indians," *William and Mary Quarterly,* 3rd ser., 46, no. 1 (1989): 94–119.

NOTES TO INTRODUCTION   161

11. Raymond Williams, *Keywords: A Vocabulary of Culture and Society*, rev. ed. (Oxford: Oxford University Press, 1985), 10.

12. Williams, *Keywords*, 22.

13. Édouard Glissant, *Poetics of Relation*, trans. Betsy Wing (Ann Arbor: University of Michigan Press, 1997), 1.

14. The literature here is vast, but key texts include James Clifford and George E. Marcus, *Writing Culture: The Poetics and Politics of Ethnography* (Berkeley: University of California Press, 1986); Renato Rosaldo, *Culture and Truth: The Remaking of Social Analysis* (Boston: Beacon, 1993); Michael A. Elliott, *The Culture Concept: Writing and Difference in the Age of Realism* (Minneapolis: University of Minnesota Press, 2002); and Lee D. Baker, *Anthropology and the Racial Politics of Culture* (Durham, N.C.: Duke University Press, 2010). More recently, for a history and defense of the concept, see Terry Eagleton, *Culture* (New Haven, Conn.: Yale University Press, 2018).

15. Glissant, *Poetics of Relation*, 169.

16. Williams, *Keywords*, 23.

17. Robert F. Berkhofer Jr., *Beyond the Great Story: History as Text and Discourse* (Cambridge, Mass.: Harvard University Press, 1995); see also Calvin Martin, ed., *The American Indian and the Problem of History* (Oxford: Oxford University Press, 1987); Devon A. Mihesuah, *Indigenous American Women: Decolonization, Empowerment, Activism* (Lincoln: University of Nebraska Press, 2003); Mihesuah, ed., *Natives and Academics: Researching and Writing about American Indians* (Lincoln: University of Nebraska Press, 1998); and Susan A. Miller and James Riding In, eds., *Native Historians Write Back: Decolonizing American Indian History* (Lubbock: Texas Tech University Press, 2011).

18. See the arguments in Eve Tuck and K. Wayne Yang, "Decolonization Is Not a Metaphor," *Decolonization* 1, no. 1 (2012): 1–40; and Manu Karuka, "Counter-sovereignty," *J19: Journal of Nineteenth Century Americanists* 2, no. 1 (2014): 142–48. The reflections that follow in this book have been inspired by many thinkers, but in key ways by the following works: Paula Gunn Allen, *Off the Reservation: Reflections on Boundary-Busting, Border-Crossing Loose Canons* (Boston: Beacon, 1998); Taiaiake Alfred, *Peace, Power, Righteousness: An Indigenous Manifesto*, 2nd ed. (Oxford: Oxford University Press, 2009); Walter Benjamin, "On the Concept of History," in *Selected Writings, Vol. 4, 1938–40* (Cambridge, Mass.: Harvard University Press, 2003); Brooks, *Our Beloved Kin*; Michel de Certeau, *The Writing of History* (New York: Columbia University Press, 1992); Clarice Lispector, "Love," in

NOTES TO INTRODUCTION

Daydream and Drunkenness of a Young Lady, trans. Katrina Dodson (New York: Penguin Classics, 2018), 17–34; Scott Richard Lyons, *X-Marks: Native Signatures of Assent* (Minneapolis: University of Minnesota Press, 2010); Saidiya Hartman, *Lose Your Mother: A Journey along the Atlantic Slave Route* (New York: Farrar, Straus and Giroux, 2008); and Robert Warrior, *Tribal Secrets: Recovering American Indian Intellectual Traditions* (Minneapolis: University of Minnesota Press, 1994). The deep patterns of professional conventionality analyzed in each of the following chapters might be thought of as what Ludwig Wittgenstein famously called "forms of life"; Wittgenstein, *Philosophical Investigations,* ed. and trans. P. M. S. Hacker and Joachim Schulte (Oxford: Wiley-Blackwell, 2009), 241.

19. On this critical "unsettling" in colonial studies, see Anna Brickhouse, *The Unsettlement of America: Translation, Interpretation, and the Story of Don Luis de Velasco, 1560–1945* (Oxford: Oxford University Press, 2014).

20. For a summa of queer pessimism, see Lauren Berlant and Lee Edelman, *Sex, or The Unbearable* (Durham, N.C.: Duke University Press, 2013); versions of Afropessimism inspiring this book can be found in Stefano Harney and Fred Moten, *The Undercommons: Fugitive Planning and Black Study* (New York: Minor Compositions, 2013); and Hartman, *Lose Your Mother.*

21. For queer temporality theory, see Elizabeth Freeman, *Time Binds: Queer Temporalities, Queer Histories* (Durham, N.C.: Duke University Press, 2010); Mark Rifkin, *Beyond Settler Time: Temporal Sovereignty and Indigenous Self-Determination* (Durham, N.C.: Duke University Press, 2017); and Jack Halberstam, *In a Queer Time and Place: Transgender Bodies, Subcultural Lives* (New York: New York University Press, 2005). Among postsecularist religious studies, see Tracy Fessenden, *Culture and Redemption: Religion, the Secular, and American Literature* (Princeton, N.J.: Princeton University Press, 2007); and John Lardas Modern, *Secularism in Antebellum America* (Chicago: University of Chicago Press, 2011). For Native American and Indigenous studies' interrogations of sovereignty and identity, see, among many others, Audra Simpson, *Mohawk Interruptus: Political Life across the Borders of the Settler States* (Durham, N.C.: Duke University Press, 2014); Mark Rifkin, *The Erotics of Sovereignty: Queer Native Writing in the Era of Self-Determination* (Minneapolis: University of Minnesota Press, 2012); Alfred, *Peace, Power, Righteousness*; and Michael F. Brown, "Sovereignty's Betrayals," in *Indigenous Experience Today,* ed. Marisol de la Cadena and Orin Starn (London: Routledge, 2007), 171–94. For irony, see Gerald Vizenor, *Man-*

ifest Manners: Narratives on Postindian Survivance (Lincoln, Neb.: Bison Books, 1999).

22. Eduardo Viveiros de Castro, "Perspectival Anthropology and the Method of Controlled Equivocation in Tipití," *Journal of the Society for the Anthropology of Lowland South America* 2, no. 1 (2004): 11, 5. The ontological turn in anthropology extends its reflexive journey since the era discussed in chapter 4; in the words of three of its practitioners, it is "a technology of description designed in the optimist (non-skeptical) hope of making the otherwise visible by experimenting with the conceptual affordances present in a given body of ethnographic materials." See Martin Holbraad, Morten Axel Pedersen, and Eduardo Viveiros de Castro, "The Politics of Ontology: Anthropological Positions," Theorizing the Contemporary, *Cultural Anthropology* website (2014), https://culanth.org/fieldsights/462-the-politics-of-ontology-anthropological-positions. See also Marisol de la Cadena, "Indigenous Cosmopolitics in the Andes: Conceptual Reflections beyond 'Politics,'" *Cultural Anthropology* 25, no. 2 (2010): 334–70; and de la Cadena, *Earth Beings: Ecologies of Practice across Andean Worlds* (Durham, N.C.: Duke University Press, 2015).

23. Glissant, *Poetics of Relation*; Siobhan Senier, *Sovereignty and Sustainability: Indigenous Literary Stewardship in New England* (Lincoln: University of Nebraska Press, 2020); Susan Howe, *The Birth-Mark: Unsettling the Wilderness in American Literary History* (Hanover, N.H.: University Press of New England, 1993); Saidiya Hartman, *Wayward Lives, Beautiful Experiments: Intimate Histories of Social Upheaval* (New York: Norton, 2019); and Brooks, *Our Beloved Kin*.

24. Simpson, *Mohawk Interruptus*, 11; Lauren Berlant, *Cruel Optimism* (Durham, N.C.: Duke University Press, 2011). My thanks to Micah Bateman for the notion of strategic pessimism.

25. Christine M. DeLucia, *Memory Lands: King Philip's War and the Place of Violence in the Northeast* (New Haven, Conn.: Yale University Press, 2018), 1.

26. DeLucia, *Memory Lands*, 9.

1. Cosmopuritanism

1. An American [Lydia Maria Child], *Hobomok, a Tale of Early Times* (Boston: Cummings, Hilliard, 1824), 6, 10.

2. Child, *Hobomok*, 11.

3. See Peter C. Mancall, *The Trials of Thomas Morton: An Anglican Lawyer, His Puritan Foes, and the Battle for a New England* (New Haven, Conn.: Yale University Press, 2019), esp. 1–17 and 179–210.

4. Nathaniel Hawthorne, "The May-Pole of Merry Mount," in *Twice-Told Tales* (Boston: American Stationers, 1837), 78.

5. Jack P. Greene, *Pursuits of Happiness: The Social Development of Early Modern British Colonies and the Formation of American Culture* (Chapel Hill: University of North Carolina Press, 1988); Greene, "Transatlantic Colonization and the Redefinition of Empire in the Early Modern Era: The British–American Experience," in *Negotiated Empires: Centers and Peripheries in the Americas, 1500–1820,* ed. Christine Daniels and Michael V. Kennedy (New York: Routledge, 2002), 267–82; David Grayson Allen, *In English Ways: The Movement of Societies and the Transferal of English Local Law and Custom to Massachusetts Bay in the Seventeenth Century* (New York: Norton, 1982); Ralph Bauer, *The Cultural Geography of Colonial American Literatures: Empire, Travel, Modernity* (Cambridge: Cambridge University Press, 2003); Douglas Anderson, *William Bradford's Books:* Of Plimmoth Plantation *and the Printed Word* (Baltimore, Md.: Johns Hopkins University Press, 2003); and Jan Stievermann, *Prophecy, Piety, and the Problem of Historicity: Interpreting the Hebrew Scriptures in Cotton Mather's* Biblia Americana (Tübingen: Mohr-Siebeck, 2016). More generally, see Alison Games, *The Web of Empire: English Cosmopolitans in an Age of Expansion, 1560–1660* (Oxford: Oxford University Press, 2008); Virginia DeJohn Anderson, *New England's Generation: The Great Migration and the Formation of Society and Culture in the Seventeenth Century* (Cambridge: Cambridge University Press, 1991); Mark Peterson, *The City-State of Boston: The Rise and Fall of an Atlantic Power, 1630–1865* (Princeton, N.J.: Princeton University Press, 2019); and Kirsten Silva Gruesz, *Cotton Mather's Spanish Lessons: Language, Race, and American Memory* (Cambridge, Mass.: Harvard University Press, 2022).

6. Lauren Berlant, "Poor Eliza," *American Literature* 70 (1998): 636, Peter Coviello, "Agonizing Affection: Affect and Nation in Early America," *Early American Literature* 37, no. 3 (2001): 439–68; Kathleen Donegan, *Seasons of Misery: Catastrophe and Colonial Settlement in Early America* (Philadelphia: University of Pennsylvania Press, 2013); Bryce Traister, ed., *American Literature and the New Puritan Studies* (Cambridge: Cambridge University Press, 2017); and Sarah Rivett and Abram Van Engen, "Postexceptionalist Puritanism," introduction to special issue edited by Rivett and Van Engen, *American Literary History* 90, no. 4 (2018): 675–92. Important

precedents for this strand of work include Andrew Delbanco, *The Puritan Ordeal* (Cambridge, Mass.: Harvard University Press, 1989); Mitchell Breitweiser, *American Puritanism and the Defense of Mourning: Religion, Grief, and Ethnology in Mary White Rowlandson's Captivity Narrative* (Madison: University of Wisconsin Press, 1990); and Sacvan Bercovitch, *The American Jeremiad* (Madison: University of Wisconsin Press, 1978).

7. Neal Salisbury, *Manitou and Providence: Indians, Europeans, and the Making of New England, 1500–1643* (Oxford: Oxford University Press, 1982), 164.

8. Craig Calhoun, "The Class Consciousness of Frequent Travelers: Toward a Critique of Actually Existing Cosmopolitanism," *South Atlantic Quarterly* 101, no. 4 (2002): 883.

9. See Bauer, *Cultural Geography*; Ed White, "Early American Nations as Imagined Communities," *American Quarterly* 56, no. 1 (2004): 49–81; and Jorge Cañizares-Esguerra, *Puritan Conquistadors: Iberianizing the Atlantic, 1550–1700* (Stanford, Calif.: Stanford University Press, 2006).

10. Joy Harjo, "In Mystic," in *Conflict Resolution for Holy Beings: Poems* (New York: Norton, 2017), 62.

11. Rob Wilson, "A New Cosmopolitanism Is in the Air: Some Dialectical Twists and Turns," in *Cosmopolitics: Thinking and Feeling beyond the Nation,* ed. Pheng Cheah and Bruce Robbins (Minneapolis: University of Minnesota Press, 1998), 355.

12. The critical literature on nationalism and cosmopolitanism is vast. Good surveys of the debate, including important contributions to it, are found in Bruce Robbins, "Introduction Part I: Actually Existing Cosmopolitanisms," in Cheah and Robbins, *Cosmopolitics,* 1–19; and Sheldon Pollock, Homi K. Bhabha, Carol A. Breckenridge, and Dipesh Chakrabarty, eds., "Cosmopolitanisms," *Public Culture* 12, no. 3 (2000). David Harvey's work is an important exception to the schematic I offer here; see Harvey, "Cosmopolitanism and the Banality of Geographical Evils," *Public Culture* 12, no. 2 (2000): 529–64. Suspicions of cosmopolitanism similar to mine are also found in Benedict Anderson, *The Spectre of Comparisons: Nationalism, Southeast Asia, and the World* (London: Verso, 1998); and Partha Chatterjee, *The Politics of the Governed: Reflections on Popular Politics in Most of the World* (New York: Columbia University Press, 2004). David A. Hollinger argues that cosmopolitanism's resurgence as a critical category in the 1990s emerged from a reaction against pluralist multiculturalism; see Hollinger, *Postethnic America: Beyond Multiculturalism* (New York: Basic Books, 1995).

13. Martha C. Nussbaum, "Patriotism and Cosmopolitanism," in *For Love of Country: Debating the Limits of Patriotism,* ed. Joshua Cohen (Boston: Beacon Press, 1996), 4.

14. The idea of "cosmopolitan democracy," despite differences in approach and emphasis, appears in Robbins, "Introduction Part I," and in Calhoun, "Class Consciousness," 869–97; see also Nussbaum, "Patriotism and Cosmopolitanism"; David Held, *Democracy and the Global Order: From the Modern State to Cosmopolitan Governance* (Stanford, Calif.: Stanford University Press, 1996); and Kwame Anthony Appiah, "Cosmopolitan Patriots," in Cheah and Robbins, *Cosmopolitics,* 91–114. Appiah distinguishes patriotism from nationalism, observing that one can be patriotic to a nonnational group or locale.

15. Chantal Mouffe, *The Democratic Paradox* (New York: Verso, 2000), 42.

16. Frantz Fanon, *The Wretched of the Earth* (New York: Grove Press, 1968), 247; see also Timothy Brennan, "Cosmopolitanism and Internationalism," *New Left Review* 7 (2001): 75–84; and Brennan, "Cosmo-Theory," *South Atlantic Quarterly* 100, no. 3 (2001): 659–91.

17. It has, however, made possible the beginnings of a critique of the academy's particular investment in speaking about cosmopolitanism. James Clifford, in "Mixed Feelings," in Cheah and Robbins, *Cosmopolitics,* 362–70, calls for "a clear-sighted awareness of institutional entanglement and a skepticism of the purifying dodges that abound in 'political' critique" based on cosmopolitanism (368).

18. Bradford quoted in Nathaniel Morton, *New-Englands Memoriall* (Cambridge, Mass.: John Usher, 1669), 144–45.

19. See also Hebrews 11:13, and I Peter 2:11. All biblical quotations in this chapter are from the Geneva Bible, 1587 edition. This poem is discussed and annotated in William Bradford, *The Collected Verse,* ed. Michael G. Runyan (St. Paul: John Colet, 1974), 238–49.

20. Here I focus on shared characteristics of separatists and Puritans in order to obtain critical leverage on cosmopolitanism. Distinctions among nonconformists are crucial to understanding the development of religious and political forms in Anglo-America. At the same time, these Calvinist religious forms shared an argument about the structure of the relationship between a believer and the larger world, rooted in the common insistence that believers have an individual relationship with God and that Christ's kingdom must be brought to earth. Property laws and church membership rules dif-

fered from colony to colony, but the structure linking these to religious imperatives through spatial and territorial metaphors or antitypes taken from the Bible was similar. Janice Knight observes a more outward-looking emphasis in the Cambridge-descended preachers of the Puritan colonies, but orthodox leaders were united in their interest in maintaining power through the sermon form and through a rigorous control over the terms of belonging to the church. See Edmund S. Morgan, *Visible Saints: The History of a Puritan Idea* (Ithaca, N.Y.: Cornell University Press, 1965); Darrett Rutman, *American Puritanism: Faith and Practice* (Philadelphia, Pa.: Lippincott, 1970); Stephen Foster, *The Long Argument: English Puritanism and the Shaping of New England Culture, 1570–1700* (Chapel Hill: University of North Carolina Press, 1991); and Philip F. Gura, *A Glimpse of Sion's Glory: Puritan Radicalism in New England, 1620–1660* (Middletown, Conn.: Wesleyan University Press, 1984).

21. Roger Williams, *The Hireling Ministry None of Christs, or A Discourse Touching the Propagating the Gospel of Christ Jesus* (London, 1652), A2v–A3r.

22. Nan Goodman, *The Puritan Cosmopolis: The Law of Nations and the Early American Imagination* (Oxford: Oxford University Press, 2018); see also Gruesz, *Cotton Mather's Spanish Lessons*.

23. "A Modell of Christian Charity" (1630?), New York Heritage Digital Collections, https://cdm16694.contentdm.oclc.org/digital/collection/p16124coll1/id/1952. See Jerome McGann's discussion of the authorship of this document in *Culture and Language at Crossed Purposes: The Unsettled Records of American Settlement* (Chicago: University of Chicago Press, 2022).

24. Cotton Mather, *India Christiana* (Boston: B. Green, 1721), 57.

25. Carrie Hyde, *Civic Longing: The Speculative Origins of U.S. Citizenship* (Cambridge, Mass: Harvard University Press, 2018), 45.

26. Hyde, *Civic Longing*, 47.

27. The political theology of American nonconformist cosmopolitanism might be seen as one of the local formations antecedent to what Mary Louise Pratt terms "planetary consciousness," a Eurocentric imagination of the relationships among individuals, nations, and the world whose persuasiveness is rooted in metaphors taken from science. Pratt, *Imperial Eyes: Travel Writing and Acculturation* (New York: Routledge, 1992), 15–36.

28. Louise Breen, *Transgressing the Bounds: Subversive Enterprises among the Puritan Elite in Massachusetts, 1630–1692* (Oxford: Oxford University Press, 2001), makes an important argument about New England cosmopolitanism that nonetheless shows the need for a more nuanced and historically

specific understanding of nonlocal thinking in the colonies. Pointing out that orthodox Puritanism was more democratic than antinomianism, Breen argues that orthodoxy appealed to those middling groups invested in local economics and politics who were likely to achieve independent landholding status. Such residents organized by various means—antinomianism, the formation of militia companies—to bring their vision of community into the political field. For Breen, "dueling versions of the good life, pitting localism against cosmopolitanism and homogeneity versus heterogeneity, competed with one another persistently throughout the entire century and beyond" (9). Yet much like homogeneity or heterogeneity, cosmopolitanism is in the eye of the beholder. If the Puritan valorization of conformity appealed, it was because of an already configured argument, made by those ministers and leaders whom Breen considers insularists, about how individuals should relate to and think about space, nation, and time in pursuit of grace. This tension may be better understood as a contest between different cosmopolitanisms.

29. Walter Mignolo, "The Many Faces of Cosmo-polis: Border Thinking and Critical Cosmopolitanism," *Public Culture* 12, no. 3 (2000): 721.

30. Scholarly work on the history of cosmopolitanism emphasizes its Enlightenment origins and in many cases depends on a Kantian conceptual vocabulary (universalism, rationality, citizenship) that coalesced in the intellectual currents of the eighteenth century. With a few exceptions, this history presumes that in the sixteenth and early seventeenth centuries there was a profound skepticism about cosmopolitanism rooted in local variation, imperial competition, religious narrow-mindedness, and protean forms of modern reason and science. For exceptions, see Tom Conley, *The Self-Made Map: Cartographic Writing in Early Modern France* (Minneapolis: University of Minnesota Press, 1996); Denis Cosgrove, "Globalism and Tolerance in Early Modern Geography," *Annals of the Association of American Geographers* 93, no. 4 (2003): 852–70; and Stephen Toulmin, *Cosmopolis: The Hidden Agenda of Modernity* (New York: Free Press, 1990).

31. Julian Yates, *Error, Misuse, Failure: Object Lessons from the English Renaissance* (Minneapolis: University of Minnesota Press, 2003), 109.

32. Sir John Mandeville's travel narrative was the central English text of this genre until the sixteenth century; see Stephen Greenblatt, *Marvelous Possessions: The Wonder of the New World* (Chicago: University of Chicago Press, 1991), 26–51. On shifts in the uses of travel narrative, see Anthony Parr, "Foreign Relations in Jacobean England: The Sherley Brothers and the 'Voyage of Persia,'" in *Travel and Drama in Shakespeare's Time*, ed. Jean Pierre

Maquerlot and Michele Willems (Cambridge: Cambridge University Press, 1996), 14–31; and Parr, ed., *Three Renaissance Travel Plays* (Manchester: Manchester University Press, 2000).

33. Bauer, *Cultural Geography,* 84.

34. Thomas Palmer, *An Essay of the Meanes How to Make Our Trauailes, into Forraine Countries, the More Profitable and Honourable* (London, 1606), A2v, 1.

35. On the Dutch commercial framework for the global connectedness with which New England Puritans contended, see Simon Schama, *The Embarrassment of Riches: An Interpretation of Dutch Culture in the Golden Age* (New York: Knopf, 1987); and Perry Miller, *The New England Mind: The Seventeenth Century* (Cambridge, Mass.: Harvard University Press, 1987). Bradford reports in *Of Plimmoth Plantation* that emigrants' motives included the preservation of the English language and customs among the separatists' children, who were rapidly adopting Dutch habits.

36. See Jonathan I. Israel, *Radical Enlightenment: Philosophy and the Making of Modernity, 1650–1750* (Oxford: Oxford University Press, 2001).

37. Anonymous [possibly Henry Ainsworth], *The Confession of Faith of Certayn English People, Living in Exile, in the Low Countreyes* (Amsterdam, 1607), A2r.

38. *Confession of Faith,* A2v.

39. Ann Kibbey, *The Interpretation of Material Shapes in Puritanism: A Study of Rhetoric, Prejudice, and Violence* (Cambridge: Cambridge University Press, 1986), 131. For analyses of Puritan preaching and oral authority, see Jane Kamensky, *Governing the Tongue: The Politics of Speech in Early New England* (Oxford: Oxford University Press, 1999); David D. Hall, *Worlds of Wonder, Days of Judgment: Popular Religious Belief in Early New England* (Cambridge, Mass.: Harvard University Press, 1990); Sandra Gustafson, *Eloquence Is Power: Oratory and Performance in Early America* (Chapel Hill: University of North Carolina Press, 2000); and Meredith Neuman, *Jeremiah's Scribes: Literary Theories of the Sermon in Puritan New England* (Philadelphia: University of Pennsylvania Press, 2013).

40. Kibbey, *Interpretation of Material Shapes,* 125.

41. Anonymous, *A Relation or Iournall of the Beginning and Proceedings of the English Plantation Setled at Plimoth* (London, 1622), 65.

42. *Relation or Iournall,* 66.

43. *Relation or Iournall,* 68, 69. For discussions of the rhetoric of settlement in relation to colonial concepts of property and sovereignty, see

Patricia Seed, *Ceremonies of Possession in Europe's Conquest of the New World, 1492–1640* (Cambridge: Cambridge University Press, 1995); Jean O'Brien, *Dispossession by Degrees: Indian Land and Identity in Natick, Massachusetts, 1650–1790* (Lincoln: University of Nebraska Press, 2003); and O'Brien, *Firsting and Lasting: Writing Indians out of Existence in New England* (Minneapolis: University of Minnesota Press, 2010).

44. *Relation or Iournall*, 68.

45. Massachusetts Bay passed laws in the 1630s requiring residents to live within a short radius of the meetinghouse, and in the following decade added other laws requiring church attendance by all residents. An "Essay on the Ordering of Towns," in the Winthrop papers, recommends that settlement be limited to a radius of no more than two miles from a town's meetinghouse. See John Winthrop, *Winthrop Papers* (Boston: Massachusetts Historical Society, 1943), 3:181–83; and Morgan, *Visible Saints,* 123.

46. See Greene, "Transatlantic Colonization"; Mark Greengrass, *Conquest and Coalescence: The Shaping of the State in Early Modern Europe* (New York: Routledge, 1991); and Jenny Hale Pulsifer, *Subjects unto the Same King: Indians, English, and the Contest for Authority in Colonial New England* (Philadelphia: University of Pennsylvania Press, 2006).

47. Jace Weaver, *The Red Atlantic: American Indigenes and the Making of the Modern World, 1000–1927* (Chapel Hill: University of North Carolina Press, 2014), 17. See also Coll Thrush, *Indigenous London: Native Travelers at the Heart of Empire* (New Haven, Conn.: Yale University Press, 2016); Anna Brickhouse, *The Unsettlement of America: Translation, Interpretation, and the Story of Don Luis de Velasco, 1560–1945* (Oxford: Oxford University Press, 2014); and Alden T. Vaughn, *Transatlantic Encounters: American Indians in Britain, 1500–1776* (Cambridge: Cambridge University Press, 2008).

48. See Salisbury, *Manitou and Providence*; Lisa Brooks, *The Common Pot: The Recovery of Native Space in the Northeast* (Minneapolis: University of Minnesota Press, 2008); and Kathleen Bragdon, *Native People of Southern New England, 1500–1650* (Norman: University of Oklahoma Press, 1996).

49. On the Pequot War, see Alfred A. Cave, *The Pequot War* (Amherst: University of Massachusetts Press, 1996); Francis Jennings, *The Invasion of America: Indians, Colonialism, and the Cant of Conquest* (New York: Norton, 1976); Richard Slotkin, *Regeneration through Violence: The Mythology of the American Frontier, 1600–1860* (Middletown, Conn.: Wesleyan University Press, 1974); Roy Harvey Pearce, *Savagism and Civilization: A Study of the Indian and the American Mind* (Baltimore, Md.: Johns Hopkins Univer-

sity Press, 1967); Alden T. Vaughan, *New England Frontier: Puritans and Indians, 1620–1675,* 3rd. ed. (Norman: University of Oklahoma Press, 1995); and Salisbury, *Manitou and Providence,* 203–24.

50. Salisbury calls this the "wampum revolution"; see *Manitou and Providence,* 147–48. See also Paul A. Robinson, "Lost Opportunities: Miantonomi and the English in Seventeenth-Century Narragansett Country," in *Northeastern Indian Lives,* ed. Robert S. Grumet (Amherst: University of Massachusetts Press, 1996), 13–28.

51. Lynn Ceci, "Native Wampum as a Peripheral Resource in the Seventeenth-Century World System," in *The Pequots in Southern New England: The Rise and Fall of an American Indian Nation,* ed. Laurence M. Hauptman and James D. Wherry (Norman: University of Oklahoma Press, 1990), 60–61. See also Kevin McBride, "The Source and Mother of the Fur Trade: Native–Dutch Relations in Eastern New Netherland," in *Enduring Traditions: The Native Peoples of New England,* ed. Laurie Lee Weinstein (Westport, Conn.: Bergin & Garvey, 1994), 33–51.

52. Edward Said, *Representations of the Intellectual* (New York: Vintage, 1996), 64.

53. Said, *Representations,* 53.

54. Bercovitch, *American Jeremiad,* 11.

55. Edward Said, *Culture and Imperialism* (New York: Vintage, 1993), 39; and see Homi K. Bhabha, "Locations of Culture," in *The Critical Tradition,* ed. David H. Richter (Boston: Bedford/St. Martin's, 1998), 1331–44.

56. George E. Tinker, *Missionary Conquest: The Gospel and Native American Cultural Genocide* (Minneapolis, Minn.: Augsburg Fortress, 1993); Alfred, *Peace, Power, Righteousness*; and Byrd, *Transit of Empire,* 117–46.

57. Homi K. Bhabha and Kwame Anthony Appiah, "Cosmopolitanism and Convergence," *New Literary History* 49, no. 2 (2018): 189; see also Homi K. Bhabha, "Unsatisfied: Notes on Vernacular Cosmopolitanism," in *Text and Nation: Cross-Disciplinary Essays on Cultural and National Identities,* ed. Laura García-Moreno and Peter C. Pfeiffer (Columbia, S.C.: Camden House, 1996), 191–207. "Some embraces can be sweet but toxic," Dorothy Wang writes. "The academic enamored of the global, transnational, cosmopolitan, and/or diasporic can be a slightly altered version of the familiar Orientalist," a narcissist "whose seeming valorization of the Oriental or subaltern thinly veils self-righteous imperialist drives." Wang, review of Kandice Chuh and Karen Shimakawa, eds., *Orientations: Mapping Studies in the Asian Diaspora,* in *Journal of Asian American Studies* 5, no. 3 (2002): 272. Similarly, see Nan

Z. Da, *Sino–U.S. Literatures and the Limits of Exchange* (New York: Columbia University Press, 2018); and Sam Knowles, "Macrocosm-opolitanism? Gilroy, Appiah, and Bhabha: The Unsettling Generality of Cosmopolitan Ideas," *Postcolonial Text* 3, no. 4 (2007): 1–11.

58. Gayatri Chakravorty Spivak—targeting Michel Foucault and Jacques Derrida at the time—made a foundational observation about the imagined cosmopolitan universalism of high critical theorists in "Can the Subaltern Speak?" See a revised version in *Can the Subaltern Speak? Reflections on the History of an Idea,* ed. Rosalind C. Morris (New York: Columbia University Press, 2010), 21–79.

59. Stephen Greenblatt, "Racial Memory and Literary History," *PMLA* 116, no. 1 (2001): 48–49.

60. Among many others, on the Jesuits, see James Axtell, *The Invasion Within: The Contest of Cultures in Colonial North America* (Oxford: Oxford University Press, 1985); on the Iroquois, Daniel K. Richter, *The Ordeal of the Longhouse: The Peoples of the Iroquois League in the Era of European Colonization* (Chapel Hill: University of North Carolina Press, 1992); and on the Society of Friends, Jane E. Calvert, "The Quaker Theory of a Civil Constitution," *History of Political Thought* 27, no. 4 (2006): 586–619.

61. Herman Melville, *The Confidence-Man: His Masquerade* (New York: Dix, Edwards, 1857), 245, 219.

62. Harjo, "In Mystic," 63.

63. Harjo, "In Mystic," 62.

2. Believing in Piety

1. N. Scott Momaday, "An Element of Piety," in *The Man Made of Words: Essays, Stories, Passages* (New York: St. Martin's, 1997), 193–95.

2. See the Southern Baptist Convention, https://www.sbc.net/ (as of September 2021).

3. James Garrison, *Pietas from Vergil to Dryden* (University Park: Pennsylvania State University Press, 1992), 258.

4. Considering the curve of Figure 1, and taking forms of the word *piety* as a proxy for devotional commitment more broadly, one wonders if what is referred to as the First Great Awakening may not have begun in the early eighteenth century and started to decline only around 1833. Max Weber, *The Protestant Ethic and the Spirit of Capitalism* (New York: Charles Scribner's Sons, 1958). Amanda Porterfield, arguing for the social power of female

piety in colonial New England in *Female Piety in Puritan New England: The Emergence of Religious Humanism* (Oxford: Oxford University Press, 1992), writes that the "religion of female piety was largely responsible for the social cohesion that existed in seventeenth-century New England," which by extension "made possible the economic success of the merchant class" (9). Respecting the skepticism of self described in the paragraphs that follow, see Andrew Delbanco, *The Puritan Ordeal* (Cambridge, Mass.: Harvard University Press, 1989).

5. Michael Kaufman, "Post-secular Puritans: Recent Retrials of Anne Hutchinson," *Early American Literature* 45, no. 1 (2010): 35.

6. "The distance, even marginality," Michael Denning writes in *Culture in the Age of Three Worlds* (New York: Verso, 2004), "of the Puritans from the canons of orthodox literary criticism, historiography, political science, sociology, and religious studies, combined with their presumed centrality to American culture, has allowed a richness of interdisciplinary work that is unparalleled in other fields of American studies" (182). On the postsecular, see in addition to the scholars cited later in this chapter John Lardas Modern, *Secularism in Antebellum America* (Chicago: University of Chicago Press, 2011).

7. For some of the scholarly landscape summarized here, see Perry Miller, *Errand into the Wilderness* (Cambridge, Mass.: Harvard University Press, 1956); Edmund S. Morgan, "The Historians of Early New England," in *The Reinterpretation of Early American History,* ed. Ray Allen Billington (San Marino, Calif.: Huntington Library, 1966), 41–63; Michael McGiffert, "American Puritan Studies in the 1960s," *William and Mary Quarterly,* 3rd ser., 27, no. 1 (1970): 36–67; David D. Hall, "On Common Ground: The Coherence of American Puritan Studies," *William and Mary Quarterly,* 3rd ser., 44, no. 2 (1987): 193–229; and Foster, *Long Argument.*

8. On white Indians, see James Axtell, *The European and the Indian: Essays in the Ethnohistory of Colonial North America* (Oxford: Oxford University Press, 1981), 168–206.

9. Douglas L. Winiarski, "Native American Popular Religion in New England's Old Colony, 1670–1770," *Religion and American Culture* 15, no. 2 (2005): 151.

10. Sir John Eliott, *Empires of the Atlantic World: Britain and Spain in America, 1492–1830* (New Haven, Conn.: Yale University Press, 2006); Jared Diamond, *Guns, Germs, and Steel: The Fates of Human Societies* (New York: Norton, 1999).

11. Winiarski, "Native American Popular Religion," 155.

12. The structure of this argument is inspired by the work of Michel Serres, in particular *The Parasite* (Baltimore, Md.: Johns Hopkins University Press, 1982), and the dialogical cosmology advocated in Kenneth M. Morrison, *The Solidarity of Kin: Ethnohistory, Religious Studies, and the Algonkian–French Religious Encounter* (Albany: State University of New York Press, 2002).

13. Vine Deloria Jr., *God Is Red: A Native View of Religion* (Golden: Fulcrum, 2003); and Deloria, *Custer Died for Your Sins: An Indian Manifesto* (New York: Macmillan, 1969).

14. Garrison, *Pietas from Vergil to Dryden*, 2. My discussion of *pietas* is indebted largely to Garrison.

15. See David Hall, "Transatlantic Passages: The Reformed Tradition and the Politics of Writing," in *Religious Transformations in the Early Modern Americas*, ed. Stephanie Kirk and Sarah Rivett (Philadelphia: University of Pennsylvania Press, 2014).

16. John Dryden, *The Works of John Dryden*, ed. Edward Niles Hooker, H. T. Swedenberg Jr., and Vinton A. Dearing, 16 vols. (Berkeley: University of California Press, 1956–2000), 5:288.

17. Virgil, *The Works of Virgil: Containing His Pastorals, Georgics, and Æneis*, trans. John Dryden (London, 1697); Cotton Mather, *Pietas in Patriam* (London, 1697). The title page of Cotton's 1697 edition features a quotation from book 12 of the *Aeneid*, "Discite Virtutem ex Hoc, verumque Laborem," or "Learn virtue/valor and true toil from this man." See an analysis rooted in the myth-symbol school in John Shields, *The American Aeneas: Classical Origins of the American Self* (Knoxville: University of Tennessee Press, 2001); an unusual treatment of *pietas* and Mather in Christopher Felker, *Reinventing Cotton Mather in the American Renaissance: Magnalia Christi Americana in Hawthorne, Stowe, and Stoddard* (Boston: Northeastern University Press, 1993); and Jane Donahue Eberwein, "'In a Book, as in a Glass': Literary Sorcery in Mather's Life of Phips," *Early American Literature* 10, no. 3 (1975): 289–300.

18. Augustine of Hippo, *De civitate Dei contra paganos*, ed. and trans. George E. McCracken et al., 7 vols. (Cambridge, Mass.: Harvard University Press, 1957), 2:82.

19. Quoted in William Bradford, *Of Plymouth Plantation, 1620–1647*, ed. Samuel Eliot Morison (New York: Modern Library, 1967), 197–98.

20. Jonathan Swift, *The Prose Works of Jonathan Swift*, ed. Herbert Davis, 14 vols. (Oxford: Oxford University Press, 1941), 11:278.

21. Perry Miller, *The New England Mind: The Seventeenth Century* (Boston: Beacon, 1968), 4, ix.

22. Walter D. Mignolo, *The Darker Side of the Renaissance: Literacy, Territoriality, and Colonization* (Ann Arbor: University of Michigan Press, 1995).

23. Janice Knight, *Orthodoxies in Massachusetts: Rereading American Puritanism* (Cambridge, Mass.: Harvard University Press, 1994); Matthew P. Brown, *The Pilgrim and the Bee: Reading Rituals and Book Cultures in Early New England* (Philadelphia: University of Pennsylvania Press, 2007), 179–207; Jordan Stein and Justine Murison, "Introduction: Religion and Method," *Early American Literature* 45, no. 1 (2010): 7. For other exemplary works on the period formed around the concept of piety, see Charles Hambrick-Stowe, *The Practice of Piety* (Chapel Hill: University of North Carolina Press, 1982); and Charles Cohen, *God's Caress: The Psychology of Puritan Religious Experience* (Oxford: Oxford University Press, 1986).

24. Saba Mahmood, *Politics of Piety: The Islamic Revival and the Feminist Subject* (Princeton, N.J.: Princeton University Press, 2005), 145.

25. Tracy Fessenden, "Religion, Literature, and Method," *Early American Literature* 45, no. 1 (2010): 185. It is illuminating when David Hall, for example, says plainly in the introduction to his edition of Hugh Amory's writing that the key thing to keep in mind as you consider his editorial effect on Amory's text is that he is a believer, and Amory was not. Hugh Amory, *Bibliography and the Book Trades: Studies in the Print Culture of Early New England*, ed. David D. Hall (Philadelphia: University of Pennsylvania Press, 2005).

26. Lyons, *X-Marks*, 96.

27. Joel W. Martin and Mark A. Nicholas, eds., *Native Americans, Christianity, and the Reshaping of the American Religious Landscape* (Chapel Hill: University of North Carolina Press, 2010), 8–9; David Silverman, *Faith and Boundaries: Colonists, Christianity, and Community among the Wampanoag Indians of Martha's Vineyard, 1600–1871* (Cambridge: Cambridge University Press, 2005). Anticipating these approaches was James P. Ronda, "Generations of the Faith: The Christian Indians of Martha's Vineyard," *William and Mary Quarterly*, 3rd ser., 38, no. 3 (1981): 369–94.

28. This is a fact that Nancy Shoemaker has also emphasized in questions

of gender, governance, and the body, and that Jill Lepore influentially argued in the case of war. See Nancy Shoemaker, *A Strange Likeness: Becoming Red and White in Eighteenth-Century North America* (Oxford: Oxford University Press, 2006); and Jill Lepore, *The Name of War: King Philip's War and the Origins of American Identity* (New York: Knopf, 1998). The argument for cultural similarity as a driver of differentiation is taken further in Erik Seeman, *Death in the New World: Cross-Cultural Encounters, 1492–1800* (Philadelphia: University of Pennsylvania Press, 2010). Seeman claims that similarity was the matrix of understanding for Europeans in the New World, and that from just after the beginning of colonization, similarities were put to exploitative use.

29. Rachel Wheeler, *To Live upon Hope: Mohicans and Missionaries in the Eighteenth-Century Northeast* (Ithaca, N.Y.: Cornell University Press, 2008), 82, 4.

30. Edward Andrews, *Native Apostles: Black and Indian Missionaries in the British Atlantic World* (Cambridge, Mass.: Harvard University Press, 2013).

31. Fessenden, "Religion, Literature, and Method," 191. See, e.g., Brown, *Pilgrim and the Bee*; Meredith Neuman, *Jeremiah's Scribes: Creating Sermon Literature in Puritan New England* (Philadelphia: University of Pennsylvania Press, 2013); and Lisa M. Gordis, *Opening Scripture: Bible Reading and Interpretive Authority in Puritan New England* (Chicago: University of Chicago Press, 2003).

32. Here I draw on Winiarski, "Native American Popular Religion." Winiarski's other works on the topic are equally rich.

33. David Hall, *Worlds of Wonder, Days of Judgment: Popular Religious Belief in Early New England* (New York: Knopf, 1989), 119.

34. Hall, *Worlds of Wonder*, 171.

35. Winiarski, "Native American Popular Religion," 149.

36. Daniel Mandell, "Eager Partners in Reform: Indians and Frederick Baylies in Southern New England, 1780–1840," in *Native Americans, Christianity, and the Reshaping of the American Religious Landscape*, ed. Joel W. Martin and Martin A. Nicholas (Chapel Hill: University of North Carolina Press, 2010), 38–66; Winiarski, "Native American Popular Religion"; and Joanna Brooks, "Hard Feelings: Samson Occom Contemplates His Christian Mentors," Martin and Nicholas, *Native Americans*, 23–37.

37. Andrews, *Native Apostles*, 228.

38. On "hand piety," see Brown, *Pilgrim and the Bee*, 102; Amory, *Bibliography*.

39. Walter Woodward, *Prospero's America: John Winthrop, Jr., Alchemy, and the Creation of New England Culture, 1606–1676* (Chapel Hill: Omohundro Institute and the University of North Carolina Press, 2010), 93–137.

40. Amory, *Bibliography*, 29; Nicholas Thomas, *Entangled Objects: Exchange, Material Culture, and Colonialism in the Pacific* (Cambridge, Mass.: Harvard University Press, 1991).

41. Kevin A. McBride, "Bundles, Bears, and Bibles: Interpreting Seventeenth-Century Native 'Texts,'" in *Early Native Literacies in New England: A Documentary and Critical Anthology*, ed. Kristina Bross and Hilary E. Wyss (Amherst: University of Massachusetts Press, 2008), 135.

42. See Seeman, *Death in the New World*.

43. See a longer discussion of the relations between kinship and systematicity in Matt Cohen, *The Networked Wilderness: Communicating in Early New England* (Minneapolis: University of Minnesota Press, 2009), especially chap. 4. On the complexities of the region's Indigenous politics in the seventeenth century, see Michael Leroy Oberg, *Uncas: First of the Mohegans* (Ithaca, N.Y.: Cornell University Press, 2006).

44. Ralph Ellison, *Invisible Man* (New York: Vintage, 1995), 13.

45. McBride, "Bundles, Bears, and Bibles," 136.

46. Frank Chouteau Brown, "'The Old House' at Cutchogue, Long Island, New York: Built in 1649," *Old-Time New England* 31, no. 1 (1940): 11–21; and John and William Blye, quoted in Robert Blair St. George, *Conversing by Signs: Poetics of Implication in Colonial New England* (Chapel Hill: University of North Carolina Press, 1998), 188.

47. George F. Horton, compiler, *Horton Genealogy, or Chronicles of the Descendants of Barnabas Horton, of Southold, L.I., 1640* (Philadelphia, Pa.: Home Circle, 1876).

48. Keith Thomas, *Religion and the Decline of Magic: Studies in Popular Beliefs in Sixteenth- and Seventeenth-Century England* (New York: Penguin, 1978). For a particularly intense version of the anti-Pequot position, see Jeff Benedict, *Without Reservation: The Making of America's Most Powerful Indian Tribe and Foxwoods the World's Largest Casino* (New York: HarperCollins, 2000).

49. Amory, *Bibliography*, 13.

50. The Pequots are the subject of a large and contentious body of writing; for a synopsis, see Cohen, *Networked Wilderness,* chap. 4.

51. Joanna Brooks, "From Edwards to Baldwin: Heterodoxy, Discontinuity, and New Narratives of American Religious-Literary History," *American Literary History* 45, no. 2 (2010): 429.

52. Foster, *Long Argument,* 305.

53. Carlo Ginzburg, *Clues, Myths, and the Historical Method,* trans. John and Anne C. Tedeschi (Baltimore, Md.: Johns Hopkins University Press, 1989), 106. Piety, it could be argued, belongs to that arsenal that Ginzburg describes as "the powerful and terrible weapon of abstraction" (115).

54. "We are always," writes Michel Serres, "simultaneously making gestures that are archaic, modern, and futuristic." Serres and Bruno Latour, *Conversations on Science, Culture, and Time,* trans. Roxanne Lapidus (Ann Arbor: University of Michigan Press, 1995), 60.

3. Waiting for the Beginning

1. *Tracts Relating to the Attempts to Convert to Christianity the Indians of New England,* Collections of the Massachusetts Historical Society, 3rd ser., vol. 4 (Cambridge, Mass.: Charles Folsom, 1834), 240. For Daniel K. Richter, *Facing East from Indian Country: A Native History of Early America* (Cambridge, Mass.: Harvard University Press, 2001), this qualification and elaboration signal evidentiary solidity: "Would the missionary have fabricated such an imperfect and inconsistent record of his big day, especially with a well-connected skeptical audience present to contradict him? Questions remain, but it seems likely that the narratives recorded in *Tears of Repentance* are a reasonably authentic record of the converts' speeches" (117). Impatience, as well as its management in the moment and in print, emerges as key here: the patience that Eliot dramatizes himself as having, in contrast even to the "graver sort," served him well at a time when Christian patience was the dominant framework for understanding such exhibitions. It seems also to have done so in the long run for the reception of his account as fact in the present.

2. *Transactions of the Buffalo Historical Society: Red Jacket* (Buffalo, N.Y.: Buffalo Historical Society, 1884), 40.

3. *Transactions of the Buffalo Historical Society: Red Jacket,* 41.

4. For a range of important work on temporality and cultural differences, see Rifkin, *Beyond Settler Time*; the notion of chrononormativity in Eliza-

beth Freeman, *Time Binds: Queer Temporalities, Queer Histories* (Durham, N.C.: Duke University Press, 2010); and Jason Farman, *Delayed Response: The Art of Waiting from the Ancient to the Instant World* (New Haven, Conn.: Yale University Press, 2019).

    5. Vine Deloria Jr., *We Talk, You Listen: New Tribes, New Turf* (New York: Dell, 1970), 62.

    6. See Marta Alda, Marta Puebla-Guedea, Baltasar Rodero, Marcelo Demarzo, Jesús Montero-Marín, Miquel Roca, and Javier García-Campayo, "Zen Meditation, Length of Telomeres, and the Role of Experiential Avoidance and Compassion," *Mindfulness* 7 (2016): 651–59; Zoë Corbyn, "Elizabeth Blackburn on the Telomere Effect: 'It's about Keeping Healthier for Longer,'" *Guardian,* January 29, 2017, https://www.theguardian.com/; and James Masters, "U.S. Scientists Awarded Nobel in Medicine for Body Clock Insights," CNN.com, October 2, 2017, http://www.cnn.com/. For Buddhists, the relationship between intersubjective understanding and the exercise of patience is causal. See Dalai Lama XIV, *Healing Anger: The Power of Patience from a Buddhist Perspective* (Ithaca, N.Y.: Snow Lion, 1997), which argues that the practice of patience is an often uncomfortable activity that cultivates compassion by way of an ability to apprehend the suffering of others. For another famous example of Native American claims about Western urgency, see the account of the treaty of Dancing Rabbit Creek in Frank Kelderman, *Authorized Agents: Publication and Diplomacy in the Era of Indian Removal* (Albany: State University of New York Press, 2019), 161–64.

    7. Robert Levine, *A Geography of Time: The Temporal Misadventures of a Social Psychologist, or How Every Culture Keeps Time Just a Little Bit Differently* (New York: Basic Books, 1997), 24.

    8. For an analysis of the "discrepant temporalities" of more recent colonial relations between Native America and the settler state, see Rifkin, *Beyond Settler Time*, 3.

    9. Walter Ong, *Orality and Literacy: The Technologizing of the Word* (New York: Methuen, 1982).

    10. James 1:4, Geneva Bible (1599 ed.).

    11. See also Ethan Shagan, *The Rule of Moderation: Violence, Religion, and the Politics of Restraint in Early Modern England* (Cambridge: Cambridge University Press, 2011): "The ubiquitous moral principle of moderation was a profoundly coercive tool of social, religious and political power" (3). Patience was, of course, one of the components of that moderation and hence was at the heart of contests over "proper" conduct and political action.

12. Lynch to Viscount Cornbury, March 29, 1672, quoted in Nuala Zahedieh, "Trade, Plunder, and Economic Development in Early English Jamaica, 1655–89," *Economic History Review,* n.s., 39, no. 2 (1986): 209.

13. Johannes Fabian, *Time and the Other: How Anthropology Makes Its Object* (New York: Columbia University Press, 1983).

14. On Williams, see Edmund S. Morgan, *Roger Williams: The Church and the State* (New York: Harcourt, Brace & World, 1967); and Edwin S. Gaustad, *Roger Williams* (Oxford: Oxford University Press, 2005).

15. Quoted in Rev. J. Lewis Diman, ed., introduction to *The Complete Works of Roger Williams,* vol. 5 (New York: Russell & Russell, 1963), vii. On the settler Quakers, see Thomas D. Hamm, *The Quakers in America* (New York: Columbia University Press, 2003).

16. Williams, *Complete Works,* title page, 3–4.

17. Williams, *A Key into the Language of America* (London: Dexter, 1643), 55.

18. Letter of Richard Scot, in George Fox and John Burnyeat, *A New-England Fire-Brand Quenched . . . ,* 2 vols. (London, 1678), 2:248.

19. Williams, *Complete Works,* 20.

20. Williams, *Complete Works,* 40.

21. "To the People Called Quakers," in Williams, *Complete Works,* p. 2, point 7.

22. Williams, *Complete Works,* 307–8.

23. Williams, *Complete Works,* 19.

24. Williams, *Complete Works,* 23.

25. Williams, *Complete Works,* 9.

26. Williams, *Complete Works,* 39.

27. Williams, *Complete Works,* 162, 34.

28. Williams, *Complete Works,* 213.

29. Fox and Burnyeat, *New-England Fire-Brand,* 1:223.

30. Fox and Burnyeat, *New-England Fire-Brand,* 2:216.

31. Fox and Burnyeat, *New-England Fire-Brand,* 1:218, 1:240.

32. Fox and Burnyeat, *New-England Fire-Brand,* 1:66.

33. Fox and Burnyeat, *New-England Fire-Brand,* 1:153, 1:130.

34. Williams, *Complete Works,* 45.

35. Fox and Burnyeat, *New-England Fire-Brand,* 1:175.

36. Williams, *Complete Works,* 218.

37. By publishing his book in Boston, and appending with it a letter to King Charles II, Williams placed this theological contest at the nexus of

earthly domains. Apparently wanting to draw as much on Williams's own words as he had on George Fox's, the Friends waited too: Fox and John Burnet did not publish their response until 1678 (in two volumes, in London). Although from internal evidence it appears that Williams composed the text not long after the conferences took place, the tome was not published until four years later, in the last phases of King Philip's War. It may be that the increasing tensions of 1674–75 delayed the book's issue. It has been speculated that Williams's text, written during the winter of 1672–73, was set in type in Boston not long after, but that the issue of the book was delayed. It is possible the book existed in sheets during the whole of the war, but it seems more likely that Williams had arranged for publication and therefore wrote his prefatory material in that expectation, with Foster waiting to set the text until funding was obtained. Williams's manuscript's being in Boston would also explain the survival of his copy despite the burning of Providence during the conflict. Governor John Leverett paid the costs of publication when it eventually appeared. See Williams, *The Correspondence of Roger Williams,* ed. Glenn LaFantasie, 2 vols. (Providence: Rhode Island Historical Society and University Press of New England, 1988), 2:688–90. In any case, it seems possible that in the wake of King Philip's War, there was at once a solace in returning to theological combat and a heightened rhetorical edge for Williams, whose accusations of Quaker similitude to Native Americans and insistence on the Friends' threat to colonial sovereignty would ring loud in the wake of the most devastating conflict the English had experienced in America.

38. Williams, *Complete Works,* 39.
39. Brooks, *Our Beloved Kin,* 115. Much of my account here is based on Brooks's extraordinary book.
40. Brooks, *Our Beloved Kin,* 126, 131.
41. Brooks, *Our Beloved Kin,* 8.
42. Williams, *Correspondence,* 2:695.
43. Williams, *Correspondence,* 2:722.
44. Williams, *Correspondence,* 2:723.
45. Williams, *Correspondence,* 2:723.
46. Williams, *Correspondence,* 2:724.
47. Brooks, *Our Beloved Kin,* 284.
48. Quoted in Noah Newman to John Cotton, March 14, 1676, Curwen Family Papers, American Antiquarian Society. See discussions of this letter in, e.g., Lepore, *Name of War,* 94–96, 283n96; and Brooks, *Our Beloved Kin,*

258–61, 403n11, where she discusses the possibility that Printer wrote the note at Nashaway leader Monoco's dictation.

49. Brooks, *Our Beloved Kin,* 287.
50. Williams, *Keywords,* 63, 116.
51. Williams, *Keywords,* 162.
52. John Underhill, *Newes from America . . .* (London, 1638), 14.
53. Proverbs 14:29, Geneva Bible (1599 ed.).
54. Underhill, *Newes from America,* 14.
55. Brooks, *Our Beloved Kin,* 4.
56. N. Scott Momaday, *House Made of Dawn* (1968; reprint, New York: Harper Perennial Modern Classics, 2010), 53; James Clifford, "Varieties of Indigenous Experience: Diasporas, Homelands, Sovereignties," in *Indigenous Experience Today,* ed. Marisol de la Cadena and Orin Starn (New York: Berg, 2007), 199; Glen Sean Coulthard, *Red Skin, White Masks: Rejecting the Colonial Politics of Recognition* (Minneapolis: University of Minnesota Press, 2014), 168.

4. Rethinking Reciprocity

1. Nathaniel Saltonstall, *A New and Further Narrative of the State of New-England* (London, 1676), 6–7. On Puritan piety and American Indians, see, e.g., Lepore, *Name of War*; and Kibbey, *Interpretation of Material Shapes.* Lepore observes that the Algonquian anti-Christian actions reported during the war bear strong similarity to Catholic anti-Protestant actions in religious riots of the era, and that their descriptions may be a result of Native reactions to the distinctive character of congregationalism in New England, or of English dissenters' rhetorical habits, or some combination of these (Lepore, *Name of War,* 286n28). Goodman Wright's story is more layered than my brief summary can indicate: Saltonstall's narrative offers him as a warning to other settlers against independent interpretation of the Bible and too much reliance on the Bible as an object of security, as opposed to investment in the common defense. On warfare and reciprocity in Algonquian societies, see, e.g., Adam J. Hirsch, "The Collision of Military Cultures in Seventeenth-Century New England," *Journal of American History* 74, no. 4 (1988): 1187–212; and Salisbury, *Manitou and Providence.*

2. John Collier, *Indians of the Americas: The Long Hope,* abridged ed. (New York: Mentor, 1960), 11.

3. On "unitary totalities," see Nicholas Thomas, *Entangled Objects: Ex-*

change, Material Culture, and Colonialism in the Pacific (Cambridge, Mass.: Harvard University Press, 1991). This identification of a culture with one of its logics in contradistinction to other cultures is reminiscent of Dumontian anthropology, which posited a contrast between South Asian (hierarchical and holistic) and Western (equalitarian and individualistic) modes of social being. See Louis Dumont, *Homo Hierarchicus: The Caste System and Its Implications* (Chicago: University of Chicago Press, 1970).

4. I am not directly engaging Nancy Fraser's controversial essay "Rethinking Recognition," from which my title takes its structure, but I take energy from her sense of the way recognition might function at cross-purposes to the long-term goals of those who invoke it. See Fraser, "Rethinking Recognition: Overcoming Displacement and Reification in Cultural Politics," in *Adding Insult to Injury: Nancy Fraser Answers Her Critics,* ed. Kevin Olson (New York: Verso, 2008), 129–41. As Glen Sean Coulthard, to take just one of many critics of Fraser's framework, puts it, "When applied to Indigenous struggles for recognition, Fraser's status model rests on the problematic background assumption that the settler state constitutes a legitimate framework within which Indigenous peoples might be more justly included, or from which they could be further excluded"—a pervasive problem in political theory. Coulthard, *Red Skin,* 36.

5. Confucius, *The Analects,* trans. Arthur Waley (New York: Random House, 1983), book 15, chap. 23. In the Bible, see in the New Testament Matthew 7:12, Luke 6:31, and many places in the Epistles; and versions of the same in the Old Testament in Leviticus 19:18 and 19:34, among other places.

6. See, e.g., Charles Taylor, *Multiculturalism: Examining the Politics of Recognition,* ed. Amy Gutmann (Princeton, N.J.: Princeton University Press, 1994); Will Kymlika, *Multicultural Citizenship: A Liberal Theory of Minority Rights* (Oxford: Oxford University Press, 1995); Aihwa Ong, *Flexible Citizenship: The Cultural Logics of Transnationality* (Durham, N.C.: Duke University Press, 1999); Fraser, "Rethinking Recognition"; Fraser and Axel Honneth, *Redistribution or Recognition? A Political-Philosophical Exchange,* trans. Joel Golb, James Ingram, and Christiane Wilke (London: Verso, 2003); Amy Gutmann, *Identity in Democracy* (Princeton, N.J.: Princeton University Press, 2003); Gutmann and Dennis Thompson, *Why Deliberative Democracy?* (Princeton, N.J.: Princeton University Press, 2004); and Selya Benhabib, *The Rights of Others* (Cambridge: Cambridge University Press, 2004).

7. Gerard de Malynes, *Consuetudo, vel, Lex mercatoria, or The Antient*

Law-Merchant (London, 1629), esp. "Of Reciprocall and double Exchanges," 404–8, at 404.

8. Articles 2–4, *The Articles of the Treaty of Peace, Signed and Sealed at Munster, in Westphalia, the 24th of October, 1648* (London: Onley, 1697), 5, 6, 4.

9. Article 112, *Articles of the Treaty of Peace*, 39.

10. See, e.g., Max Savelle, *The Origins of American Diplomacy: The International History of Anglo-America, 1492–1763* (New York: Macmillan, 1967); Andreas Osiander, "Sovereignty, International Relations, and the Westphalian Myth," *International Organization* 55, no. 2 (2001): 251–87; Edward Keene, *Beyond the Anarchical Society: Grotius, Colonialism and Order in World Politics* (Cambridge: Cambridge University Press, 2002); and Nan Goodman, *The Puritan Cosmopolis: The Law of Nations and the Early American Imagination* (Oxford: Oxford University Press, 2018), 143. The cultural and political consequences of these developments have of course been vast. "Treaties of reciprocity," Hannah Arendt observes in *The Origins of Totalitarianism* (New York: Shocken, 2004), "have woven a web around the earth" that makes citizens' legal status portable (373). Yet without a state framework, she argues, that status evaporates; rights are only actionable under some state regime that substantiates them. The history of Native people in, under, and in relation to the United States powerfully evidences this generative paradox of modern liberal statehood.

11. In the nineteenth century and into the present, scientific uses of the term "reciprocity" in mathematics and physics would follow this economic logic as well; this likely reflects the original use of the term "reciprocate" from the field of logic, where it signals transposability or reversibility of definitions, dating at least to the early sixteenth century, according to the *Oxford English Dictionary*. But consider also the case of what Audra Simpson in *Mohawk Interruptus: Political Life across the Borders of the Settler States* (Durham, N.C.: Duke University Press, 2014) calls "nested sovereignties," induced by the complex layers of group agency in the reserve and reservation systems in Canada and the United States. "Sovereignty may exist within sovereignty," she writes. "One does not entirely negate the other, but they necessarily stand in terrific tension and pose serious jurisdictional and normative challenges to each other" (10). Given the refusals of the Mohawks of Kahnawà:ke (in Simpson's case) and many other Native nations to operate exclusively within Westphalian models of sovereignty, it seems reasonable to assert, as Simpson does, that "there is more than one *political* show in town," and that "Indige-

nous sovereignties and Indigenous political orders prevail within and apart from settler governance" (11).

12. Robert O. Keohane, "Reciprocity in International Relations," *International Organisation* 40, no. 1 (1986): 1–27.

13. John Locke, *The Second Treatise of Government* and *A Letter Concerning Toleration* (1689; reprint, New York: Dover, 2002), 2.

14. Thomas Hobbes, *Leviathan, or The Matter, Forme, & Power of a Common-Wealth Ecclesiasticall and Civill* (London, 1651), 48.

15. See Georg Wilhelm Friedrich Hegel, *The Phenomenology of Spirit*, trans. and ed. Terry Pinkard (Cambridge: Cambridge University Press, 2018); and Immanuel Kant, *The Metaphysics of Morals*, trans. Mary Gregor, ed. Lara Denis (Cambridge: Cambridge University Press, 2017).

16. Gutmann and Thompson, *Why Deliberative Democracy?*, 98. Consider Chickasaw critic Jodi Byrd's warning against "the syllogistic traps of participatory democracy born out of violent occupation of lands." In Byrd, *Transit of Empire*, xii.

17. Gutmann and Thompson, *Why Deliberative Democracy?*, 98.

18. Gutmann, in *Identity in Democracy*, sketches a fairly precise role for reciprocity in deliberative democracy, but elsewhere refers to reciprocity as a "social good," describing it as "the generalized form of mutual aid" (113). She also asserts, following Charles Taylor (following Hegel), that it is essential to establishing minority group recognition, or the "public recognition of the value of some cultural particularities that are not universally valued" (43).

19. "Reciprocity" has become a key term of art in evolutionary anthropology. In the study of the history of cooperation—whether for mutual benefit or for altruism—reciprocity has been hailed as an evolved trait of human societies. Unlike other animals, researchers claim, humans cooperate instinctively and in wider social circles than other animals do, even with complete strangers. See Michael Tomasello with Carol Dweck, Joan Silk, Brian Skyrms, and Elizabeth S. Spelke, *Why We Cooperate* (Cambridge, Mass.: MIT Press, 2009). "Norms of cooperation," Tomasello writes, were built on top of evolved tendencies to work together, "on reciprocity and respect for others as beings like oneself" (106). That said, evolutionary anthropologists also seem to agree that reciprocity as they understand it does not operate free of potential selfishness or deception—what they term "contingent reciprocity" is premised on continued mutual benefit. These scientists would argue, then, that antecedent to any cosmological or political traditions of reciprocity is a deep-rooted, universal human willingness to help each other.

For many anthropologists, as for Hegel's theory of subject formation, reciprocity just happens—first at the level of human subjective formation, then somewhere in the chain of need and response of social belonging or seeking. "It is through these reciprocal processes and exchanges of recognition," Glen Coulthard summarizes, that for Hegel "the condition of possibility for freedom emerges," as individuals recognize each other and imagine their identities through an emergent and transforming relationship (*Red Skin*, 25). Frantz Fanon criticized Hegel's notion of a guaranteed reciprocity of subject formation compactly in *Black Skin, White Masks* (New York: Grove, 1967): "For Hegel there is reciprocity," he writes. "Here the master laughs at the consciousness of the slave. What he wants from the slave is not recognition but work" (220n8). For Fanon, reciprocity's relationship to equality is at best unclear; reciprocity can sometimes be a shell game, and sometimes it can exist in the eye of the beholder.

20. Claude Lévi-Strauss, *Tristes Tropiques,* trans. John Russell (New York: Criterion Books, 1961), 179.

21. Lévi-Strauss, *Tristes Tropiques,* 230–31.

22. Lévi-Strauss, *Tristes Tropiques,* 97–98.

23. Soumhya Venkatesan, Jeanette Edwards, Rane Willerslev, Elizabeth Povinelli, and Perveez Mody, "The Anthropological Fixation with Reciprocity Leaves No Room for Love: 2009 Meeting of the Group for Debates in Anthropological Theory," *Critique of Anthropology* 31, no. 3 (2011): 210–50.

24. David Aberle, *The Peyote Religion among the Navaho* (Chicago: Aldine, 1966); Walter Holden Capps, ed., *Seeing with a Native Eye: Essays on Native American Religion* (New York: Harper Forum, 1976); Barre Toelken, "Seeing with a Native Eye: How Many Sheep Will It Hold?," in Capps, *Seeing with a Native Eye,* 9–24; Kenneth Lincoln, *Native American Renaissance* (Berkeley: University of California Press, 1983), 16.

25. Brooks, *Common Pot*; Brooks, "Digging at the Roots: Locating an Ethical, Native Criticism," in *Reasoning Together,* ed. Craig S. Womack, Daniel Heath Justice, and Christopher B. Teuton (Norman: University of Oklahoma Press, 2008), 234–64.

26. Ned Blackhawk, *Violence over the Land: Indians and Empires in the Early American West* (Cambridge, Mass.: Harvard University Press, 2006); Daniel K. Richter, *Facing East from Indian Country: A Native History of Early America* (Cambridge, Mass.: Harvard University Press, 2001); Salisbury, *Manitou and Providence.*

27. Abram Van Engen, *Sympathetic Puritans: Calvinist Fellow Feeling in Early New England* (Oxford: Oxford University Press, 2015), 3.

28. See, e.g., David D. Hall, *Worlds of Wonder, Days of Judgment: Popular Religious Belief in Early New England* (Cambridge, Mass.: Harvard University Press, 1990).

29. John Cotton, *Christ the Fountaine of Life* (London, 1651), 35; see also Perry Miller's discussion of this passage in *Errand into the Wilderness* (Cambridge, Mass.: Harvard University Press, 1956), 61.

30. John Smith, *The Generall Historie of Virginia, New-England, and the Summer Isles . . .* (London, 1624), book 3, chap. 2, 44.

31. Anne Bradstreet, *The Tenth Muse Lately Sprung Up in America . . .* (London, 1650), 40.

32. Woodward, *Prospero's America*, 19.

33. Georges Bataille, *The Accursed Share: An Essay on General Economy* (New York: Zone Books, 1988). See also Ethan Shagan, *The Rule of Moderation: Violence, Religion and the Politics of Restraint in Early Modern England* (Cambridge: Cambridge University Press, 2011). Shagan observes that the quest for balance was more broadly characteristic of early modern English governance and society—a middling-way ideal enforced by extremes of violence and social control. "The middle ages were nothing if not Aristotelian," he reminds us, "and besides numerous attempts to reconcile Peripatetic ethics with Christianity, concepts of 'balance' or 'equilibrium' brought moderation to the core of medieval science and economics" (3).

34. See, e.g., Matthew Dennis, *Cultivating a Landscape of Peace: Iroquois–European Encounters in Seventeenth-Century America* (Ithaca, N.Y.: Cornell University Press, 1993): "In general, the Five Nations lacked a means to achieve peaceful relations with those not tied to them by consanguinity or affinity. The archaeological record suggests that, from an ancient time, their response to the dangers posed by the proximity of hostile outsiders was to transform them symbolically and physically into kinspeople. Unpredictable raiding activity that raged back and forth, even if sporadically, created a cycle of violence and chaos, which left no one secure" (8).

35. Brooks, *Our Beloved Kin*, 215.

36. Seth Mallios, *The Deadly Politics of Giving: Exchange and Violence at Ajacan, Roanoake, and Jamestown* (Tuscaloosa: University of Alabama Press, 2006), 4.

37. As Brooks puts it, discussing the Cascoak raid, the abstracting or

erasing of names and families of the victims of war "occurs on both sides, shifting our perspective as readers of history." Brooks, *Our Beloved Kin,* 212.

38. Claude Lévi-Strauss, "Reciprocity and Hierarchy," *American Anthropologist,* n.s., 46 (1944): 267.

39. Julie A. Fisher and David J. Silverman, *Ninigret, Sachem of the Niantics and Narragansetts: Diplomacy, War, and the Balance of Power in Seventeenth-Century New England and Indian Country* (Ithaca, N.Y.: Cornell University Press, 2014), 17. See also Thomas Morton's observations about Native burial styles being differentiated by "noble, and of ignoble, or obscure, or inferior discent" of the deceased in *New English Canaan* (Amsterdam: Stam, 1637), 51.

40. Jenny Hale Pulsipher, *Subjects unto the Same King: Indians, English, and the Contest for Authority in Colonial New England* (Philadelphia: University of Pennsylvania Press, 2005), 12.

41. See Michael Leroy Oberg, *Uncas: First of the Mohegans* (Ithaca, N.Y.: Cornell University Press, 2003).

42. Joan Silk, "Forum," in Tomasello et al., *Why We Cooperate,* 118. See also Samuel Bowles and Herbert Gintis, *A Cooperative Species: Human Reciprocity and Its Evolution* (Princeton, N.J.: Princeton University Press, 2011).

43. On the *Cowwéwonck* or dream soul and interpretation, see Fisher and Silverman, *Ninigret,* 5.

44. Arjun Appadurai, "Introduction: Commodities and the Politics of Value," in *The Social Life of Things: Commodities in Cultural Perspective,* ed. Appadurai (Cambridge: Cambridge University Press, 1986), 10–11. He cites as an example of such fetishization Michael Taussig's discussion of the transformation of reciprocity-based exchange into commodity exchanges among Bolivian miners. Taussig, *The Devil and Commodity Fetishism in South America* (Chapel Hill: University of North Carolina Press, 1980), esp. 224.

45. "Acts of kindness from indigenous ancestors passed being reciprocated nearly 200 years later through blood memory and interconnectedness," writes Vanessa Tulley in a post appended to "Navajo and Hopi Families COVID-19 Relief Fund," GoFundMe.com, May 3, 2020, http://www.gofundme.com/f/NHFC19Relief.

46. Thomas, *Colonialism's Culture: Anthropology, Travel and Government* (Princeton, N.J.: Princeton University Press, 1994), 2.

47. In Venkatesan et al., "Anthropological Fixation," Elizabeth Povinelli notes, following Maurice Godelier, that "Mauss's logic of the gift is striated with affective powers: rather than understanding the gift from the point of

view of the demand to give, receive and reciprocate, we can understand the gift as dependent upon the power to persuade, seduce, wait and make others wait, a waiting that increases the desire for the love object" (223). This suggests a way of looking at reciprocity that isn't exactly economic and that identifies part of its complex temporality. How many times have you done something for someone—a kind of gift—and that someone didn't notice? If you can count the times, if you haven't forgotten them, do those instances constitute latent reciprocity? And if you have forgotten them, is it the same, or are they gifts?

48. Taiaiake Alfred, *Peace, Power, Righteousness: An Indigenous Manifesto* (Oxford: Oxford University Press, 1999), 133.

49. Deloria, *God Is Red*, 3, 1–2.

50. Deloria, *We Talk, You Listen*, 196.

51. Paula Gunn Allen, *Off the Reservation: Reflections on Boundary-Busting, Border-Crossing Loose Canons* (Boston: Beacon, 1998), 142.

52. Coulthard, *Red Skin*, 61.

53. Coulthard, *Red Skin*, 60.

54. Coulthard, *Red Skin*, 35, 48.

55. Eva Marie Garroutte, *Real Indians: Identity and the Survival of Native America* (Berkeley: University of California Press, 2003).

56. Lyons, *X-Marks*, 58.

57. Lyons, *X-Marks*, 58, 58.

58. Gerald Vizenor with Colleen Eils, Emily Lederman, and Andrew Uzendoski, "'You're Always More Famous When You Are Banished': Gerald Vizenor on Citizenship, War, and Continental Liberty," *American Indian Quarterly* 39, no. 2 (2015): 226–27.

59. Vizenor, "You're Always More Famous," 227.

5. Beyond Understanding

1. Perry Miller, *Errand into the Wilderness* (New York: Harper Torchbook, 1964), ix.

2. Miller, *Errand*, 153.

3. "UNESCO Constitution (1945–46)," UNESCO.org, https://en.unesco.org/.

4. Ryan Enos, *The Space between Us: Social Geography and Politics* (Cambridge: Cambridge University Press, 2017). Such observations have a long

history; see, e.g., Randolph Bourne, "Trans-National America," *Atlantic* 118 (July 1916): 86–97.

5. Seward Darby, "White Supremacy Was Her World. And Then She Left," *New York Times,* July 17, 2020, https://www.nytimes.com/; see also Darby, *Sisters in Hate: American Women on the Front Lines of White Nationalism* (New York: Little, Brown, 2020).

6. Deloria, *Custer Died,* 5, 27.

7. Deloria, *We Talk, You Listen,* 15–16.

8. Donald Fixico, "Ethics and Responsibilities in Writing American Indian History," in *Natives and Academics: Researching and Writing about American Indians,* ed. Devon A. Mihesuah (Lincoln: University of Nebraska Press, 1998), 93.

9. Fixico, "Ethics and Responsibilities," 92.

10. Fixico, "Ethics and Responsibilities," 93.

11. Saidiya Hartman, "Venus in Two Acts," *small axe* 26 (June 2008): 12.

12. Harjo, *Conflict Resolution,* 55.

13. Richard White, "Creative Misunderstandings and New Understandings," *William and Mary Quarterly,* 3rd ser., 63, no. 1 (2006): 9. White himself has, according to that essay, been misunderstood by many of the scholars influenced by *The Middle Ground: Indians, Empires, and Republics in the Great Lakes Region, 1650–1815* (Cambridge: Cambridge University Press, 1991). Anna Brickhouse argues that "strategic" or motivated mistranslation by Indigenous peoples underwrote "a long history of American unsettlement." That is, deliberate mistranslation characterized the colonial political scene broadly, rather than being a unique tactic of European empires. Brickhouse, *The Unsettlement of America: Translation, Interpretation, and the Story of Don Luis de Velasco, 1560–1945* (Oxford: Oxford University Press, 2014), 8. See also Eric Cheyfitz, *The Poetics of Imperialism: Translation and Colonization from "The Tempest" to "Tarzan"* (Philadelphia: University of Pennsylvania Press, 1997). Anthropologist Anna L. Tsing argues in *Friction: An Ethnography of Global Connection* (Princeton, N.J.: Princeton University Press, 2005) that productive misunderstandings are in fact constitutive of global interconnections in a world of integrated markets.

14. Nancy Shoemaker, *A Strange Likeness: Becoming Red and White in Eighteenth-Century North America* (Oxford: Oxford University Press, 2004), 3.

15. Céline Carayon, *Eloquence Embodied: Nonverbal Communication among French and Indigenous Peoples in the Americas* (Chapel Hill: Omo-

hundro Institute of Early American History and Culture and the University of North Carolina Press, 2019), 30.

16. Carayon, *Eloquence Embodied*, 7. "We have really everything in common with America nowadays," Oscar Wilde once wrote, "except, of course, language." Wilde, *The Canterville Ghost* (Boston: J. W. Luce, 1906), 6.

17. Carayon, *Eloquence Embodied*, 73.

18. Christopher Columbus, *Select Letters of Christopher Columbus*, ed. and trans. R. H. Major (London: For the Hakluyt Society, 1847), 9.

19. Cartier, in 1541, quoted in Carayon, *Eloquence Embodied*, 232.

20. Abram Van Engen, *Sympathetic Puritans: Calvinist Fellow Feeling in Early New England* (Oxford: Oxford University Press, 2015), 18; see also Norman Fiering, "Will and Intellect in the New England Mind," *William and Mary Quarterly* 29, no. 4 (1972): 515–58.

21. Isaac Ambrose, *Media: The Middle Things, in Reference to the First and Last Things . . .* (London, 1649), 27.

22. Ambrose, *Media*, b2.5, 152.

23. Miller, *Errand*, 51.

24. Thomas Shepard, *The Sincere Convert* (London, 1641), A4.5. This stance has been updated for evangelicals in the age of science by C. S. Lewis, in his widely read *Mere Christianity*. "A man can eat his dinner without understanding exactly how food nourishes him. A man can accept what Christ has done without knowing how it works: indeed, *he certainly would not know how it works until he has accepted it.*" C. S. Lewis, *Mere Christianity* (New York: HarperCollins, 2001), 55. That which surpasseth understanding holds understanding in its offered hand on the other side. Understanding is not eliminated but promised, as long as you can let go of it.

25. Shepard, *Sincere Convert*, 165.

26. Eliot quoted in *The Eliot Tracts: With Letters from John Eliot to Thomas Thorowgood and Richard Baxter*, ed. Michael P. Clark (Westport, Conn.: Praeger, 2003), 85.

27. On Eliot's translation shop, see Brown, *Pilgrim and the Bee*, 179–207; and Brooks, *Our Beloved Kin*, 72–106.

28. Ives Goddard and Kathleen Bragdon, *Native Writings in Massachusett* (Philadelphia, Pa.: American Philosophical Society, 1988), 586.

29. Thomas Shepard with Grindal Rawson, *Sampwutteahae Quinnuppekompauaenin*, trans. John Eliot et al. (Cambridge, Mass. Bay Colony, 1689), A2.1. Williams, in his *Key into the Language of America*, records several phrases using the term "understand," most of which feature the *wah-* stem.

But he also records a phrase for "I understand you"—*Cuppíttous*—with a different stem, which may be a lesser-known term or a phrase peculiar to the Narragansetts, with whose dialect Williams was most familiar (8, 56).

30. Mashpee petition quoted in Van Engen, *Sympathetic Puritans,* 162; Goddard and Bragdon, *Native Writings,* 177.

31. Thomas Hobbes, *Leviathan, or The Matter, Forme, and Power of a Common-Wealth Ecclesiasticall and Civill* (London, 1651), 12.

32. Hobbes, *Leviathan,* 18.

33. Hobbes, *Leviathan,* 31.

34. Immanuel Kant, *Critique of Judgment* (1790), trans. Werner S. Pluhar (Indianapolis, Ind.: Hackett, 1987), 62.

35. William James, *Pragmatism* (1907; reprint, New York: Dover, 1995), 5. For an introduction to these philosophical questions focused on the problem of understanding, see Josef Bleicher, *Contemporary Hermeneutics: Hermeneutics as Method, Philosophy, and Critique* (Boston: Routledge & Kegan Paul, 1980).

36. German, of course, has many ways of speaking of "understanding," a few of which Gadamer focalizes: *gemeiner Verstand* or *gesunder Menschenverstand* indicate good sense; *verstehen* is everyday intersubjective agreement; and *Verständigung* a sense of coming to agreement about something. See, e.g., Hans-Georg Gadamer, *Truth and Method,* trans. Joel Weinsheimer and Donald G. Marshall, 2nd rev. ed. (New York: Continuum, 2004), 180.

37. Gadamer, *Truth and Method,* 484. Glissant, *Poetics of Relation,* 117.

38. Gadamer, *Truth and Method,* 11.

39. For a recent treatment of this fact in the colonial Northeast, see Christine DeLucia, *Memory Lands: King Philip's War and the Place of Violence in the Northeast* (New Haven, Conn.: Yale University Press, 2018). On precolonial imperial historiography, see, e.g., Jorge Cañizares-Esguerra, *How to Write the History of the New World: Histories, Epistemologies, and Identities in the Eighteenth-Century Atlantic World* (Stanford, Calif.: Stanford University Press, 2001).

40. Irving Hallowell, "Ojibwa Ontology, Behavior, and Worldview," in *Readings in Indigenous Religions,* ed. Graham Harvey (New York: Continuum, 2002), 20.

41. Olaudah Equiano, *The Interesting Narrative of the Life of Olaudah Equiano, or Gustavus Vassa, the African,* 9th ed. (London: For the author, 1794), 303.

42. Equiano, *Interesting Narrative,* 303. For more on Equiano and the Mosquito Coast venture, see Vincent Carretta, *Equiano, the African: Biography of a Self-Made Man* (New York: Penguin, 2007). Some contextualization in this section is drawn from C. Napier Bell, *Tangweera: Life and Adventures among Gentle Savages* (London: Edward Arnold, 1899); George Henderson, *An Account of the British Settlement of Honduras . . . ,* 2nd ed. (London, 1811); Alden Vaughan, *Transatlantic Encounters: American Indians in Britain, 1500–1776* (Cambridge: Cambridge University Press, 2006), 219–20; and Eric Rodrigo Meringer, "*Miskitu Takaia*: Miskito Identity and Transformation, 1600–1979" (PhD diss., Arizona State University, 2007), esp. 22–90. See also Robert Berkhofer's contemplations on the paradoxes of studying Miskito history—whom is the ethnohistorian to believe, in reconstructing a heavily politicized Miskito past in the wake of their rebellion against the Sandinistas?—in Robert F. Berkhofer Jr., *Beyond the Great Story: History as Text and Discourse* (Cambridge, Mass.: Harvard University Press, 1995), 181. For a comparative look at Atlantic missionizing, see, e.g., Jorge Cañizares-Esguerra, *Puritan Conquistadors: Iberianizing the Atlantic, 1550–1700* (Stanford, Calif.: Stanford University Press, 2006).

43. Equiano, *Interesting Narrative,* 304–6.

44. Equiano, *Interesting Narrative,* 306.

45. Srinivas Aravamudan, *Tropicopolitans: Colonialism and Agency, 1688–1804* (Durham, N.C.: Duke University Press, 1999), 235. While the hottest recent debate about Equiano has been about whether he was or was not Indigenous—actually born in Africa or in South Carolina—the meaning of cross-racial interactions in the *Interesting Narrative* would have depended less, I suspect, on the resolution of that question than on the connection between a former heathen and a current one. In the eighteenth century, Equiano defended himself against similar claims that his origins were not African. See Carretta, *Equiano*; and a summary of the debate in Jennifer Howard, "Unraveling the Narrative," *Chronicle of Higher Education,* September 9, 2005.

46. Ian Finseth, "Irony and Modernity in the Early Slave Narrative: Bonds of Duty, Contracts of Meaning," *Early American Literature* 48, no. 1 (2013): 40–41.

47. Yael Ben-Zvi, "Equiano's Nativity: Negative Birthright, Indigenous Ethic, and Universal Human Rights," *Early American Literature* 48, no. 2 (2013): 401–2. For Ben-Zvi, it is significant that Equiano compares his African past with the Miskito cultural present, praises the fact that the Miskitos build houses for him "exactly like Africans, by the joint labor of men, women,

and children," and dwells with the Indigenous people (309). Yet such comparisons had a long foreground in the rhetoric of English colonial writing, and there was much precedent in the English colonial past alone for Natives and colonists living side by side. See, e.g., Morton, *New English Canaan*; for an expansion of Ben-Zvi's argument, see Ben-Zvi, *Native Land Talk: Indigenous and Arrivant Rights Theories* (Lebanon, N.H.: Dartmouth College Press, 2018). In the case of the Zambo Miskito group, from which Prince George came, Equiano's comparisons may have had more concrete foundations, given "a high level of African miscegenation" in the chiefdom resulting from successive nearby shipwrecks from which slaves had escaped to the Mosquito coast. Meringer, "*Miskitu Takaia*," 83–84.

48. Peter Linebaugh and Marcus Rediker, *The Many-Headed Hydra: Sailors, Slaves, Commoners, and the Hidden History of the Revolutionary Atlantic* (Boston: Beacon, 2000), 243.

49. Linebaugh and Rediker, *Many-Headed Hydra*, 336.

50. Joanna Brooks, *American Lazarus: Religion and the Rise of African-American and Native American Literatures* (Oxford: Oxford University Press, 2003), 60.

51. Henry Louis Gates Jr.'s arguments about the book format in relation to the presentation of black subjectivity on the one hand, and Homi Bhabha's about the paradoxes of the book in colonialism on the other, have deeply shaped scholarly discussions of literacy, the book, and the colonized. See Gates, *The Signifying Monkey: A Theory of African-American Literary Criticism* (New York: Oxford, 1988), 127–69; and Bhabha, *The Location of Culture* (New York: Routledge, 1994), 102–22.

52. Thomas Wilson, *An Essay towards an Instruction for the Indians* (1740); anonymous [signed Laurence Harlow], *The Conversion of an Indian, in a Letter to a Friend* (London, 1774). Several editions were published in the eighteenth century and a German translation in 1796 in Lancaster.

53. *Conversion of an Indian*, 9.

54. *Conversion of an Indian*, 13.

55. See, e.g., John Foxe, *Acts and Monuments of Matters Most Speciall and Memorable...* (London: Islip, Kingston, and Young, 1632).

56. For a discussion of the popularization of Foxe's book of martyrs—how it came to be adopted by Protestants of otherwise radically differing theologies and how it helped shape a complex contest over Englishness itself—see Jesse M. Lander, *Inventing Polemic: Religion, Print, and Literary Culture*

in Early Modern England (Cambridge: Cambridge University Press, 2006), 56–79.

57. Quoted in Linebaugh and Rediker, *Many-Headed Hydra,* 266.

58. Equiano, *Interesting Narrative,* 306.

59. Stefano Harney and Fred Moten, *The Undercommons: Fugitive Planning and Black Study* (New York: Minor Compositions, 2013), 96.

60. Audre Lorde, "The Master's Tools Will Never Dismantle the Master's House," in *Sister Outsider: Essays and Speeches* (Trumansburg, N.Y.: Crossing Press, 1984), 111. Other theorizations like Carayon's that decenter understanding include the concept of *cha'anil* in Genner Llanes-Ortiz, "Yaan muuk' ich cha'anil/El potencial de Cha'anil: Un concepto maya para la revitalización lingüística," *Ichan Teolotl/La Casa del Tecolote* 26, no. 301 (2015): 28–30; and Inga Clendinnen's reference to the surrendering of the act of interpretation that grounds this version of "understanding" as "a heroic act of renunciation" confessing the limitations of our knowledge in her magnificent essay "'Fierce and Unnatural Cruelty': Cortés and the Conquest of Mexico," in *New World Encounters,* ed. Stephen Greenblatt (Berkeley: University of California Press, 1993), 18.

61. David Treuer, *The Translation of Dr Apelles* (New York: Vintage, 2008), 167.

62. See Marisol de la Cadena, "Indigenous Cosmopolitics in the Andes: Conceptual Reflections beyond 'Politics,'" *Cultural Anthropology* 25, no. 2 (2010): 334–70; and Simpson, *Mohawk Interruptus.* As Simpson shows, among the many examples of North American Indigenous opacity, Mohawk refusals to assimilate to Canadian governmental and commercial languages, laws, and forms of recognition exemplify an insistence on the right not to be understood or to agree on terms as a concrete form of Native community and maintenance of sovereignty. The Black refusal referenced by Harney and Moten is further elaborated on by members of the Practicising Refusal Collective; see, e.g., Tina Campt, "Black Visuality and the Practice of Refusal," *Women and Performance* 29, no. 1 (2019): 79–87. See also the question of silence explored at the human–animal boundary in Kalpana Rahita Seshadri, *HumAnimal: Race, Law, Language* (Minneapolis: University of Minnesota Press, 2012).

63. De la Cadena, "Indigenous Cosmopolitics," 351.

64. Glissant, *Poetics of Relation,* 189–90.

65. Glissant, *Poetics of Relation,* 190.

66. Glissant, *Poetics of Relation,* 192.

67. Glissant, *Poetics of Relation,* 155.

68. Kimberly Theidon, *Intimate Enemies: Violence and Reconciliation in Peru* (Philadelphia: University of Pennsylvania Press, 2013), 12.

69. Theidon, *Intimate Enemies,* 245; Hannah Arendt, *The Human Condition* (Chicago: University of Chicago Press, 1958).

70. Harjo, *Conflict Resolution,* 82.

Index

Aberle, David, 112
Acts and Monuments (Foxe), 149
Aeneas, 58
Aeneid (Virgil), 58
Afropessimism, 12
Agamemnon (Greek mythology), 122
alchemy, 116–17
Alfred, Taiaiake, 43, 123
Algonquian peoples, 39, 59, 139–40, 156; converts, 79–80, 114; cosmology, 60; reciprocity, 103–4, 116, 120–21; traditions, 68, 71, 74, 87–88, 100, 115–16, 118
Allen, Paula Gunn, 124–25
altruism, 106
Ambrose, Isaac, 137–38, 141
American Jeremiad, The (Bercovitch), 42
American thought, 129–30
Amory, Hugh, 68–70, 73–74
Analects, The (Confucius), 106
Andrews, Edward, 64–65, 67
"Anthropologists and Other Friends" (Deloria), 4–5
anthropology, 4–5, 9, 13, 107, 109–10, 112, 121
anticolonialism, 54

Appadurai, Arjun, 121
Aravamudan, Srinivas, 147
Arendt, Hannah, 157
Ascham, Roger, 33–34
authenticity, 67

Baker, Richard, 148, 152
Baldwin, James, 75
Bataille, Georges, 117
Bauer, Ralph, 34
bear paw. *See* bundle
benevolence, 105
Ben-Svi, Yael, 147–48
Bercovitch, Sacvan, 24, 42–43
Berkhofer, Robert, Jr., 10–11
Berlant, Lauren, 15, 24
Bhabha, Homi, 41, 43
Bible, 25, 68–69, 76, 103–4, 148
Bishop, Bridget, 71–72
Blackburn, Elizabeth, 82
Black Hills, 122
bodies, 82, 104
Bororo, 111
Bradford, William, 29–30, 32, 34, 41
Bradstreet, Ann, 116
Bragdon, Kathleen, 139–40
Brazil, 110–12
Brooks, James, 3

INDEX

Brooks, Joanna, 66, 75, 149
Brooks, Lisa, 14, 31, 55, 60, 96–97, 99, 100, 101, 113, 118, 124
Brown, Frank, 71–72
Brown, Matthew, 60
bundle, ritual burial, 68–70, 73–74
Bureau of Indian Affairs, 104
Burnet, John, 91
Bush, George W., 23
Byrd, Jodi, 7, 43

Calhoun, Craig, 25
Calvinism, 15, 22, 60, 73
capitalism, 51, 104
Carayon, Céline, 135–36
Cartier, Jacques, 136
Cassacinamon, Robin, 69
Ceci, Lynn, 40
charity, 31
Cheah, Pheng, 28
Child, Lydia Maria, 21–23
Christianity, 5, 6–7
Christian universalist, 25
chromosome health, 82
Church of England, 24
civilizing mission, 33, 40, 100
class, 10
Clement, Cotton, 85
Clifford, James, 28
Clinton, Bill, 44
Clinton, George W., 80
Clytaemnestra (Greek mythology), 122
Cold War, 26
collectivity, 67–68
Collier, John, 104, 112
colonialism, 5, 6–7, 9, 52, 56, 58–59, 123; French, 135

Columbus, Christopher, 136
Common Pot, The (Brooks), 113, 115
communication systems, 4
comprehension, 129–30
Confession of Faith of Certayn English People (Ainsworth), 35
Confidence-Man, The, 21, 45–46
Confucius, 106, 114
Connecticut Colony, 116
Constitution of the United States, 54
Conversion of an Indian, in a Letter to a Friend, The, 149, 150
converts, Native Christian, 23, 31, 36–37, 55, 63, 69, 114, 138–39, 148
Coryate, Thomas, 34
cosmography, 40–41
cosmology, 2, 8, 23, 56, 86, 105
cosmopolitanism, 3, 5, 8, 16, 18, 23, 25, 26–28, 31, 40, 46; academic, 44–45; dialogical, 43; secular, 33–34
cosmopuritanism, 32–33, 47–48
Cotton, John, 36, 115
Coulthard, Glen, 102, 125–26
covenant, 31
Cowboy–Indian Alliance, 157
Creole, 53
Crudities (Coryate), 34
culture, 3–4, 5, 7, 9–10, 59–60, 73, 84; distinctiveness, 66; reciprocity and, 104, 118–19, 125–26
Cushman, Robert, 37–38, 41
Custer Died for Your Sins (Deloria), 57

INDEX

Danforth, Samuel, 36–37, 38
Darby, Seward, 131
"Declaration of the Lords and Commons Assembled at Oxford, A," 103
decolonization, 11, 13, 82
deeds, land, 31
de la Cadena, Marisol, 154–55
Deloria, Vine, Jr., 4–5, 57, 79, 82, 123, 125, 131–33
DeLucia, Christine, 17
democracy, 27–28, 109–10, 117
Diamond, Jared, 55
displacement, Indigenous, 7
dispossession, 17, 31, 37–38, 50, 95
Dryden, John, 58

Easton, John, 96
economic systems, 39, 53, 86, 104–5, 127
Edmundson, William, 79, 91, 94, 100
Edwards, Jonathan, 130
"Element of Piety, An" (Momaday), 49
Eliot, John (missionary), 79, 84, 85, 87, 114, 137–38
Eliott, Sir John, 55
Elizabeth I, Queen, 33
Ellison, Ralph, 70
emotion, 83–84
Enos, Ryan, 131
equality, 27
Equiano, Olaudah, 1–3, 5, 16, 19, 23, 64, 86, 134, 145–47, 148–53, 154, 156
equivocation, 13–14, 18

Essay of the Meanes How to Make Our Trauailes (Palmer), 34
Essay towards an Instruction for the Indians, An (Wilson), 149, 150
ethnocentrism, 6
Euthyphro (Plato), 59
exceptionalism, 24, 25, 50, 59
exchange, economic, 39–40, 118
exile, 29–31
exile theory, 41–43
Exodus 6:4, 29
exploitation, 27

Fabian, Johannes, 87
faculties, mental, 141
Faith and Boundaries (Silverman), 63–64
Fanon, Frantz, 28, 126
Faulkner, William, 14
feminism, 60
Fessenden, Tracy, 61–62, 65
Finseth, Ian, 147–48
Fixico, Donald, 132–33
Foster, Stephen, 49, 75
Fox, George, 88, 89
Foxe, John, 149
French colonialism, 135
Friends. *See* Society of Friends
friendship, 147–48, 151–52
Fuentes, Carlos, 44
future orientation, 13, 37, 53, 104, 122

Gadamer, Hans-Georg, 141–43, 144
Garrison, James, 50, 58
Garroutte, Eva, 126
George, King, 148

George, Prince, 1–3, 5, 16, 19, 23, 64, 86, 134, 145–46, 148–53, 156
George Fox Digg'd Out of His Burrows (Williams), 79, 90, 91–93
gift giving, 110, 121, 127
Ginzburg, Carlo, 76
Giving Tree, The (Silverstein), 16
Glissant, Édouard, 6, 9–10, 14, 143, 155–56
globalization, 26
Goddard, Ives, 139–40
God Is Red (Deloria), 57, 123
Golden Rule, 106, 114
Gordimer, Nadine, 44
grace, gift of, 114
Greenblatt, Stephen, 43–45, 137
Greider, Carol W., 82
Guanahaní peoples, 136
Gulliver's Travels (Swift), 59
Gutmann, Amy, 109–10, 117

Hackney, Sheldon, 27
Hall, David, 65
Hall, Jeffrey C., 82
Hallowell, Irving, 144–45
Harjo, Joy, 26, 46–47, 134, 158
Harney, Stefano, 154, 158
Harris, William, 91
Hartman, Saidiya, 14, 133
Haudenosaunee, 122
Hawthorne, Nathaniel, 22, 23
Hegel, Georg Wilhelm Friedrich, 107, 109, 110, 123
Heidegger, Martin, 142
hierarchicalism, 118–20
historiography, 2–3, 6, 9, 14, 54, 55, 68, 102, 136–37

Hobbes, Thomas, 109, 140–41, 142
Hobomok, a Tale of Early Times (Child), 21–23
Hopi, 122
Horton, Benjamin, 71, 73
House Made of Dawn (Momaday), 50, 129
Howe, Susan, 14
humanism, 28, 81, 86, 137
Hutchinson, Anne, 56
Hyde, Carrie, 32

identification, 14
identity, 7, 13, 27, 54–55, 67, 126
imagination, 8, 10
impatience, 82–83
imperialism, 7
"Indian question," 80
Indigenous refusal, 154
individualism, 110, 134, 143, 147
information technology, 4
inner light, 88–90, 92–93
Interesting Narrative (Equiano), 145–46, 152
Invention of Culture, The (Wagner), 129
Irish, 122
Islam, 60
Itinerary Written by Fines Morrison, Gent. (Morrison), 34

Jacket, Red, 80, 87
Jamaica, 1–2, 86, 145
James (Biblical figure), 85
James, William, 142
jeremiad, 42, 45, 62
Jesuits, 25, 127
Jews, 31

Job (Biblical figure), 85–86
John 15.14, 115
justice, 18, 27, 122, 157

Kant, Immanuel, 141–42
Kauffman, Michael, 51
Keohane, Robert, 108
Key into the Language of America, A (Williams), 18, 30, 90, 100
Keywords, 7–9
Kibbey, Ann, 36
King Philip's War, 31, 96, 103, 118, 119
Kings 4:29, 140
Kings 18:21, 146
kinship, 7, 18, 58, 85, 86, 104, 110, 112, 120
Knight, Janice, 60
Kutquen (Kwinitekw), 99

land repatriation, 11
language, 1–3, 8, 11, 18, 81, 87, 126–27, 138–39, 142
Leiden, 34–35, 37, 59
Leviathan (Hobbes), 109, 140–41
Levine, Robert, 83
Lévi-Strauss, Claude, 103, 105, 107, 110–12, 115, 119
liberalism, 27–28, 54, 146
Lincoln, Kenneth, 112
Linebaugh, Peter, 148
literacy, 2, 4, 150–51
"Locating an Ethical Native Criticism" (Brooks), 113
Locke, John, 108
Lorde, Audre, 154, 158
Low Countries, 35
Luis de Velasco, Don, 127

Lynch, Thomas, 86
Lyons, Scott Richard, 63, 126–27

magical world, 72–73, 74–75
Mahmood, Saba, 60
Malinowski, Bronislaw, 110
Mallios, Seth, 118
Mandell, Daniel, 66
Man Made of Words, The, 1
Many-Headed Hydra, The (Linebaugh and Rediker), 148
Marrant, John, 75
marriage, 86
Martha's Vineyard, 63
Martin, Joel, 63, 66
Mashpee, 140
Massachusett language, 120, 139–40
Massachusetts Bay, 30, 61
Massasoit (Wampanoag), 37
mass communication, 131
Mather, Cotton, 30–31, 41
Mauss, Marcel, 107, 110
McBride, Kevin, 68, 69–70, 74
Media (Ambrose), 137–38
Melville, Herman, 21, 45–46
Merrell, James, 8, 10
Metacom (Wampanoag), 95–96
Middle Ground, The (White), 135
Mignolo, Walter, 60
millennium, 31
Miller, Perry, 59–60, 129–30, 138
Miskito, 5, 150
Miskito Prince. *See* George, Prince
missionary work, 6, 50, 54, 64, 79
misunderstanding. *See under* understanding

INDEX

"Modell of Christian Charity, A," 31, 119
Mohican, 64
Momaday, N. Scott, 1, 8, 10, 49–50, 76, 102, 129, 130
Monequassun (Algonquian convert), 79–80, 87
Morning Star, 1–3, 5, 154
Morrison, Kenneth, 6, 17
Morton, Thomas, 22, 23, 42–43
mortuary rituals, 69–70
Moten, Fred, 154, 158
Mouffe, Chantal, 27
Murison, Justine, 60
Mvskoke Creek, 46
Mystic river, 39–40

Nameaug plantation, 69
Narragansett, 30, 88–89, 90, 97, 99–100
Nashe, Thomas, 34
Natick (Massachusetts Bay), 79
nationalism, 28, 34, 40, 43, 44, 126; Christian, 32–33
Native American Renaissance (Lincoln), 112
Native Americans, Christianity, and the Reshaping of the American Religious Landscape (Martin and Nicholas), 63
Native Studies Keywords, 7–9
Navajo, 122
New-England Fire-Brand Quenched, A (Society of Friends), 93–94
Nicholas, Mark, 63, 66
Nipmuc, 97
nonconformist settler Christians, 21–22, 23, 24–25, 32, 47, 94, 113–14, 156
nonhuman agents, 117, 123–24
Nussbaum, Martha, 27

Occom, Samson, 18, 75
Oceti Sakowin, 122
Off the Reservation (Gunn Allen), 124
"Of the foure Humours in Mans constitution" (Bradstreet), 116
Ojibwe, 126–27, 144
Old House in Cutchogue, 71–72
Ong, Walter, 85
ontological turn, 13
Oresteia (Aeschylus), 122
Ortiz, Simon, 16
Oxford English Dictionary, 60, 86–87, 107

Palmer, Thomas, 34
Paracelsianism, 116–17
parasitical objects, 68–71, 74–75
Parker, Ely, 87
Parks, Rosa, 82
patience, 3, 5–6, 8, 18, 85–88, 98–102, 156; Quaker, 16, 89, 90–92, 94–95, 97; time and, 79–80, 81–85
patriarchy, 56
Paul (Biblical figure), 30
Peace of Westphalia, 107, 110
People of the Dawnland, 118, 120, 130
Pequot, 16, 40, 68–70, 73, 100, 117
Pequot War of 1637, 39–40, 46, 69, 73

Peru, 156–57
Petonowowet (Benjamin), 96
Peyote Religion among the Navaho, The (Aberle), 112
phenomenology, 145
Phenomenology of Spirit, The (Hegel), 107, 109
Philip, King. *See* Metacom
piety, 3, 5, 49–50, 74, 76; definition, 60; history of, 53–56, 57–59, 61–62; incidence rate, 51; Indigenous, 52, 70; popular, 65–66; resistance and, 62–68
pilgrim, figure of, 29–30, 32
Plato, 59
Plymouth Colony, 29–32, 96, 129
Pocahontas, 127
Pocasset, 95–96
poetry, 14, 29, 32, 34, 41, 46, 156
Politics of Piety (Mahmood), 60
Ponca, 157
poppets, 71–73, 74, 76
Posey, Alexander, 49–50, 63
postmodernism, 11
poststructuralism, 4
power, 103, 106
prayer, 138–39
Prince George. *See* George, Prince
Printer, James, 99
Proverbs 4:5, 140
Providence Plantations, 16, 88–89, 91, 94, 95, 98
Psalm 98, 71
psychology, 137–38
Pulsipher, Jenny, 119–20
Puritans, 15, 21–22, 24–25, 31, 40, 137, 158; knowledge and, 51–52, 129; piety and, 59–60, 62

Quakers. *See* Society of Friends
queer theory, 12, 13
Quin, Daniel, 148
Quran, 60

race, 10, 64, 131
radical indigenism, 126
Real Indians (Garroutte), 126
"Reasons and Considerations" (Cushman), 37
reciprocity, 3, 5, 8, 16, 18, 110–11, 113, 121–22, 125, 127; settler, 106–9, 112, 114–16, 117; violent, 4, 18, 104–5, 118–20
Rediker, Marcus, 148
Red Power, 132
relationality, 113
religious experiences, Indigenous, 62–63
repatriation, land, 11
Representations of the Intellectual (Said), 21
resistance, 7, 11, 22, 53, 62–68, 87, 119, 154
Riding, Laura, 1
Robbins, Bruce, 28
Robinson, John, 59
Romans 12:15, 114
Rorty, Richard, 27
Rosbash, Michael, 82
Rowlandson, Mary, 99

sacred, 1, 18
Said, Edward, 21, 41–42

INDEX

Salem witch trials, 70–71
Salisbury, Neal, 24
salt, sharing of, 115
savage, figure of, 40, 56
Scarlet Letter, The (Hawthorne), 22
School-master, The (Ascham), 33
Scrooby congregation, 34–35
Scudder, Henry, 85
Seeing with a Native Eye (Toelken), 112
Sendero Luminoso, 156
Seneca, 80, 87
Senier, Siobhan, 14
September 11, 2001, attacks, 23–24
settlement, 36–38, 55
sexuality, 86
Shepard, Thomas, 138–39, 141
Shoemaker, Nancy, 135
silence, 152–53, 154
Silk, Joan, 120
Silverman, David, 63–64, 112–13, 119
Silverstein, Shel, 16
Simpson, Audra, 15, 154
Sincere Convert, The (Shepard), 138–39
slavery, 146–47, 150
Smith, John, 127
Society of Friends, 16, 25, 88–91, 93–94, 95, 97–98
Sopranos, The, 120
Southern Baptist Convention (SBC), 50
sovereignty, 13, 15, 68, 96, 97, 108, 117, 123, 128, 132, 155
Stein, Jordan, 60

St. George, Robert, 71–73
Strange Likeness, A (Shoemaker), 135
Swift, Jonathan, 59
sympathy, 113–14
Szostak, Jack W., 82

Tanderup, Art, 157
Tears of Repentance (Eliot), 79–80
Telling, The (Riding), 1
temporality. *See* time
Theidon, Kimberly, 156–57
Thirty Years' War, 107
Thomas, Keith, 73
Thomas, Nicholas, 69, 123
Thompson, Dennis, 109–10
Throckmorton, John, 91–92
time, 6, 14, 34, 73, 81–85, 97–98, 121–22, 127–28, 133
Time and the Other (Fabian), 87
Tinker, George, 43, 50
Tisquantam (Patuxet), 39
Toelken, Barre, 112
To Live upon Hope (Wheeler), 64
Translation of Dr Apelles, The (Treuer), 154
travel accounts, 33–34
treaties, 6, 30, 31, 107–8
Treuer, David, 154
tribal recognition, 62–63
Tristes Tropiques (Lévi-Strauss), 103, 110–11
trust, 6
Truth and Method (Gadamer), 141
Truth and Reconciliation Commission (Peru), 156–57
typology, 25

Underhill, John, 100
understanding, 3, 5, 6–7, 8, 18, 130–32, 139–40, 154–58; definition of, 137; knowledge and, 133, 141–44; misunderstanding, 4, 129, 134, 135–37, 144
UNESCO, 130–31
Unfortunate Traveller (Nashe), 34
universalism, 31, 47
utopia, 133

Van Engen, Abram, 114, 137
vanishing Indian myth, 23
Virgil (poet), 58
virtues, 85
Viveiros de Castro, Eduardo, 13
Vizenor, Gerald, 13, 128

Wabanaki, 118
Wagner, Roy, 129, 140
Wakely, John, 118
Wampanoag, 37, 63, 95–97, 99, 112–13
Wampum, 40, 73
war practices: European, 40; Native, 99–100, 104

Water Protectors, 119
Weaver, Jace, 38–39
Weber, Max, 50–51
Weetamoo, 95–97
We Talk, You Listen (Deloria), 79, 124
Wheeler, Rachel, 64
White, Richard, 135
wilderness, 32
Williams, Raymond, 8–9, 10
Williams, Roger, 16, 18, 30, 61, 79, 88–95, 97–100
Wilson, Rob, 26
Wilson, Thomas, 149
Winiarski, Douglas, 54, 65–66
Winslow, Edward, 34
Winthrop, John, Jr., 69, 116
Wituwamat (Massachusett man), 59
Woodward, Walter, 116
Wright, Goodman, 103–5, 118

xenophobia, 23, 28–29, 47

Yellowknives Dene, 125
Young, Michael W., 82
Younge, Richard, 85

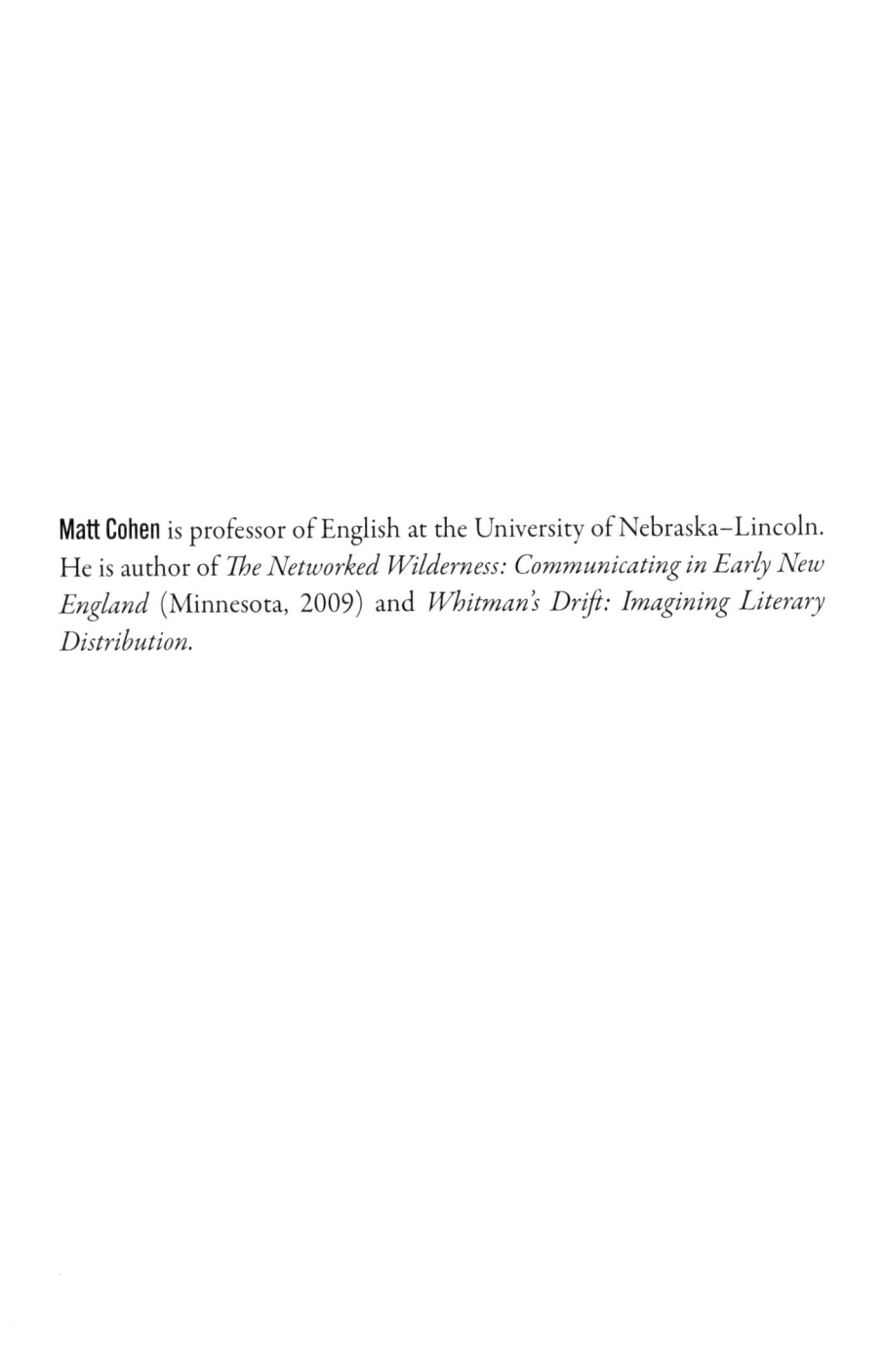

Matt Cohen is professor of English at the University of Nebraska–Lincoln. He is author of *The Networked Wilderness: Communicating in Early New England* (Minnesota, 2009) and *Whitman's Drift: Imagining Literary Distribution.*